UNITED STATES POSTAL SERVICE — SO-ACC-087

The Postal Service Guide to U.S. Stamps

12th Edition
U.S. Stamps in Full Color
1986 Stamp Values

United States Postal Service
Washington, D.C.   20260-6355
Item No. 822

IMPORTANT INFORMATION

The United States Postal Service sells only the commemoratives released during the past few years and current regular and special stamps and postal stationery.

Prices listed in this book are called "catalog prices" by collectors and serve only as a guide to market prices for Fine specimens when offered by an informed dealer to an informed buyer.

Prices in regular type for single unused and used stamps are taken from the latest Scott 1986 Standard Postage Stamp Catalogue, Volume I © 1985, whose editors have based these values on the current stamp market. Prices quoted for unused and used stamps are for "Fine" condition, except where Fine is not available. If no value is assigned, market value is individually determined by condition of the stamp, scarcity and other factors.

Prices for Plate Blocks, Line Pairs, First Day Covers, Stamped Envelopes and Postal Cards are taken from Scott's Specialized Catalogue of U.S. Stamps, 1985 Edition, © 1984. The Scott numbering system for stamps is used in this book.

Prices for Souvenir Cards have been taken from the Catalog of United States Souvenir Cards, by Franklin R. Bruns, Jr., and James H. Bruns, published by Washington Press.

Prices for American Commemorative Panels are from Frank Riolo, Delray Beach, Florida. Souvenir Pages prices are from Charles D. Simmons of Buena Park, California.

Prices of actual stamp sales are dependent upon supply and demand, changes in popularity, local custom, quality of the stamp itself and many other factors.

Copyright © 1985 U.S. Postal Service

The stamp numbering system, certain values and quotations contained herein are owned exclusively by Scott Publishing Co. © 1984, 1985. All rights thereto are reserved by Scott Publishing Co. under Pan American and Universal Copyright conventions and such materials are reproduced and used herein under license from Scott Publishing Co.

The designs of stamps and postal stationery issued since January 1, 1978, are the subject of individual copyrights by the United States Postal Service.

Library of Congress Catalogue Card Number 85-51082.
ISBN: 0-9604756-5-6
Printed in the United States of America

Editorial and Design: Mobium Corporation for Design and Communication, Chicago, IL
Printing: R.R. Donnelley and Sons Co., Crawfordsville, IN
Photo Credits: Milt and Joan Mann, Cover Inset
               Frank Cezus, pages 22-23

TABLE OF CONTENTS

HOW TO USE THE POSTAL SERVICE GUIDE TO U.S. STAMPS

The Postal Service Guide to U.S. Stamps is a color catalog of postage stamps of the United States, designed to put all the vital information you need in one handy reference line.

Each line listing contains the following information:

	Un	U	PB/LP	#	FDC	Q
2145 22¢ AMERIPEX '86, May 25	.00	.00	0.00	(4)	0.00	000,000,000

Scott Catalog Number — Denomination — Description — First Day of Issue — Unused Catalog Price — Used Catalog Price — Plate Block Price or Line Pair Price — # of stamps in Plate Block — First Day Cover Price — Quantity Issued

2145

The Postal Service Guide to U.S. Stamps also lists philatelic details such as watermarks, perforations and years of issue. These will aid you in identifying stamps of similar design. Watermarks (Wmk.) are designs incorporated in the paper on which certain stamps are printed. Perforations are the number of small holes in a two centimeter space on the edge of the stamp. A stamp which has 12 such holes is listed as Perf. 12 (perforated 12), while a stamp with no perforations is listed as Imperf. (imperforate). Coil stamps are perforated on two sides only, either horizontally or vertically. **When a perforation, year of issue, or watermark is mentioned, the description applies to all succeeding issues until a change is noted.**

Illustration Numbers. Some of the stamps cataloged in this book are not shown. The illustrations for such stamps are identified by a number in parentheses. For example, in the listings which appear below, Scott No. 247 has the same illustration as Scott No. 246.

246   1¢ Franklin
247   1¢ blue Franklin (246)

How to Order Stamps. When ordering stamps from a dealer, identify items wanted by country of issue, Scott No., and condition (unused or used).

Condition is an important factor of price. Prices are for stamps in fine condition. Off center, heavily cancelled, faded or stained stamps usually sell at large discounts. Values in italics indicate latest auction prices, infrequent sales or fluctuating market values.

Suppose someone asked you, "What is the most popular hobby in the world?" Since you're reading this book, you can probably guess the answer. That's right. It's stamp collecting. In the United States alone, about 22 million people are stamp collectors. And there are millions more around the world.

What makes stamps so fascinating? Some people think of stamps as tiny windows on the world. Most countries have stamps that show people or things or events that their citizens think are very important, or valuable, or beautiful. So when you look at a postage stamp, you learn something about the country it comes from.

Another reason people like to collect stamps is that many stamps are really works of art. Talented artists and photographers design the stamps. They are printed with great care and skill. Having a collection of beautiful stamps is like having an art gallery of your own.

Another thing that makes stamp collecting so popular is that there is no special age for it. You can enjoy stamp collecting just as much when you're 70 years old as when you're 10. In stamp collecting, you never run out of something to do. If you started now, and collected stamps for the rest of your life, you'd probably not be able to collect all the stamps in the world. The first postage stamp was issued in 1840. Since then, hundreds of thousands of different stamps have been issued by the countries of the world. But rather than trying to collect as many different kinds of stamps from as many places as you can, you'll probably find some types of stamps that are particularly interesting to *you*—and concentrate on collecting those.

Stamps can help with schoolwork. They can be used in special projects in classes like history, geography, and science. Also, stamp collecting is a merit badge activity for Scouts.

Stamp collecting doesn't have to be an expensive hobby. Of course, you could spend many thousands of dollars on stamps, but you can also be a collector without spending much money at all.

You can start out by asking your family and your friends to save used stamps for you. Just ask them to save the used stamps on envelopes they receive in the mail at their homes or businesses. As you gather stamps, you'll want to put them in order so you can show them to other people. A ring binder with loose leaf paper can be your first stamp album. But don't paste or tape your stamps into the album! That would destroy their value.

You'll find out how to handle your stamps throughout this section. But first, look at the next page. There you'll discover some stamps that are very famous or very rare. If you are just starting to collect stamps, this bit of history will give you a feeling for the past and for some of the interesting stories you'll discover as you continue collecting.

SELECTING STAMP SUBJECTS

Governments all over the world, the United States included, have long recognized postage stamps as an effective means of communicating to a worldwide audience. Fixed tightly to envelopes, packages and postcards, U.S. commemorative stamps are highly visible as they recall outstanding individuals and events of historical significance, celebrate important current events and focus attention on important social issues.

The U.S. Postal Service Stamps Division is responsible for the commemorative stamps program that began in 1893 with the Columbian issues. Each week the division receives hundreds of suggestions for commemorative stamps; of these, very few are selected. To help in the enormous job of sorting through the suggestions and making final subject recommendations, the Postmaster General in 1957 established a Citizens' Stamp Advisory Committee. This committee, made up of historians, artists, businessmen, stamp collectors and others interested in American history and culture, is guided by a set of Standards for Stamp Selection.

The standards dictate that a person may be portrayed on a stamp only ten years after his or her death and that the stamp should be issued on a significant birth anniversary. U.S. Presidents are excepted from this rule. They may be honored with a stamp on their first birthdate following their death.

Historical anniversaries are considered as stamp subjects on even-date anniversaries, preferably starting with the 50th year and continuing at 50-year intervals. Themes and events are considered only if they are judged to be of widespread national interest and appeal. No stamps are issued to honor charitable, fraternal, political, sectarian or service organizations or commercial enterprises or products. Similarly, anniversaries of cities, towns, municipalities, counties and schools are considered too regional in nature to qualify as subjects for postage stamps.

So what's left to portray on stamps? The supply of subjects that do qualify as appropriate for commemorative stamps seems virtually inexhaustible. They have included, in addition to Presidents, statesmen and other prominent persons, themes that have ranged from religious freedom to the importance of dental health to a recognition of the American woman.

Yes, postage stamps are communicators. A good example is a single stamp, "Giving Blood Saves Lives", issued in 1971. This stamp was credited by the American Association of Blood Banks with inspiring enough blood donations to stock American blood banks with a six-month supply.

The wide variety of commemorative stamps issued enables collectors to carve out areas of specialization and helps make stamp collecting a hobby of continuing interest. More importantly, commemorative stamps give the nation a special avenue for keeping alive the lessons of the past.

TYPES OF STAMPS

Many people who know about stamp collecting suggest that you shouldn't decide right away what kind of stamps you are going to collect. At first, they say, just get together as many different stamps as you can. United States stamps. Stamps from some other countries. Stamps that feature special subjects—birds, dogs, famous women, or Scouts, for example. (Stamps of this type are called *topicals*, because they are about one *topic*.) Then, after you've been collecting for a while, you'll have a better idea about what kind of stamps you want to specialize in. Just be sure to pick a type that has a lot of stamps, so you'll be able to get enough for a good-sized collection. U.S. commemoratives are an easy way to start.

Regular or Definitive Stamps These are the stamps you'll find on most mail. They are printed in unlimited quantities and sold by the Postal Service for long periods of time—several years, usually.

Regular or Definitive

Commemorative Stamps These stamps are issued to honor an important event, person, or special subject. They are usually larger and more colorful than definitives. They are sold for only a certain length of time—a few months, maybe, and are printed in limited quantities.

Coil Stamps These stamps are issued in rolls. Each stamp has two straight edges and two perforated edges.

Coil

Commemorative

Airmail Stamps U.S. airmail stamps are used for sending mail overseas.

Postage Due Stamps Postage due stamps are put on mail at the post office to show that the postage already paid was not enough. The amount shown on the stamp must be paid by the receiver of the mail.

Airmail

Postage Due

ALBUMS/STAMP COLLECTING EQUIPMENT

A simple ring binder with loose-leaf pages will do very nicely for your first album. But after a while you may want to buy a special stamp album. It's usually best to buy an album with loose-leaf pages. Then you can add more pages as your collection grows.

There is a kind of album that does not have pictures of the stamps that are to go on the pages. It just has plastic pockets on the pages. This type of album is called a *stock book*. The pages can be placed in a binder. You can buy as many pages as you need to hold your stamps.

How to Remove Stamps from Covers

To get stamps off paper, you'll need a small pan with some warm (not hot) water in it, some newspapers or paper towels, and your tongs. Place a few stamps face down in the water. Wait a little while, until the stamps float off the paper. The stamps will sink to the bottom. The paper will float. As soon as the stamps are free, lift them out with the tongs, one by one. Place them face down on the newspaper or paper towel. If they dry flat, you can put them in your album. Follow carefully the next directions. If the stamps are curled up when they are dry, put them between the pages

of a telephone directory or another big, heavy book. Put another heavy book or some other kind of weight on top. Leave the stamps overnight. The next day they should be flat and ready to place in your album.

Putting Stamps in Your Album

You can use either folded or unfolded hinges to put stamps in your album. The shiny side is the gummed side. If you are using a folded hinge, lightly touch your tongue to the short side. Then, press the short side to the back of the stamp. Next, while holding the stamp with your tongs, touch your tongue to the long side of the hinge. Now put the stamp in its place on the album page, pressing it down with a blotter. (*Never* handle stamps with your fingers. Even if your hands are clean, oil from your skin may damage the stamps.) Finally, gently lift the corners of the stamp with the tongs to be sure it has not stuck to the page.

If you are collecting unused (called *uncancelled or mint*) stamps, you should use plastic mounts to put them in your album. Mounts will protect your stamps better than hinges. A mount is a small envelope that covers the whole stamp. It keeps air, grease, and dirt from damaging the stamp.

Suppose you have begun collecting stamps—from friends, family, businesses, and visiting the post office to look for new U.S. issues. You also have some kind of album. What else will you need for your hobby?

A. Tongs for moving a stamp from one place to another, especially when handling unused stamps, to prevent damage.

B. Hinges for attaching stamps to the pages of your album. Hinges come either folded or unfolded.

C. Mounts are small plastic envelopes. They cost more money than hinges, but are necessary to protect unused stamps.

D. A package of glassine (glass-ene) **envelopes** to hold different kinds of stamps until you are ready to put them in an album. Glassine is a special kind of thin paper that keeps grease and air from damaging stamps.

E. Stamp catalog to help you identify stamps and give you other information about them, including their value, used and unused.

F. Magnifying glass, four- or six-power, to help you distinguish stamps that seem to be the same.

G. Perforation gauge to help you identify stamps. It is used to measure the size and number of perforations (cuts or holes along the edges) on stamps.

H. Watermark fluid and a watermark tray of black glass or plastic. The stamp is placed face down in the tray and covered with a few drops of the watermark fluid. Then the watermark shows up. Watermark fluid can be dangerous, so be careful in following the directions.

Adhesive A gummed stamp made to be attached to mail.

Aerophilately The hobby of collecting airmail stamps, covers and other postal materials that are delivered by balloon, airplane, or other types of aircraft.

APS Abbreviation for American Philatelic Society.

Approvals Stamps sent by a dealer to a collector for examination. Approvals must either be bought or returned to the dealer within a certain time.

ATA Abbreviation for American Topical Association.

Autographed Cover A cover sheet or envelope signed by a person who had something to do with the event that is being commemorated— for example, the pilot of the plane that carried the material. Or an envelope addressed to a famous person, and signed by that person.

Block An attached group of stamps at least two stamps high and two stamps wide.

Booklet Pane A small sheet of stamps especially cut and printed to be sold in booklets.

Cachet (ka-shay') A design on a first day cover (envelope).

Cancellation A mark placed on a stamp to show that the stamp has been used.

Centering The position of the design on a postage stamp. On perfectly centered stamps the design is exactly in the middle of the stamp.

Coils Stamps issued in rolls for use in dispensers, affixers or vending machines.

Commemoratives Stamps that honor anniversaries, important people, or special events. Commemoratives are usually sold for only a certain length of time.

Condition The state of a stamp in regard to such things as centering, freshness, color, gum, and hinge marks.

Cover The envelope or wrapping in which a letter has been sent through the mail.

Definitives Regular issues of stamps—not commemoratives. Regular issues are usually sold over long periods of time.

Face Value The value of a stamp as printed on the stamp.

First Day Cover An envelope with a new stamp and a cancellation showing the date the stamp was first sold.

Gum The adhesive on the back of a stamp.

Hinges Small strips of paper gummed on one side and used by collectors to put their stamps in albums.

Imperforate Stamps Stamps printed in sheets without perforations or other means of separating them. Users had to cut the stamps apart with scissors or a knife. These stamps were usually early issues. They were printed before machines to make perforations had been invented.

Mint Sheet A sheet of unused stamps.

Mint Stamp A postage stamp that is in the same condition as when it was purchased from a post office.

Overprint A regular issue stamp that has some printing on top of the original design. Sometimes stamps are overprinted when there has been a change of government or when one country takes over another in a war.

Pane Part of an original large printed sheet of stamps. Sheets are cut into panes so that they are easier to handle and sell at post offices.

Pen Cancellation A cancellation made before modern post office equipment was used. Postmasters drew a line in ink across stamps, initialed them, or wrote their names on them.

Perforations Lines of small cuts or holes between two rows of stamps so that the stamps are easy to separate.

Philately (fi-lat'-el-lee) The collecting and study of postage stamps and other postal material.

Plate The metal base from which stamps are printed.

Plate Block (or number plate block) A block of stamps with the plate number or numbers in the margin.

Postal Stationery Envelopes, postal cards, aerogrammes, and wrappers with stamps printed or embossed on them.

Postmark A mark put on envelopes and other mailing pieces, showing the date and the name of the post office where it was mailed.

Postmaster Provisionals Stamps made by local postmasters. They were used before the government of the country began issuing stamps, or when the post office ran out of regular stamps.

Precancels Stamps with cancellations applied before the material was mailed.

Reissue An official reprinting of a stamp that was no longer being printed.

Revenue Stamps Stamps issued for use in collecting taxes on special papers or products. Not used for postage.

Selvage The paper around panes of stamps. Sometimes called the margin.

Se-tenant An attached pair, strip or block of stamps which differ in value, design or surcharge.

Surcharge An overprint which alters or restates the face value or denomination of the stamp to which it is applied.

Tagging Marking stamps with chemicals to be read by machines that sort mail and turn letters face-up for cancellation.

Thin Spot A thinning of the paper on the back of a stamp where a hinge was carelessly removed.

Tied On A stamp is "tied on" when the cancellation or postmark goes across the stamp to the envelope.

Topicals A group of stamps all with the same subject—space travel, for example.

Unused A stamp with or without original gum that has no cancellation or other sign of use.

Used A stamp that has been cancelled.

Want List A list of stamp numbers or philatelic items needed by a collector.

Watermark A design or pattern pressed into paper during its manufacture.

Overprint

Precancel

Perforate

Se-tenant

Imperforate

Coils

Surcharge

Specialty collecting hasn't anything to do with the subject matter of the stamps you collect. (Collecting stamps that have a particular subject is called **topical** collecting.) A specialty collection is a particular form of stamps, such as:

Blocks of Four A square block of four unused (mint), unseparated stamps, with two stamps above and two below. A block can come from anywhere on a pane of stamps. This is the easiest block to collect.

Plate Blocks Usually plate blocks are four corner stamps with the printing plate number in the margin (selvage) of the pane. On January 1, 1981, the Postal Service started a new plate number system. Each color plate first used in the production of a stamp is represented by a number 1 in the group of numbers in the margin. Whenever a plate is worn out and replaced during the printing process, a number 2 replaces the number 1. The color of the number is the same as the color of the plate it stands for.

Copyright Blocks The U.S. Postal Service now copyrights all new stamp designs. The copyright C in a circle, followed by "United States Postal Service" or "USPS" and the year, appears in the margin of each sheet of stamps. The first copyright notice appeared January 6, 1978, in the margin of sheets of the Carl Sandburg stamp. Most copyrights are collected in blocks of four.

Booklet Panes Stamp booklets were first issued in 1898. Usually six or more of the same stamps are on a page, called a pane. Several pages of stamps are stapled in a cover. Most collections are of an entire pane.

Covers Covers (envelopes) stamped and postmarked with the date of the stamp's first day of issue are collected by a large number of people. On page 20 you'll find more information about first day covers and how to order them.

Souvenir Cards These 6″ x 8″ cards are issued as souvenirs of the philatelic (stamp collecting) events. They are distributed by the United States Postal Service, or the Bureau of Engraving and Printing. Some are available cancelled. They cannot be used for postage. Of special interest to American stamp collectors is the annual souvenir card for National Stamp Collecting Month each October, first issued in 1981.

Mr. ZIP Blocks The Zoning Improvement Plan—better known as ZIP Code—helps the Postal Service handle and deliver mail quickly. A Mr. ZIP cartoon and slogan were first printed on the Sam Houston stamp of 1964. Mr. ZIP blocks have become quite popular with collectors.

The U.S. Postal Service encourages people to collect stamps and helps them with their hobby. One of the ways it does this is through the Benjamin Franklin Stamp Clubs. These are clubs that are sponsored by the U.S. Postal Service in schools and libraries across the country. They are for students in third through seventh grade.

Benjamin Franklin Stamp Clubs were first started in 1974. Since then more than 5 million students have been introduced to stamp collecting through these clubs. There are about 50,000 Ben Franklin Stamp Clubs now. Why are these clubs named after Benjamin Franklin? Because he was a leader in organizing our postal system. He was the first Postmaster General, in 1775.

1474

How does a Benjamin Franklin Stamp Club get started?
At the beginning of the school year, a person who works for the U.S. Postal Service in your area telephones schools and libraries to see if they are interested in having a stamp club. If the answer is yes, the person goes to the school or library to tell the teachers, librarians, and students about the Ben Franklin clubs. Sometimes a film about stamp collecting is shown. Usually a teacher, librarian, or parent agrees to be the club's advisor.

The U.S. Postal Service gives some materials to the Benjamin Franklin Stamp Clubs. Each of the members gets a free Treasury of Stamps album every year. This album has places for most of the new U.S. postage stamps that will be issued during the school year. Each member also gets a membership card. And every month during the school year, a newsletter called *Stamp Fun* is sent to the club. The advisor gets other free materials to help get the club started and keep it going. Films, slide-tape programs, and filmstrips are also available free from the Postal Service. The Postal Service representative will give other help to the club as it needs it.

What are some activities of the Ben Franklin Stamp Clubs?
If possible, the club meets every week. One of the most important activities, of course, is collecting, showing, and trading stamps. The club might arrange to have a stamp show. There might be a trip to visit a post office. Older stamp collectors in the community might visit the club, show their collections, and talk about them. Stamp dealers are often invited to meet with the clubs.

A new activity of the Benjamin Franklin Stamp Clubs is the Pen Pal Program. Clubs that want to write letters to other Ben Franklin clubs send their club names, addresses, and identification numbers to the Benjamin Franklin Stamp Club headquarters in Washington, D.C. A club can say in which states it wants Ben Franklin club pen pals. Then headquarters will send to the club addresses of pen pals in those states. Clubs write letters to their pen pal clubs about their activities. They also exchange "want lists" of stamps members need for their collections. Stamps can be traded or even bought this way.

Landsat views the Earth.

©USPS 1985

USA 36

AEROGRAMME • VIA AIRMAIL • PAR AVION

② Second fold

③ Seal top flap last

⑤

Do not use tape or stickers to seal — No enclos

← ① Fold first at notches

Additional message area

© USPS 1985

aerogramme

Three items of postal stationery are popular with stamp collectors. These are embossed stamped envelopes, postal cards, and aerogrammes. You can buy these items at post offices.

Stamped Envelopes On stamped envelopes, the stamp is not printed separately. It is printed and embossed (made with a raised design) right on the envelope. Stamped envelopes are made for the Postal Service by a private contractor. They are made in several sizes and styles, including the window type. The embossed designs are sometimes commemoratives in more than one color.

Stamped envelopes were first issued in 1853. Today the average issue of stamped envelopes in one year is more than 1 million.

Postal Cards Postal cards are made of a heavier paper than envelopes. Plain and simple one-color postal cards were first issued in 1873. They stayed plain and simple until 1956. Then the first U.S. commemorative postal card came out. Usually several different postal cards are issued during a year. About 800 million are printed each year.

Aerogrammes An aerogramme (air letter) is a flat sheet of paper that's made to be a letter and an envelope in one. It's specially stamped, marked for folding, and gummed. After you write your letter, fold up the aerogramme and seal it. It's meant for foreign air mail only. An aerogramme will carry your message anywhere in the world at a lower postage rate than regular airmail.

Just as is the case with stamped envelopes and postal cards, the Postal Service has in recent years increased the use of commemorative designs on aerogrammes.

postal card

stamped envelope

The value of a stamp depends mostly on two things: how rare it is—that is, how few of them there are—and what condition it's in. You can get an idea of how rare a stamp is by the price listed for it in a catalog. But a stamp may sell for more or less than the catalog price, depending on its condition. A very rare stamp may be quite expensive even though it's in poor condition. For a while anyway, you'll probably be collecting stamps that aren't very expensive. But still, you should try to get stamps that are in the best condition you can.

Here are some of the things to look for when you are judging the condition of a stamp. Look at the front of the stamp. Are the colors bright? Or is the stamp dirty, stained, or faded? Is the design in the center of the paper, or is it a little crooked or off to the side? Are the edges in good condition? Or are some of the perforations missing? A stamp with a light cancellation mark is in better condition than one with heavy marks across it.

Now look at the back of the stamp. Is there a thin spot in the paper? It may have been caused by careless removal of paper or a hinge. Can you see marks from hinges? Stamps that have the original gum and have never been hinged are more valuable.

Stamp dealers put stamps into categories according to their condition. The worst is "Poor" or "Spacefiller." Most stamps you see will be in the categories "Superb," "Fine," and "Good." You can look at the examples on the next page to see the differences among stamps in these big categories.

Catalog prices listed in *The Postal Service Guide to U.S. Stamps* are for used and unused stamps in Fine condition that have been hinged. A stamp that has not been hinged and has excellent centering and color will cost more. A stamp in less than Fine condition that has been heavily cancelled will cost less than the catalog price.

You may see a stamp listed as mint. A mint stamp is one that is in the same condition as it was when purchased from the post office. An unused stamp is one that has not been cancelled. It may not have any gum on it or it may be damaged in some way. Stamps in mint condition are usually more valuable than in unused condition.

Light Cancel-Very Fine   Medium Cancel-Fine   Heavy Cancel

Superb   Very Fine

Fine   Good

Most stamp catalogs are printed only in black and white, not colors. That makes it hard to imagine what the stamps really look like, because most of them are in colors. Sometimes, to help you, the catalogs give the names of the colors on the stamps shown.

On these pages are some popular names for stamp colors, along with examples of stamps that are printed in those colors. The stamp colors shown here are not 100% accurate because printing processes such as the one used for this **Guide** don't use the same kinds of inks and paper as the original stamps. So the colors here may not look quite the same.

When you become an experienced stamp collector, you'll be able to recognize a stamp whose color makes it rare and valuable. In the meantime, you can use this guide to get a better idea of what stamps in a catalog really look like.

Bright Blue

Blue

Dark Blue

Ultramarine

Purple

Violet

Carmine

Rose Lake

Peach Blossom

Red

Henna Brown

Bistre Brown

Brown

Sepia

Gray Brown

Dark Gray

Black

Light Green

Green

Olive

Light Olive Green

Blue Green

Yellow Gold

Orange

Deep Orange

Yellow-Black-Green

A first day cover is an envelope that has a new stamp cancelled with the date of the first day it was issued. For each new postal stamp or stationery issue, the Postal Service names one post office that is related in some way to the subject of the stamp. First day cover ceremonies are conducted at this post office to honor the subject of the stamp.

Here's how you can get a first day cover through the Postal Service. You will get faster service if you buy the stamp yourself, and then send it to the first day post office for cancellation. When a new stamp goes on sale at your post office (usually the next day after the first day of issue), you can buy one and put it on your own envelope. Put the address in the lower right-hand corner. Leave plenty of room for the stamp and the cancellation. You can use a peelable address label if you don't want the address to remain on the envelope. Put your first day envelope inside another envelope. Mail it to "Customer Affixed Envelopes" in care of the postmaster of the first day city. The post office will cancel your envelope and return it to you through the mail. You may do this for 30 days after the issue date of the stamp.

Or, you can send an envelope addressed to yourself, but without a stamp. Put the addressed envelope into another envelope. Address the outside envelope to the name of the stamp, in care of the postmaster of the first day city. You must also include payment for the stamp or stamps that are to be put on your envelope. Do not send cash. You may send a check, a bank draft, or a U.S. Postal money order. Make it out to the U.S. Postal Service.

Do not send requests more than 60 days prior to the issue date. Usually you will receive your cancelled cover within three weeks after the first day of issue. If you don't, write to the postmaster of the first day city. Tell how the envelope was addressed, what kind of design or cachet it had, and how many stamps were ordered. If you ever get a first day cover that is damaged, send it back to the postmaster. A new one will be sent to you.

The U.S. Postal Service tries to get the first day covers into the mail just as soon as possible. To do this, it sends a special team of workers to a first day post office. Their job is just to work on first day covers. Of course, they can't do all that work on one day. Often it takes weeks. When there's an especially popular stamp issue, it may take even longer than usual to get all the first day covers out. For example, for the 1982 State Birds and Flowers issue 12,070,206 first day covers were cancelled.

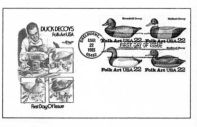

The Bureau of Engraving and Printing in Washington, D.C. prints U.S. stamps and money. The Bureau has tours for visitors, and is a popular spot with tourists. To see the printing presses in operation can be very interesting, especially for stamp collectors. Stamps produced in the United States are the most carefully made and inspected in the world.

Several types of printing are used in the production of stamps.

Typography, or letterpress In this process, the design that is to appear on the stamp is raised above the metal printing plate. It is coated with ink and then pressed against the paper to print the design.

Intaglio (in-tal′-yo) In this type of printing, the design is cut into the metal printing plate. The ink flows down into the lines. Then damp paper is forced onto the plate to pick up the ink.

Gravure This process is a form of intaglio. The design is photographed through a very fine screen. The screen breaks the image up into patterns of small dots. The photograph is then cut into a metal plate. The tiny dots made by the screen become holes that catch and hold the ink. The deeper the holes are, the more ink they will hold. When paper is pressed against the printing plate, it collects the ink from the holes. In this way, the design is printed on the paper.

Offset This printing process is based on the fact that water and grease do not mix. The stamp design is put on a metal printing plate by a photographic process. The part of the design that is to print (the image area) is made so that it will accept the greasy ink. The plate is wet with acid and water. When the plate is inked, the greasy ink sticks only to the image area. If paper were pressed against the plate at this point, the design would print backward. So the design is first "offset" onto a rubber blanket, and then onto the paper.

In all these processes, a separate printing plate is made for each color in the stamp.

Sometimes when a stamp is complicated, different printing processes are combined. For example, the Love Special issue of 1984 was printed by a combination of intaglio and gravure presses. The intaglio colors in this stamp are black and red. The gravure colors are red, orange, green, blue and violet.

2072

A Walk Down Main Street and More

Plans are being finalized, and organizers are working at a fevered pitch; countless details are being tracked, and the logistics are falling into place for what is expected to be one of the largest international philatelic exhibitions to date—AMERIPEX '86. The AMERIPEX '86 steering committee, formed in 1976 after the last U.S. international exhibition in Philadelphia, will see a decade of planning and organizing effort culminate in a virtual "world's fair of stamps" at the O'Hare Exposition Center near Chicago from May 22 through June 1, 1986.

The numbers associated with AMERIPEX '86 are staggering. The exhibition space covers an area the size of seven football fields. The U.S. Postal Service area alone encompasses 90,000 square feet, making the U.S.P.S. exhibit one of the largest ever planned for any trade show anywhere. Some 4,000 specially-designed frames will be erected for the displays of 800 qualifying individual exhibitors. More than 55 countries have appointed representative commissioners to travel to the show. The world's largest and most prestigious dealers will be in attendance. And, of course, there will be millions of stamps, covers, postal cards, postal stationery items and more—a philatelic fantasy for collectors of every age, speciality and nationality.

AMERIPEX '86 organizers recom-

MAY 22 - JUNE 1

mend that visitors plan at least two days to adequately cover the highlights of this enormous event. Now, we'll take an imaginary whirlwind tour over the floor of AMERIPEX '86 to trace the excitement that the spring of 1986 will bring to philatelists from all over the world as they assemble in Chicago for 11 days of "stamp mania."

A Royal Welcome for Every Visitor
AMERIPEX '86 is organized around the theme "international cooperation through stamp collecting," and the exhibition will literally roll out the red carpet for philatelists. The spacious entrance will welcome participants with some 15,000 square yards of scarlet flooring.

As visitors enter the show, they will receive a copy of the AMERIPEX '86 daily newspaper. The paper will supply a map of the exhibit floor and will detail the

special events scheduled each day, along with covering breaking news at the exhibition. In keeping with its philosophy of remaining one of the most democratic of international stamp shows, AMERIPEX '86 will open all of its events to the public at a single daily admission price of $2.50, or $20.00 for a run-of-the-show admission. As a courtesy to the host country, every U.S. Postal Service employee and family will be admitted to AMERIPEX '86 free of charge.

Floor plan in hand, we file past a parade of flags, each from a different participating country, that beckons us to the excitement within the exhibit hall.

Main Street—A Super Highway
AMERIPEX '86's 22-foot wide main aisle is dubbed "Main Street." Here

CHICAGO

we find the super booths; most of the world's largest philatelic dealers have paid from $12,000 to $20,000 each for the privilege of purveying their inventories to AMERIPEX '86 visitors. Their offerings range from some of the world's rarest, most expensive and coveted stamps, to inexpensive items that more than likely will be treasured finds for some collectors.

Among the super booth holders are six auction firms which have been designated the official auctioneers for AMERIPEX '86. Each of the firms has agreed to conduct one single-session unreserved public auction sale. AMERIPEX '86 is the first international exhibition in the United States at which such auctions are to be held. Many valuable philatelic items are expected to be consigned by their owners for these auctions, making the bidding an exciting experience for all philatelists even though the thought of purchasing these stamps may only be a dream.

Philatelic Rarities

A left turn off Main Street brings us to the Court of Honor, an unprecedented collection of rare and valuable stamps and old collectibles to be housed in an area of the highest security imaginable. Each frame in the Court of Honor will display the rare, the unique and the unusual.

The Aristocrats of Philately to be exhibited include the 5-cent blue Postmaster Provisional of Alexandria, the Sweden 1855 3-Skilling Banco error and the se-tenant strip of the 30r and 60r Bulls Eyes of Brazil. The Old Collectibles area will offer a special review of the Beginnings of the Mail. Here, visitors will be transported back in time as they view and learn about a 4,000-year-old clay tablet and a quipu of the Incas. Fragments of papyrus letters along with letters on parchment and early paper also will be on display. Early Roman letter forms will be seen in intricate detail on a replica of the famous Trajan Inscription on loan from Mobium Corporation of Chicago.

Another Court of Honor highlight is illuminated pages lent from the Cardinal Spellman collection. It is said that the Cardinal enhanced and maintained his magnificent collection

The O'Hare Exposition Center is perhaps the largest arena ever to house an international philatelic exhibit. Thousands of rooms in nearby hotels have been set aside for AMERIPEX '86 visitors.

Shown here is the official logo of the Chicago International Philatelic Exhibition, Inc. —AMERIPEX '86.

with the help of many volunteers. Their intricate work is evident in the pages to be exhibited. Selected pieces from the collection of Her Majesty Queen Elizabeth II will travel to AMERIPEX '86 under the watchful eye of The Keeper of the Royal Collection.

Private collectors will contribute a complete collection of presidential free franks to the Court of Honor exhibit. These highlights of this fascinating area by no means cover all the rarities to be exhibited in the Court of Honor. AMERIPEX '86 visitors will be awestruck at the actual presence of many of the world's most famous philatelic materials.

The Business of Philately

Next on the tour is a walk through the regular booth area in which more than 200 dealers from the world over will man their booths for buying, selling and trading. The International Hall in this area will house dealer booths from at least 63 countries. Each will be offering the stamps and other philatelic products of his country at face value. Every collector, generalist and specialist alike, is certain to discover items of great interest here.

Adjacent to the regular dealer booths are the municipal service areas of what will be coined "AMERIPEX '86 City." AMERIPEX '86 City will provide banking services for changing currency and cashing travellers checks, will house a lost and found and message center, and will provide a computer service for making reservations for tours, banquets and other functions.

The Heart of Philately

Eight hundred individual exhibitors will display the results of their devotion to philatelic endeavors; international exhibitions like AMERIPEX '86 are their opportunity to proudly exhibit the fruits of their research, collection, preservation and maintenance of things philatelic. Each exhibitor is allowed four to eight frames for his or her exhibit, and, as a group, these 4,000 frames will cradle the cream of philately from all over the world.

More than 50 countries have appointed commissioners whose charge is to accompany exhibits from their country to AMERIPEX '86. To qualify as an exhibitor, a person's collection must have won a vermeil or better in a national show. As a result, shows leading up to AMERIPEX '86 have been and will continue to be swamped with competitors attempting to qualify for the international exhibit.

To add interest to the individual exhibit area and attract the new

collector, AMERIPEX '86 organizers have reserved 800 frames for collectors who have never exhibited at an international exhibition before. And in another departure from tradition, prize winners will be announced and awards displayed on exhibitor frames prior to the awards dinner that will be held at the end of AMERIPEX '86. The enormous space devoted to individual exhibits will be organized according to each specialty within geographic designations.

The Future of Philately

Young collectors will be a primary focus of AMERIPEX '86. High attendance by youths will be fostered by funds earmarked by the show organizing committee for transporting thousands of youngsters from the midwestern United States to AMERIPEX '86.

Ben Franklin Clubs will enjoy 9,000 square feet of display area, hosted

Above: *The 5¢ blue Alexandria, also known as the "Alexandria Blue Boy", was sold at auction in 1981 for one million dollars.*
Below: *Tiny clay tablets like this one served as letters for the Incas of Peru some 4,000 years ago. The tablet is part of "The Beginnings of the Mail" exhibit.*

by U.S.P.S. living characters—
Natalie Philately, Stan The Answer
Stamp and Ben Franklin himself. A
series of presentations for youth
will cover many different aspects
of stamp collecting, including
cancelling covers, specialization in
collecting, maintaining a collection
and more. The presentations will be
in a variety of entertaining forms,
from slide shows and films, to
interactive, hands-on video
game-oriented exhibits.

Winners of the U.S.P.S.-sponsored
Youths Exhibiting Stamps (Y.E.S.)
project will exhibit. And two special
booths will be devoted exclusively to
the needs of philatelic enthusiasts
under age 18. One booth, sponsored
by Dr. Robert Friedman of Joliet,
Illinois, will offer a minimum of five
million stamps priced at 5 cents each.
The other, sponsored by Barrett &
Worthen of Lexington, Massachusetts, will offer a minimum of 250,000
special event covers priced at 25
cents each. (Prices may change.)

In addition to promoting the
fun of stamp collecting to youth,
AMERIPEX '86 will devote a special
section to the education of pros-
pective collectors of every age.

Fifty frames have been set aside to
dramatically illustrate the variety and
enjoyment that anyone can gain by
pursuing philately as a hobby. The
frames will contain 16 pages each
to show the diversity of ways that
stamps can be collected.

Each frame will concentrate on a
different area of interest, such as
cinderellas, picture postcards,
maximum cards, town cancels,
special event pictorial cancels, coins
on stamps, folk lore and much more.
The frames will all display title pages
along with pages explaining the
purpose of each one-frame exhibit
and an estimate of the dollar amount

These il-
luminated
pages from
the Cardinal
Spellman col-
lection are hand-
lettered and high-
lighted with gold
leaf. They will be dis-
played along with other
antique philatelic pieces
in the AMERIPEX '86 Old
Collectibles section.

spent. Each frame is limited to a
maximum expenditure of $25.00.

Nearby, collectors active in stamp
clubs will man a booth entitled "Join a
Stamp Club." These ambassadors of
philately will have available a listing
of more than 1,500 stamp clubs in the
U.S. AMERIPEX '86 visitors will be
able to visit the booth to find out about
stamp clubs in their area and when
and where the clubs meet.

**United States Postal Service Plans
a Spectacular**
The back of the huge AMERIPEX
'86 hall will be devoted entirely to

U.S.P.S. exhibits. The Postal Service displays are planned according to three separate focal areas. The first is the Ben Franklin Clubs youth area. In addition to the youth-oriented exhibits, the U.S.P.S. will unveil a general exhibit and a retail booth.

The U.S.P.S. general exhibit will center on an ambitious and stunning multi-media presentation of the history of the United States as seen through stamps and other philatelic products. The presentation will utilize state-of-the-art visual arts technology and promises to be unlike any presentation seen before at an international exhibition.

The Postal Service retail booth will be manned throughout the run of AMERIPEX '86 by 20 postal clerks. (All current U.S. stamps, postal stationery and philatelic products will be sold.) Each day of AMERIPEX '86 will have a different theme, such as President's Day, Philatelic Literature Day, Young Collector's Day and Stamp Dealer's Day, among others. Cancellations will be chosen from designs submitted to the AMERIPEX '86 cancellation competition. Each will be used on its corresponding day only at the AMERIPEX '86 postal station.

Just the Iceberg's Tip
We must close our imaginary AMERIPEX '86 tour, and we haven't even touched on areas devoted to the various philatelic societies, the postal administration competition, the philatelic literature areas, and much, much more. It's apparent that philatelists will be kept busy at AMERIPEX '86 for the entire 11 days of the exhibition.

These papyrus fragments are among the oldest known examples of letters. They are from the collection of Robson Lowe of London and will be shown as part of "The Beginnings of the Mail" exhibit.

An Exciting Chicago Awaits AMERIPEX '86 Visitors

Chicago, the capital of the Midwest, will offer excitement and interest to the AMERIPEX '86 visitor who takes the time to see the city. To get visiting philatelists started, the organizers of AMERIPEX '86 have arranged for some very interesting tours. These include the following:

Ethnic Tours. Chicago is one of the most ethnically heterogeneous cities in the U.S. AMERIPEX '86 visitors can experience Chicago's ethnic character as they tour the city's neighborhoods, learning about many cultures from well-trained, multi-lingual guides. A special evening tour will offer opportunities to visit the city's finest ethnic restaurants.

Architectural Tours. These tours will offer a close-up view of Chicago's famous dazzling skyline. Visitors will come to know the work of architectural giants such as Ludwig Mies van der Rohe, Louis Sullivan and Frank Lloyd Wright. A separate tour will visit the Chicago suburb of Oak Park, where visitors will see Wright's home and studio along with some 32 Wright-designed homes.

AMERIPEX '86 visitors can also explore the city on their own. The following review of Chicago's most famous and respected museums is just the beginning of a "don't miss" list of things to see and do.

The Adler Planetarium. One of the world's largest collections of antique stargazing instruments, a navigation display, space photography, Sky Theatre star shows.

The Art Institute of Chicago. Renowned for medieval masterpieces, a stunning French Impressionist collection, plus room after room of art treasures from all periods and cultures. Frequent special exhibits.

Field Museum of Natural History. Halls of animal dioramas, plant models, ethnological displays, Hall of Gems, the Egyptian Hall featuring walk-through tombs, Hall of Chinese Jades, special exhibits.

Museum of Science and Industry. Interactive exhibits in this, perhaps the city's most fun museum, uncover the secrets of physics, communications, industry, electronics, agriculture and more.

John G. Shedd Aquarium. Life beneath the sea unfolds in six galleries encompassing 5,000 specimens of aquatic life. The Coral Reef exhibit features divers who talk to visitors as they hand-feed colorful South Sea fish.

Most of these museums, plus many more sights and sounds of Chicago, cluster near the city's downtown lakefront. Most are easily accessible from AMERIPEX '86 by public transportation or by car.

Young People Say Y.E.S. To USPS

Late in 1984, the U.S. Postal Service inaugurated an exciting project for youthful philatelists called Youth Exhibiting Stamps, or Y.E.S. The Y.E.S. project's objective is to introduce young people to stamp collecting and exhibiting as an absorbing and rewarding pastime. Along with the fun and fascination offered by stamp collecting itself, Y.E.S. participants also enjoy taking a project from the concept stage, doing research and creatively assembling their own completed philatelic exhibit.

The deadline for receipt of exhibits by USPS Management Sectional Centers (MSC) was March 31, 1985. Throughout 1985, exhibits will be judged across the nation; winning exhibits will progress from the local MSC level to state and regional competition and finally to the national level.

Six Grand National Winners will be announced by the Postmaster General in conjunction with National Stamp Collecting Month in October. These six will receive all-expense-paid trips with their families to AMERIPEX '86 in Chicago. There, exhibits will be displayed in a special area.

Y.E.S. exhibitors competed at three age levels and entered as either novice or experienced exhibitors. Novice and experienced exhibitors aged 11 and younger prepared four 8½" x 11" album pages for display; all others submitted eight-page exhibits. While the subject area of the exhibits was unrestricted, Y.E.S. entrants were required to center their displays around U.S. or foreign stamps in mint or used condition, or around first day or other covers. Other philatelic materials were not eligible for competition.

As judging progresses this year, Y.E.S. entries will be evaluated according to criteria in five categories. A neat, clean presentation and well-planned format are important, as is the condition and adequacy of the material presented. Exhibits are also judged on their content and originality.

Each Y.E.S. entrant already is a winner. All participants received a participation certificate and philatelic prize. Other prizes will be awarded to state and regional winners, including definitive and commemorative mint sets, stamp albums and collecting kits. However, the most important reward for all the young people competing in the Y.E.S. project may be a solid introduction to stamp collecting, a hobby for life.

Baseball Stamps

Baseball originated in Cooperstown, New York, in 1839.

Babe Ruth holds the all-time record of 60 home runs in a 154 game major league season.

Jackie ... black ... major lea...

...ente was famo... ...o could hit ...of pitch...

In 1869 the first professional baseball team ... organized in Cincinnati.

Santa Claus ...
Designed by John ...

...sledding, building a snowman, skating and decorating a Christmas tree.
Designed by Dolli Tingle.

A New Way to Keep Up With U.S. Commemoratives

Whether your stamp collection is well-established or you're just beginning, it's important to keep up with U.S. commemorative stamp issues. Commemorative stamps can help round out a specialty collection, or they can inspire a collector to explore a new area of concentration. Gathering a good variety of commemoratives also can strengthen a collector's position for trading at shows and other philatelic meetings.

In 1984, the United States Postal Service began a new program designed specifically to help philatelists stay current on U.S. commemorative issues. The program, the U.S. Postal Service Commemorative Stamp Club, can help any collector make sure he or she doesn't miss an issue.

Membership in the U.S. Postal Service Commemorative Stamp Club offers collectors an advance announcement of every U.S. commemorative stamp. A specially-designed Commemorative Stamp Club album can be ordered, and, every other month, members receive stamp album pages for current commemorative issues.

Each album page has space to mount two issues. The pages detail the background behind why the stamp was issued and its date and the place of first issue, along with a history of the stamp. Commemorative Stamp Club members also can elect to have the stamps themselves mailed to them as the commemoratives are issued.

Commemorative stamps were first issued by the United States beginning in 1893 with a series of stamps marking the historic World's Columbian Exposition in Chicago. The 16 Columbian stamps issued that year were not only the first U.S. commemorative stamps, they also were among the first U.S. stamps to feature pictorial matter other than portraits of famous people.

The huge success of the Columbian issue prompted the U.S. Postal Service to continue offering stamps to mark historic occasions. Later, the concept of commemoratives was expanded to include social issues of note as well, such as conservation, employment of the handicapped and the importance of higher education.

Commemorative stamps are printed by the U.S. Postal Service in limited quantities and are offered for sale in local post offices for designated periods of time. They can be obtained after that time from the Philatelic Sales Branch until supplies run out. Once the printed supplies of a commemorative issue are sold out, these stamps enter the realm of buying, selling and trading by philatelists.

The U.S. Postal Service Commemorative Stamp Club makes certain that its members are aware of all commemorative stamps issued; members may then decide to purchase the stamps or not. For more information on the Club, contact the U.S. Postal Service Philatelic Sales Division, Commemorative Stamp Club, Washington, D.C. 20265-9980.

Philatelic Societies

American Air Mail Society
102 Arbor Rd.
Cinnaminson, NJ 08077-3859
Specializes in aerophilately, and periodically presents the Conrath Award to a member of the society in the name of Walter Conrath, one of its founders.

American First Day Cover Society
Mrs. Monte Eiserman
Membership Chairman
14359 Chadbourne
Houston, TX 77079-6611

American Philatelic Society
Box 8000
State College, PA 16803-8000
A full complement of services and resources for the philatelist. Membership offers: American Philatelic Research Library; expertizing service; estate advisory service; translation services; a stamp theft committee which functions as a clearing house for stamp theft information; a speakers' bureau and a monthly journal, "The American Philatelist," sent to all members.

American Society of Philatelic Pages and Panels
1138 Princeton Drive
Richardson, TX 75081-3615

American Stamp Dealer's Association
5 Dakota Dr.
Suite 102
Lake Success, NY 11042-1109
Association of dealers engaged in every facet of philately, with eleven regional chapters nation wide. Sponsors national and local shows, seminars for member and non-member dealers, credit information service, monthly newsletter and ASDA membership directory.

American Topical Association
P.O. Box 630
Johnstown, PA 15907-0630
A service organization concentrating on the specialty of topical collecting. Offers handbooks on specific topics; an exhibition award; *Topical Time*, a bi-monthly publication dealing with topical interest areas; a slide and film loan service; information, translation, biography and sales services; and an heirs' estate service.

Black American Philatelic Society
% Walt Robinson
9101 Taylor Street
Landover, MD 20785-2554
For collectors interested in the study of black Americans on postage stamps.

Bureau Issues Association
4630 Greylock Street
Boulder, CO 80301-4207

Collectors Club, Inc.
22 East 35th Street
New York, NY 10016-3806
Regular services include library and reading rooms, a publication and lectures on philatelic subjects. The group also honors a great American collector annually and actively supports national and international exhibitions.

Council of Philatelic Organizations
P.O. Box COPO
State College, PA 16803-8340
A non-profit organization comprised of more than 200 national, regional and local stamp clubs, organizations, societies and philatelic business firms. The objective of COPO is to promote and encourage the hobby of stamp collecting. Membership is open only to organizations; COPO uses a variety of methods to promote stamp collecting including an on-going publicity campaign, a quarterly newsletter and joint sponsorship (with the USPS) of National Stamp Collecting Month.

Errors, Freaks and Oddities Collectors Club
Box 1125
Falls Church, VA 22041-0125
Includes an exhibit critique service.

Junior Philatelists of America
P.O. Box 15329
San Antonio, TX 78212-8529
Provides an auction department, library service, tape and slide service, stamp identification and translation services. Publishes a bi-monthly, illustrated publication titled the *Philatelic Observer*.

Maximum Card Study Club
Bill Kelleher
Box 375
Bedford, MA 01730-0375

Mobile Post Office Society
5030 Aspen Drive
Omaha, NE 68157-2267
A non-profit organization concentrating on transit markings and the history of postal transit routes. The Society is engaged in documenting and recording transit postal history by publishing books, catalogs and monographs, as well as a semi-monthly journal.

Modern Postal History Association
% Psychology Department
Pace University
Pleasantville, NY 10570-2799

National Association of Precancel Collectors
5121 Park Blvd.
Wildwood, NJ 08260-1454

The Perfins Club
2163 Cumbre Place
El Cajon, CA 92020-1005
Send SASE for information.

Philatelic Foundation
270 Madison Ave.
New York, NY 10016-0656
   A non-profit organization known for its excellent expertization service. The Foundation's broad resources, including extensive reference collections, 5,000-volume library and Expert Committee, provide collectors with comprehensive consumer protection. It also publishes educational information. Slide and cassette programs are available on such subjects as the Pony Express, Provisionals, Confederate Postal History and special programs for beginning collectors.

Plate Block Collector Club
Box 937
Homestead, FL 33090-0937

Plate Number Society
9600 Colesville Rd.
Silver Spring, MD 20901-3144

Postal History Society
Box 20
Bayside, NY 11361-0020

Post Mark Collectors Club
Wilma Hinrichs
4200 SE. Indianola Rd.
Des Moines, IA 50320-1555

Precancel Stamp Society
David A. Coates, Secretary
2500 Wisconsin Avenue, N.W. #829
Washington, D.C. 20007-4561

Souvenir Card Collectors Society
P.O. Box 4155
Tulsa, OK 74159-4155

Souvenir Page & Commemorative Panel Society
1138 Princeton Drive
Richardson, TX 75081-3615

United Postal Stationery Society
Mrs. J. Thomas
Box 48
Redlands, CA 92373-0601

The United States Possessions Philatelic Society
141 Lyford Drive
Tiburon, CA 94920-1652

The Universal Ship Cancellation Society
P.O. Box 13
New Britain, CT 06050-0013
   Specializing in naval ship cancellations.

Catalogs

Brookman Price List of U.S. Stamps
91 South 9th Street
Minneapolis, MN 55402-3295

Catalogue of United States Souvenir Cards
The Washington Press
2 Vreeland Rd.
Florham Park, NJ 07932-1587

First Day Cover Catalogue (U.S.-U.N.)
The Washington Press
2 Vreeland Rd.
Florham Park, NJ 07932-1587

Perfins of the World
9801 Dewey Drive
Garden Grove, CA 92641-1344

Souvenir Pages Price List
(Please send self-addressed stamped envelope to receive current listings.)
Charles D. Simmons
P.O. Box 6238
Buena Park, CA 90622-6238

Noble Official Catalog of United States Bureau Precancels, 64th Edition
P.O. Box 931
Winter Park, FL 32789-0931

Stamps of the World 1982 Catalogue
Stanley Gibbons Publications. Available through dealers only. All the stamps of the world from 1840 to date. Over 1,900 pages feature more than 200,000 stamps (47,900 illustrations) from over 200 issuing countries.

Commemorative Panel Price List
(Please send self-addressed stamped envelope to receive current listings.)
Frank Riolo
P.O. Box 1540
Delray Beach, FL 33447-1540

Fleetwoods Standard First Day Cover Catalog
Unicover Corporation
Cheyenne, WY 82008-0001

Harris Illustrated Postage Stamp Catalog
H.E. Harris & Co., Inc.
Boston, MA 02117-0810

Minkus New World Wide Stamp Catalogue
116 West 32nd Street
New York, NY 10001-3284

American Air Mail Catalogue
American Air Mail Society
Cinnaminson, NJ 08077-3859

Scott Standard Postage Stamp Catalogue
911 South Vandemark Road
Sydney, OH 45367-8959

U.S. Postal Card Catalog, 1980
Box 48
Redlands, CA 92373-0601

Magazines and Newspapers

Linn's Stamp News
Box 29
Sidney, OH 45365-0029

Mekeel's Weekly Stamp News
Box 1660
Portland, ME 04104-1660

Minkus Stamp Journal
41 West 25th Street
New York, NY 10010-2021

Scott's Monthly Stamp Journal
911 South Vandemark Road
Sydney, OH 45367-8959

Stamps
153 Waverly Place
New York, NY 10014-3849

Stamp Collector
Box 10
Albany, OR 97321-0006

Stamp Review
1839 Palmer Ave.
Larchmont, NY 10538-3099

COMMEMORATIVE MINT SETS

Enjoy the Colorful World of U.S. Commemoratives

The ongoing series of U.S. Postal Commemorative Mint Sets make the collecting of commemoratives fun, informative and convenient. Each annual Mint Set contains all the U.S. commemoratives issued for that year in protective mounts that help you display and preserve your collection. Each Set also includes an attractive folder that brings you the background behind the subjects being commemorated.

New collectors will find this an absorbing way to learn both about stamps and the people, places and events chosen for commemoration. Experienced philatelists find that they make an attractive addition to their other collecting efforts. Commemorative Mint Sets are available at your local post office.

1984 Commemorative Mint Set—Includes 31 issues and 43 separate stamps representing all 1984 commemoratives. Of special interest are blocks of four covering the Winter Olympics, Summer Olympics, Orchids and Dogs. Also includes Christmas stamps and new issues in the Black Heritage and American Sports series. $10.25.

1985 Commemorative Mint Set—Consists of all the new commemorative issues, including Abigail Adams, Winter Special Olympics and Rural Electrification Administration. Also with blocks of four of Duck Decoys and Horses. $8.00.

37

Beginning Your First Collection?

It's actually very easy for a new collector to begin enjoying the fun and excitement of stamp collecting. Just stop in your local post office and ask for a U.S. Postal Service Stamp Collecting Kit—an inexpensive and educational way to join the millions of Americans who now enjoy the world's most popular hobby.

With the USPS Kits you can begin collecting some of the most interesting stamps in the world. Each year the Postal Service issues a new Commemorative Stamp Collecting Kit which includes a selection of genuine, colorful stamps; plastic mounts for all 1985 Commemorative issues; and the informative book, *Introduction to Stamp Collecting*.

The 1985 Commemorative Stamp Collecting Kit features 7 stamps commemorating Jerome Kern, Mary McLeod Bethune, Winter Special Olympics and Folk Art (block of four). The 1986 edition will be available early in 1986.

The USPS Stamp Collecting Kits can be purchased at any post office. Still available at certain locations are Stamp Collecting Kits on special topics like space, sports or aviation; you may wish to check with more than one post office in your area.

1984 DEFINITIVE MINT SETS

Receive the Entire Year's Issue

USPS Definitive Mint Sets are the convenient way for collectors to insure they receive every definitive item issued by the USPS in a given year, including all varieties of postal stationery. Begun in 1980, this program has proven to be of increasing importance to philatelists with each successive issue. The exceptional demand for these sets is enhanced by the limited production of only 170,000 for each year.

Each set comes complete with an attractive display album filled with illustrations, photographs and articles providing the historical background of each stamp topic, the stamp designer and the date and place of issue.

The colorful 1984 Definitive Mint Set includes the stamp honoring Harry S. Truman, the colorful 1984 Love stamp, two new entries in the popular Transportation Series, as well as other stamps, postal cards and Postal Service envelopes. $4.00.

The Mint Set for 1984 is now available at the more than 15,000 Post Offices across the nation and at all Philatelic Centers. It can also be ordered by mail from the Postal Service's Philatelic Sales Division, Washington, D.C. 20265-9997.

An Exciting Limited Edition Subscription Service

The U.S. Postal Service Souvenir Page Program provides a colorful and informative way to follow the year's stamp issues. These attractive display pages are printed in a limited edition for every definitive and commemorative U.S. stamp issued in a given year, including airmails, coil pairs and booklet panes.

Each Souvenir Page includes the featured stamp, postmarked with a "First Day of Issue" cancellation and mounted on an 8½" by 10½" page of brightly colored paper. A large black and white enlargement of the stamp is followed by

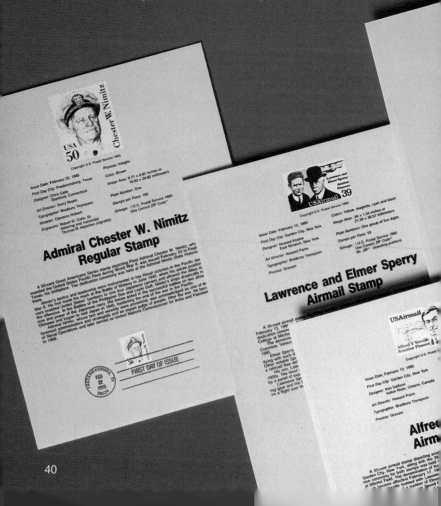

its relevant philatelic specifications and a lively historical narrative about the stamp's subject. All collectors will find the Souvenir Page Program a convenient, informative setting for their U.S. issues.

Increasingly important as philatelic collectibles, Souvenir Pages are available only on an advanced subscription basis and only on a first-come first-served basis. Write now for full details from the U.S. Postal Service, Philatelic Sales Division, Souvenir Pages Subscription Program, Washington, D.C. 20265-9980.

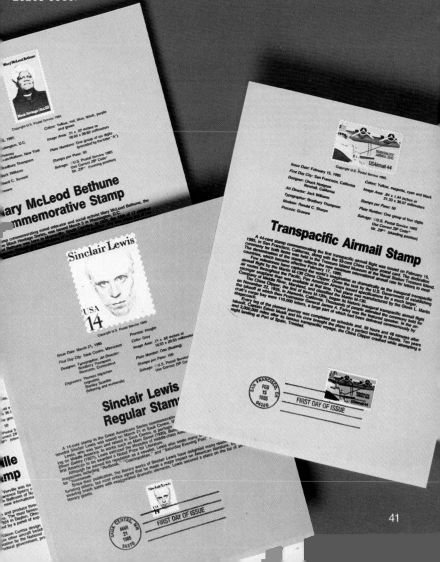

A Treasured Bit of History

Exquisite stamp art, magnificent engravings, lively historical narrative... these are some of the qualities that have made thousands of collectors become regular subscribers to the limited edition USPS American Commemorative Panels series since its inception in 1972.

Each panel is devoted to a separate commemorative stamp and is a work of art in itself, worthy of framing, exhibiting and sharing. A block of four, newly issued, mint condition stamps are mounted on an 8½" by 11¼" panel of heavy, high-quality paper. Then the rich tradition behind the stamp's subject is portrayed in word and picture.

Special intaglio-printed reproductions of historical engravings, many over 100 years old and some reproduced for the first time since their original engraving, illustrate the panel, while carefully researched articles help you share in the fascinating heritage depicted on the stamp. Objects of true workmanship, the American Commemorative Panels are becoming increasingly popular and increasingly valuable.

The Panels are printed in limited editions and are only available on an advanced subscription basis. For full details on subscribing to this unique collection, write the Philatelic Sales Division, Commemorative Panel Program, Washington, D.C. 20265-9993.

Service Offers Superior Panes of Stamps

Panes collectors can now make sure they receive mint condition panes of superior quality. Panes ordered through the Panes Subscription Service are individually selected at the U.S. Bureau of Engraving on the basis of exceptional paper, gum, color and registration quality, as well as exact centering, perforations and marginal markings.

The panes are delivered in safe, attractive acetate mounts. Most importantly, the USPS guarantee allows you to return any panes that do not meet your expectations within 30 days for a full refund.

As a subscriber, you choose the type of service you want: Order a full set of commemoratives, a full set of definitives or both, and choose from one of three levels of service. Advance deposits are for the first six stamp issues—subsequent issues are prebilled at the face value of the stamps.

Service A—Includes one full pane of each stamp issued in your category. Deposit: $60.

Service B—Includes four panes with matching plate block numbers of each stamp issued in your category. Deposit: $240.

Service C—For the exacting collector, includes four panes with four-position matching plate block numbers for each plate block number made available to the Philatelic Sales Division. Deposit: $240.

You may subscribe at any time and receive superior quality panes for a full year from the time your account is opened. For full details about the Panes Subscription Service, write to the Philatelic Sales Division, Washington, D.C. 20265-9997.

1¢ Franklin Types I-IV of 1851-56

5

Bust of **5**

Detail of **7** Type II
Lower scrollwork incomplete (lacks little balls).
Side ornaments are complete.

11

Bust of **5**

Detail of **6** Type Ia
Top ornaments and outer line partly cut away.
Lower scrollwork is complete.

Bust of **5**

Detail of **8** Type III
Outer lines broken in the middle.
Side ornaments are complete.

Detail of **8A** Type IIIa
Outer lines broken top or bottom but not both.

Detail of **11**
THREE CENTS.
Type I. There is an outer frame line at top and bottom.

Bust of **5**

Detail of **5** Type I
Has curved, unbroken lines outside labels.
Scrollwork is complete, forms little balls at bottom.

Detail of **5A** Type Ib
Lower scrollwork is incomplete, the little balls are not so clear.

Bust of **5**

Detail of **9** Type IV
Outer lines recut top, bottom, or both.

Detail of **12**
FIVE CENTS.
Type I. There are projections on all four sides.

12

10¢ Washington Types I-IV of 1855

15

Bust of **15** ↓

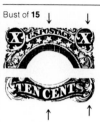

Detail of **13**
Type I. The "shells" at the lower corners are practically complete. → The outer line below the label is very nearly complete. The outer lines are broken above the middle of the top label and the "X" in each upper corner.

Bust of **15** ↓

Detail of **14**
Type II. The design is complete at the top. The outer line at the bottom is broken in the middle. The shells are partly cut away.

Detail of **15**
Type III. The outer lines are broken above the top label and the "X" numerals. The outer line at the bottom and the shells are partly cut away, as in Type II.

Bust of **15** ↓

Detail of **16**
Type IV. The outer lines have been recut at top or bottom or both.
Types I, II, III and IV have complete ornaments at the sides of the stamps and three pearls at each outer edge of the bottom panel.

Bust of **5**

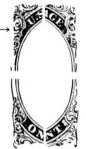

Detail of **24**
ONE CENT FRANKLIN
Type V. Similar to Type III of 1851-56 but with side ornaments partly cut away.

Bust of **11**

Detail of **26**
THREE CENTS WASHINGTON
Type II. The outer frame line has been removed at top and bottom. The side frame lines were recut so as to be continuous from the top to the bottom of the plate.

30A

Detail of **30A**
FIVE CENTS JEFFERSON
Type II. The projections at top and bottom are partly cut away.

Detail of **35**
TEN CENTS WASHINGTON
(Two typical examples).
Type V. Side ornaments slightly cut away. Outer lines complete except over right X.

55   57

Detail of **67**
5¢. A leaflet has been added
to the foliated ornaments at
each corner.

Detail of **64**
3¢. Ornaments at corners have
been enlarged and end in a
small ball.

Issue of 1861

Detail of **55**

Detail of **57**

56   58   68   69

63   67

Detail of **56**

Detail of **68**
10¢. A heavy curved line has
been cut below the stars and an
outer line has been added
to the ornaments above them.

Detail of **58**

Detail of **69**
12¢. Ovals and scrolls have
been added to the corners.

Issue of 1861-62

Detail of **63**
1¢. A dash has been added
under the tip of the ornament
at right of the numeral in upper
left corner.

62   64

72

Detail of **62**

Detail of **72**
90¢. Parallel lines from an angle above the ribbon with "U.S. Postage"; between these lines a row of dashes has been added and a point of color to the apex of the lower pair.

Detail of **134**

Detail of **138**

135   **136**   **139**   **140**

118

Detail of **118**
FIFTEEN CENTS.
Type I. Picture unframed.

Detail of **135**

Detail of **139**

Detail of **119**
Type II. Picture framed.
Type III. Same as Type I but without fringe of brown shading lines around central vignette.

Detail of **136**

Issue of 1870-71:
Printed by the National Bank Note Company.
Issued without secret marks (see Nos. 156-163).

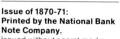
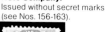

137   **138**   **141**

134

Detail of **137**

Detail of **141**

1873: Printed by the Continental Bank Note Co.

Designs of the 1870-71 Issue with secret marks on the values from 1¢ to 15¢ as described and illustrated below.

159   160

Detail of **159**
6¢. The first four vertical lines of the shading in the lower part of the left ribbon have been strengthened.

Detail of **160**
7¢. Two small semi-circles are drawn around the ends of the lines which outline the ball in the lower right hand corner.

161   162

Detail of **161**
10¢. There is a small semi-circle in the scroll, at the right end of the upper label.

Detail of **162**
12¢. The balls of the figure "2" are crescent shaped.

163

Detail of **163**
15¢. In the lower part of the triangle in the upper left corner two lines have been made heavier forming a "V". This mark can be found on some of the Continental and American (1879) printings, but not all stamps show it.
Secret marks were added to the dies of the 24¢, 30¢ and 90¢ but new plates were not made from them. The various printings of these stamps can be distinguished only by the shades and paper.

206   207

Detail of **206**
1¢. Upper vertical lines have been deepened, creating a solid effect in parts of background. Upper arabesques have lines of shading.

Detail of **207**
3¢. Shading at sides of central oval is half its previous width. A short horizontal dash has been cut below the "TS" of "CENTS".

208   209

Detail of **208**
6¢. Has three vertical lines instead of four between the edge of the panel and the outside of the stamp.

Detail of **209**
10¢. Has four vertical lines instead of five between left side of oval and edge of the shield. Horizontal lines in lower part of background have been strengthened.

2¢ Washington
Types I-III of 1894

Triangle of **248-250**
Type I. Horizontal lines of uniform thickness run across the triangle.

251

Triangle of **251**
Type II. Horizontal lines cross the triangle, but are thinner within than without.

Triangle of **252**
Type III. The horizontal lines do not cross the double frame lines of the triangle.

$1 Perry
Types of 1894

261

 ←

Detail of **261**
Type I. The circles enclosing $1 are broken.

 ←

Detail of **261A**
Type II. The circles enclosing $1 are complete.

282C

 ←

Detail of **282C**
TEN CENTS
Type I. The tips of the foliate ornaments do not impinge on the white curved line below "TEN CENTS."

283

 ←

Detail of **283**
Type II. The lips of the ornaments break the curved line below the "E" of "TEN" and the "T" of "CENTS."

Watermark **191**

USPS
Watermark **190**

USPS
Watermark **191**

1847-1875

1

2

3

4

5

11

12

15

17

30A

37

39

	Un	U
Issues of 1847 to 1894 are Unwatermarked, Issue of 1847, Imperf.		
1	5¢ Benjamin		
	Franklin, July 1	4,500.00	750.00
2	10¢ George		
	Washington,		
	July 1	18,500.00	2,200.00
Issue of 1875, Reproductions of 1 & 2		
3	5¢ Franklin	1,500.00	—
4	10¢ Washington	1,850.00	—

Reproductions. The letters R. W. H. & E. at the bottom of each stamp are less distinct on the reproductions than on the originals.

5¢. On the original the left side of the white shirt frill touches the oval on a level with the top of the "F" of "Five." On the reproduction it touches the oval about on a level with the top of the figure "5."

10¢. On the reproduction, line of coat at left points to right of "X" and line of coat at right points to center of "S" of CENTS. On the original, line of coat points to "T" of TEN and between "T" and "S" of CENTS.

On the reproduction the eyes have a sleepy look, the line of the mouth is straighter, and in the curl of hair near the left cheek is a strong black dot, while the original has only a faint one.

	Issue of 1851-56, Imperf.		
5	1¢ Franklin, type I	100,000.00	21,500.00
5A	1¢ Same, type Ib	11,500.00	4,000.00
	Nos. 6-9: Franklin (5)		
6	1¢ dark blue,		
	type Ia	14,500.00	4,750.00
7	1¢ blue, type II	450.00	85.00
8	1¢ blue, type III	4,750.00	1,350,00
8A	1¢ pale blue,		
	type IIIA	1,700.00	575.00
9	1¢ blue, type IV	300.00	75.00
10	3¢ orange brown Washington,		
	type I (11)	1,200.00	65.00
11	3¢ Washington, type I	130.00	7.00

		Un	U
12	5¢ Jefferson, type I	9,500.00	1,350.00
13	10¢ green Washington,		
	type I (15)	8,000.00	700.00
14	10¢ green, type II (15)	1,600.00	275.00
15	10¢ Washington, type III	1,650.00	285.00
16	10¢ green, type IV (15)	10,000.00	1,450.00
17	12¢ Washington	1,850.00	250.00

		Un	U
Issue of 1857-61, Perf. 15			
Nos. 18-24: Franklin (5)			
18	1¢ blue, type I	675.00	350.00
19	1¢ blue, type Ia	9,000.00	2,250.00
20	1¢ blue, type II	425.00	135.00
21	1¢ blue, type III	3,750.00	1,050.00
22	1¢ blue, type IIIa	600.00	210.00
23	1¢ blue, type IV	1,650.00	275.00
24	1¢ blue, type V	120.00	22.50

		Un	U
Nos. 25-26: Washington (11)			
25	3¢ rose, type I	650.00	27.50
26	3¢ dull red, type II	50.00	2.75
Nos. 27-29: Jefferson (12)			
27	5¢ brick red, type I	7,000.00	950.00
28	5¢ red brown, type I	1,350.00	275.00
28A	5¢ Indian red, type I	8,500.00	1,300.00
29	5¢ brown, type I	700.00	225.00
30	5¢ orange brown		
	Jefferson, type II (30A)	750.00	900.00
30A	5¢ Jefferson, type II	450.00	170.00
Nos 31-35: Washington (15)			
31	10¢ green type I	4,850.00	525.00
32	10¢ green, type II	1,550.00	160.00
33	10¢ green, type III	1,650.00	170.00
34	10¢ green, type IV	13,000.00	1,450.00
35	10¢ green type V	175.00	57.50
36	12¢ black Washington		
	(17)	325.00	75.00
37	24¢ Washington	650.00	200.00
38	30¢ Franklin	800.00	285.00
39	90¢ Washington	1,450.00	2,750.00
	90¢ Same, with pen cancel	—	1,000.00

Note: Beware of forged cancellations of No. 39. Genuine cancellations are rare.

	1875: Government Reprints, Perf. 12, White Paper, Without Gum		
40	1¢ bright blue Franklin (5)	550.00	—
41	3¢ scarlet Washington (11)	2,850.00	—
42	5¢ orange brown		
	Jefferson (30A)	950.00	—
43	10¢ blue green		
	Washington (15)	2,250.00	—

		Un	U
1875 continued			
44	12¢ greenish black		
	Washington (17)	2,600.00	—
45	24¢ blackish violet		
	Washington (37)	2,850.00	—
46	30¢ yel. org. Franklin		
	(38)	2,850.00	—
47	90¢ deep blue		
	Washington (39)	4,250.00	—
Issue of 1861, Perf. 12			

Following the outbreak of the Civil War, the U.S. Government demonetized all previous issues.

		Un	U
55	1¢ Franklin	16,500.00	—
56	3¢ Washington	700.00	—
57	5¢ brown Jefferson	12,000.00	—
58	10¢ Washington	5,000.00	—
59	12¢ Washington	35,000.00	—
60	24¢ dk. vio. Washington		
	(70)	5,500.00	—
61	30¢ red org. Franklin		
	(71)	16,000.00	—
62	90¢ dull blue		
	Washington (72)	20,000.00	—
62B	10¢ dark green		
	Washington (58)	5,000.00	450.00

Nos. 55-62 were not used for postage and do not exist in a cancelled state. The paper they were printed on is thin and semi-transparent, that of the following issues is more opaque.

		Un	U
Issue of 1861-62, Perf. 12			
63	1¢ Franklin	100.00	17.50
64	3¢ Washington	3,250.00	250.00
65	3¢ rose Washington (64)	45.00	1.10
66	3¢ lake Washington (64)	1,500.00	—
67	5¢ Jefferson	4,000.00	375.00
68	10¢ Washington	235.00	25.00
69	12¢ Washington	425.00	50.00
70	24¢ Washington	475.00	67.50
71	30¢ Franklin	450.00	60.00
72	90¢ Washington	1,200.00	250.00
Issue of 1861-66, Perf. 12			
73	2¢ Andrew Jackson		
	("Black Jack")	110.00	20.00

		Un	U
74	3¢ scarlet Washington		
	(64)	4,000.00	—
75	5¢ red brown Jefferson		
	(67)	1,200.00	190.00
76	5¢ brn. Jefferson (67)	275.00	47.50
77	15¢ Abraham Lincoln	450.00	60.00
78	24¢ lilac Washington (70)	250.00	47.50

No. 74 was not regularly issued.

Grills on U.S. Stamps

Between 1867 and 1870, postage stamps were embossed with grills to prevent people from re-using cancelled stamps. The pyramid-shaped grills absorbed cancellation ink, making it virtually impossible to remove a postmark chemically.

		Un	U
Issue of 1867, With Grills, Perf. 12			
Grills A, B, C: Points Up			
A. Grill Covers Entire Stamp			
79	3¢ rose Washington		
	(64)	1,650.00	425.00
80	5¢ brn. Jefferson (67)	40,000.00	—
81	30¢ org. Franklin (71)	—	32,500.00
B. Grill about 18x15 mm.			
82	3¢ rose Washington (64)	—	35,000.00
C. Grill about 13x16 mm.			
83	3¢ rose Washington (64)	1,500.00	350.00
Grills, D, Z, E, F: Points Down			
D. Grill about 12x14 mm.			
84	2¢ blk. Jackson (73)	2,500.00	800.00
85	3¢ rose Washington (64)	1,150.00	350.00
Z. Grill about 11x14 mm.			
85A	1¢ bl. Franklin (63)	—	110,000.00
85B	2¢ blk. Jackson (73)	1,000.00	300.00
85C	3¢ rose Washington (64)	2,750.00	825.00
85D	10¢ green Washington		
	(68)	—	23,500.00
85E	12¢ black Washington		
	(69)	1,450.00	500.00
85F	15¢ blk. Lincoln (77)	—	35,000.00
E. Grill about 11x13 mm.			
86	1¢ blue Franklin (63)	650.00	225.00
87	2¢ black Jackson (73)	300.00	65.00
88	3¢ rose Washington (64)	210.00	9.50
89	10¢ grn. Washington (68)	1,000.00	160.00
90	12¢ blk. Washington (69)	1,200.00	175.00

55   56   57   58   59

62   63   64   67   68   69

2   113   114   115   116

7   118   120   121   122

4   135   136   137   138

1867 continued		Un	U
91	15¢ black Lincoln (77)	2,500.00	425.00
	F. Grill about 9x13 mm.		
92	1¢ blue Franklin (63)	265.00	90.00
93	2¢ black Jackson (73)	110.00	22.50
94	3¢ red Washington (64)	75.00	2.50
95	5¢ brown Jefferson (67)	750.00	200.00
96	10¢ yellow green		
	Washington (68)	550.00	90.00
97	12¢ black Washington		
	(69)	600.00	95.00
98	15¢ black Lincoln (77)	600.00	100.00
99	24¢ gray lilac		
	Washington (70)	1,150.00	425.00
100	30¢ orange Franklin (71)	1,300.00	350.00
101	90¢ blue Washington		
	(72)	3,750.00	900.00

**Reissues of 1861-66 in 1875,
Without Grill, Perf. 12**

102	1¢ blue Franklin (63)	*475.00*	*650.00*
103	2¢ black Jackson (73)	*2,500.00*	*3,250.00*
104	3¢ brown red		
	Washington (64)	*3,000.00*	*4,000.00*
105	5¢ brown Jefferson (67)	*1,600.00*	*1,850.00*
106	10¢ grn. Washington (68)	*2,100.00*	*2,850.00*
107	12¢ blk. Washington (69)	*3,000.00*	*3,750.00*
108	15¢ black Lincoln (77)	*3,000.00*	*4,000.00*
109	24¢ deep violet		
	Washington (70)	*4,000.00*	*5,500.00*
110	30¢ brownish orange		
	Franklin (71)	*4,250.00*	*7,000.00*
111	90¢ blue Washington (72)	*5,750.00*	*14,000.00*

**Issue of 1869, With Grill Measuring
9½x9 mm., Perf. 12**

112	1¢ Franklin	225.00	60.00
113	2¢ Post Horse & Rider	160.00	25.00
114	3¢ Locomotive	135.00	5.50
115	6¢ Washington	775.00	85.00
116	10¢ Shield and Eagle	850.00	95.00
117	12¢ S.S. Adriatic	750.00	85.00
118	15¢ Columbus		
	Landing, type I	1,750.00	235.00
119	15¢ brown and blue		
	Columbus Landing,		
	type II (118)	850.00	115.00

		Un	U
119b	Center		
	inverted	*130,000.00*	*17,000.00*
120	24¢ Declaration of		
	Independence	2,500.00	500.00
120b	Center		
	inverted	*100,000.00*	*16,500.00*
121	30¢ Shield, Eagle		
	and Flags	2,250.00	250.00
121b	Flags inverted	115,000.00	*45,000.00*
122	90¢ Lincoln	8,000.00	1,250.00

**Reissues of 1869 in 1875, Without
Grill, Hard White Paper, Perf. 12**

123	1¢ Buff (112)	325.00	225.00
124	2¢ brown (113)	375.00	325.00
125	3¢ blue (114)	3,000.00	1,400.00
126	6¢ blue (115)	850.00	500.00
127	10¢ yellow (116)	1,400.00	1,000.00
128	12¢ green (117)	1,500.00	1,000.00
129	15¢ brown and blue		
	Columbus Landing,		
	type III (118)	1,300.00	500.00
130	24¢ grn. & vio. (120)	1,250.00	500.00
131	30¢ bl. & car. (121)	1,750.00	1,000.00
132	90¢ car. & blk. (122)	5,500.00	*7,000.00*

**Reissues of 1869 in 1880, Soft,
Porous Paper, Perf. 12**

133	1¢ buff (112)	200.00	135.00

**Issue of 1870-71, With Grill, White Wove
Paper, Perf. 12**

134	1¢ Franklin	450.00	50.00
135	2¢ Jackson	300.00	30.00
136	3¢ Washington	250.00	9.50
137	6¢ Lincoln	1,500.00	250.00
138	7¢ Edwin M. Stanton	1,000.00	225.00
139	10¢ Jefferson	1,350.00	375.00
140	12¢ Henry Clay	*11,500.00*	1,500.00
141	15¢ Daniel Webster	1,650.00	675.00
142	24¢ General Winfield		
	Scott	—	*10,500.00*

It is generally accepted as fact that the
Continental Bank Note Co. printed and delivered
a quantity of 24¢ stamps. They are impossible to
distinguish from those printed by the National
Bank Note Co.

	Un	U
1870-71 continued		
143 30¢ Alexander		
Hamilton	3,750.00	800.00
144 90¢ Commodore Perry	5,000.00	700.00
Without Grill, White Wove Paper, Perf. 12		
145 1¢ ultra. Franklin (134)	145.00	6.50
146 2¢ red brn. Jackson		
(135)	45.00	4.50
147 3¢ green Washington		
(136)	90.00	.50
148 6¢ carmine Lincoln (137)	185.00	12.00
149 7¢ verm. Stanton (138)	300.00	50.00
150 10¢ brown Jefferson (139)	185.00	12.00
151 12¢ dull violet Clay (140)	475.00	50.00
152 15¢ bright orange Webster		
(141)	450.00	50.00
153 24¢ purple W. Scott (142)	525.00	75.00
154 30¢ black Hamilton (143)	900.00	80.00
155 90¢ carmine Perry (144)	1,100.00	150.00
Issue of 1873, Without Grill, Perf. 12, White Wove Paper, Thin to Thick		
156 1¢ Franklin	45.00	1.75
157 2¢ Jackson	130.00	7.00
158 3¢ Washington	35.00	.15
159 6¢ Lincoln	175.00	8.00
160 7¢ Stanton	375.00	55.00
161 10¢ Jefferson	175.00	9.00
162 12¢ Clay	550.00	60.00
163 15¢ Webster	500.00	45.00
165 30¢ Hamilton (143)	500.00	45.00
166 90¢ Perry (144)	1,150.00	170.00
Issue of 1875, Special Printing, Hard, White Wove Paper, Without Gum		
167 1¢ ultra. Franklin (156)	6,000.00	—
168 2¢ dark brown		
Jackson (157)	3,000.00	—
169 3¢ blue green		
Washington (158)	8,500.00	—
170 6¢ dull rose Lincoln		
(159)	7,500.00	—
171 7¢ reddish vermilion		
Stanton (160)	1,850.00	—
172 10¢ pale brown		
Jefferson (161)	6,500.00	—

	Un	U
173 12¢ dark violet Clay		
(162)	2,500.00	—
174 15¢ bright orange		
Webster (163)	7,000.00	—
175 24¢ dull purple		
W. Scott (142)	1,650.00	—
176 30¢ greenish black		
Hamilton (143)	6,500.00	—
177 90¢ violet car. Perry		
(144)	6,500.00	—
Although perforated, these stamps were usually cut apart with scissors. As a result, the perforations are often much mutilated and the design is frequently damaged.		
Yellowish Wove Paper		
178 2¢ vermilion Jackson		
(157), June 21	125.00	4.50
179 5¢ Zachary Taylor,		
June 21	150.00	8.00
Special Printing, Hard, White Wove Paper, Without Gum		
180 2¢ carmine verm.		
Jackson (157)	17,000.00	—
181 5¢ bright blue Taylor		
(179)	32,500.00	—
Issue of 1879. Printed by the American Bank Note Company. Soft, Porous Paper Varying from Thin to Thick.		
182 1¢ dark ultramarine		
Franklin (156)	90.00	1.20
183 2¢ vermilion Jackson		
(157)	45.00	1.20
184 3¢ green Washington		
(158)	40.00	.10
185 5¢ blue Taylor (179)	190.00	7.50
186 6¢ pink Lincoln (159)	400.00	10.00
187 10¢ brown Jefferson (139)		
(no secret mark)	650.00	13.00
188 10¢ brown Jefferson (161)		
(with secret mark)	375.00	14.00
189 15¢ red orange		
Webster (163)	150.00	14.00
190 30¢ full black Hamilton		
(143)	450.00	25.00
191 90¢ carmine Perry (144)	1,000.00	140.00

43   144   156   157   158   159

60   161   162   163   179

Watermark 191

205 206 207 208 209

210 211 212 219 219D

221 222 223 224 225 226

15 30 90

	Un	U
Issue of 1880, Special Printing, Soft, Porous Paper, Without Gum		
192 1¢ dark ultramarine		
Franklin (156)	8,500.00	—
193 2¢ black brown		
Jackson (157)	5,000.00	—
194 3¢ blue green		
Washington (158)	12,500.00	—
195 6¢ dull rose Lincoln		
(159)	8,750.00	—
196 7¢ scarlet vermilion		
Stanton (160)	2,000.00	—
197 10¢ deep brown		
Jefferson (161)	8,000.00	—
198 12¢ blackish purple		
Clay (162)	4,000.00	—
199 15¢ orange Webster		
(163)	7,500.00	—
200 24¢ dark violet		
W. Scott (142)	2,500.00	—
201 30¢ greenish black		
Hamilton (143)	6,500.00	—
202 90¢ dull car. Perry (144)	6,500.00	—
203 2¢ scarlet vermilion		
Jackson (157)	16,000.00	—
204 5¢ deep blue Taylor		
(179)	27,500.00	—
Issue of 1882		
205 5¢ Garfield, Apr. 10	90.00	4.00
Special Printing. Soft, Porous Paper, Without Gum		
205C 5¢ gray brown (205)	16,500.00	—
Issue of 1881-82, Designs of 1873 Re-engraved.		
206 1¢ Franklin	30.00	.40
207 3¢ Washington	35.00	.12
208 6¢ Lincoln	210.00	45.00
209 10¢ Jefferson	67.50	2.25
Issue of 1883		
210 2¢ Washington, Oct. 1	28.50	.08
211 4¢ Jackson, Oct. 1	130.00	7.50
Special Printing. Soft, Porous Paper.		
211B 2¢ pale red brown		
Washington (210)	700.00	—

	Un	U
211D 4¢ deep blue green		
Jackson (211) no gum	13,000.00	—
Issue of 1887		
212 1¢ Franklin	45.00	.65
213 2¢ green Washington		
(210)	20.00	.08
214 3¢ vermilion		
Washington (207)	42.50	35.00
Issue of 1888, Perf. 12		
215 4¢ carmine Jackson		
(211)	130.00	10.00
216 5¢ indigo Garfield (205)	110.00	6.00
217 30¢ orange brown		
Hamilton (143)	325.00	70.00
218 90$p07¢ purple Perry(144)		700.00
130.00		
Issue of 1890-93, Perf. 12		
219 1¢ Franklin	18.50	.10
219D 2¢ Washington	150.00	.45
220 2¢ carmine (219D)	16.50	.05
1890-93 continued		
221 3¢ Jackson	50.00	4.50
222 4¢ Lincoln	50.00	1.50
223 5¢ Ulysses S. Grant	50.00	1.50
224 6¢ Garfield	50.00	15.00
225 8¢ William T. Sherman	35.00	8.50
226 10¢ Webster	90.00	1.75
227 15¢ Clay	140.00	15.00
228 30¢ Jefferson	210.00	18.50
229 90¢ Perry	350.00	90.00

	1893 continued	Un	U	PB/LP	#	FDC	Q
	Columbian Exposition Issue, 1893, Perf. 12						
230	1¢ Columbus Sights Land	25.00	.30	450.00	(6)	*2,750.00*	449,195,550
231	2¢ Landing of Columbus	22.50	.06	400.00	(6)	*2,100.00*	1,464,588,750
232	3¢ The Santa Maria	45.00	15.00	750.00	(6)	*6,000.00*	11,501,250
233	4¢ Fleet of Columbus ultramarine	65.00	6.00	1,100.00	(6)	*6,000.00*	19,181,550
233a	4¢ blue (error) (233)	*6,500.00*	*2,500.00*				
234	5¢ Columbus Seeking Aid	75.00	7.00	1,500.00	(6)	*6,250.00*	35,248,250
235	6¢ Columbus at Barcelona	65.00	20.00	1,200.00	(6)	*6,750.00*	4,707,550
236	8¢ Columbus Restored to Favor	45.00	8.00	750.00	(6)		10,656,550
237	10¢ Columbus Presenting Indians	115.00	6.50	3,250.00	(6)	*7,500.00*	16,516,950
238	15¢ Columbus Announcing						
	His Discovery	200.00	65.00	*5,250.00*	(6)		1,576,950
239	30¢ Columbus at La Rabida	300.00	90.00	*8,000.00*	(6)		617,250
240	50¢ Recall of Columbus	350.00	140.00	*11,000.00*	(6)		243,750
241	$1 Isabella Pledging Her Jewels	1,000.00	550.00	*22,000.00*	(6)		55,050
242	$2 Columbus in Chains	1,150.00	500.00	*23,500.00*	(6)	*14,000.00*	45,550
243	$3 Columbus Describing His						
	Third Voyage	2,400.00	1,000.00	*50,000.00*	(6)		27,650
244	$4 Isabella and Columbus	3,250.00	1,400.00	*100,000.00*	(6)		26,350
245	$5 Portrait of Columbus	3,500.00	1,650.00	*110,000.00*	(6)		27,350

The SSSS

The Columbian Exposition issue of 1893 (#230-245) gained fame as a "first" in many respects. It was the first series of commemorative stamps issued by the United States, it included higher face value stamps than previous issues, it contained more denominations, and it was issued in greater numbers than any other series.

When the stamps were issued, there was an uproar among stamp collectors. This series of stamps, with a face value of $16.34, was probably two or three times the average weekly salary of most Americans. Letters to the editor of stamp magazines were vehement in their denunciation of the Post Office for daring to issue so many stamps with high values. Editorials predicted that this would be the end of philately. Petitions were signed by collectors vowing that they would not buy this series of stamps.

A new stamp society was born during this period, the Society for the Suppression of Speculative Stamps (SSSS). The group had tremendous acceptance for a short period of time, then quietly passed into oblivion. Today, the set of Columbian Exposition stamps is eagerly sought after, and brings high prices at stamp auctions. An interesting comparison would be to add up the current catalog value of the series and then compare this figure to the $16.34 original cost of the stamps. Christopher Columbus left his mark on stamp collectors, as well as historians.

1893

230

231

232

233

234

235

236

237

238

239

240

241

242

243

244

245

246

251

253

254

255

256

257

258

259

260

261

262

263

		Un	U	PB/LP	#	FDC		Q

Bureau Issues
Starting in 1894, the Bureau of Engraving and Printing at Washington has produced all U.S. postage stamps except Nos. 909-921 (Overrun Countries), 1335 (Eakins painting), 1355 (Disney), 1410-1413 (Anti-Pollution), 1414-1418 (Christmas, 1970), 1789 (John Paul Jones), 1804 (Benjamin Banneker), 1825 (Veterans Administration), 1833 (American Education), 2023 (Francis of Assisi), 2038 (Joseph Priestley), 2065 (Martin Luther), 2066 (Alaska Statehood) and 2080 (Hawaii Statehood).

Issue of 1894, Perf. 12, Unwmkd.

		Un	U	PB/LP	#
246	1¢ Franklin	21.00	3.00	325.00	(6)
247	1¢ blue Franklin (246)	52.50	1.25	650.00	(6)
248	2¢ Washington, type I	17.50	2.00	225.00	(6)
	Nos. 249-252; Washington (251)				
249	2¢ carmine lake, type I	125.00	1.35	1,250.00	(6)
250	2¢ carmine, type I	21.00	.25	325.00	(6)
251	2¢ carmine, type II	165.00	2.50	2,500.00	(6)
252	2¢ carmine, type III	85.00	3.25	1,200.00	(6)
253	3¢ Jackson	80.00	6.25	1,000.00	(6)
254	4¢ Lincoln	90.00	2.50	1,250.00	(6)
255	5¢ Grant	75.00	3.50	875.00	(6)
256	6¢ Garfield	140.00	14.00	1,600.00	(6)
257	8¢ Sherman	100.00	10.00	1,000.00	(6)
258	10¢ Webster	175.00	6.50	2,750.00	(6)
259	15¢ Clay	250.00	45.00	4,250.00	(6)
260	50¢ Jefferson	350.00	75.00	7,000.00	(6)
261	$1 Commodore Perry, type I	900.00	250.00	*16,500.00*	(6)
261A	$1 black Perry, type II (261)	1,850.00	475.00	*27,500.00*	(6)
262	$2 James Madison	2,250.00	600.00	*40,000.00*	(6)
263	$5 John Marshall	3,500.00	1,050.00	—	(6)
	Issue of 1895, Perf. 12, Wmkd. 191				
264	1¢ blue Franklin (264)	6.00	.10	185.00	(6)
	Nos. 265-267; Washington (251)				
265	2¢ carmine, type I	25.00	.65	375.00	(6)
266	2¢ carmine, type II	22.50	2.50	350.00	(6)
267	2¢ carmine, type III	4.50	.05	125.00	(6)
268	3¢ purple Jackson (253)	32.50	1.00	650.00	(6)
269	4¢ dk. brown Lincoln (254)	32.50	1.10	650.00	(6)
270	5¢ chocolate Grant (255)	32.50	1.75	650.00	(6)
271	6¢ dull brn. Garfield (256)	65.00	3.50	1,250.00	(6)
272	8¢ vio. brn. Sherman (257)	35.00	1.00	700.00	(6)
273	10¢ dk. green Webster (258)	50.00	1.20	1,300.00	(6)
274	15¢ dark blue Clay (259)	165.00	8.25	3,500.00	(6)
275	50¢ orange Jefferson (260)	250.00	20.00	6,750.00	(6)
276	$1 black Perry, type I (261)	575.00	65.00	*11,500.00*	(6)
276A	$1 blk. Perry, type II (261)	1,250.00	125.00	*23,500.00*	(6)
277	$2 brt. blue Madison (262)	950.00	275.00	*21,000.00*	(6)
278	$5 dk. grn. Marshall (263)	2,000.00	400.00	*60,000.00*	(6)

	Issue of 1898, Perf. 12	Un	U	PB/LP	#	FDC	Q
279	1¢ dp. green Franklin (246)	10.00	.06	175.00	(6)		
279B	2¢ red Washington, type III (251)	9.00	.05	175.00	(6)		
280	4¢ rose brn. Lincoln (254)	30.00	.70	600.00	(6)		
281	5¢ dark blue Grant (255)	35.00	.65	700.00	(6)		
282	6¢ lake Garfield (256)	45.00	2.00	1,100.00	(6)		
282C	10¢ Webster, type I	160.00	2.00	3,000.00	(6)		
283	10¢ Webster, type II	90.00	1.75	1,700.00	(6)		
284	15¢ olive green Clay (259)	120.00	6.75	2,500.00	(6)		
	Trans-Mississippi Exposition Issue, June 17, Perf. 12						
285	1¢ Marquette on the Mississippi	27.50	5.50	240.00	(4)	5,250.00	70,993,400
286	2¢ Farming in the West	25.00	1.50	225.00	(4)	4,500.00	159,720,800
287	4¢ Indian Hunting Buffalo	140.00	22.50	1,250.00	(4)		4,924,500
288	5¢ Fremont on the Rocky Mts.	120.00	20.00	1,150.00	(4)	5,500.00	7,694,180
289	8¢ Troops Guarding Train	170.00	40.00	2,000.00	(4)	8,000.00	2,927,200
290	10¢ Hardships of Emigration	190.00	20.00	2,500.00	(4)		4,629,760
291	50¢ Western Mining Prospector	725.00	165.00	16,000.00	(4)	9,250.00	530,400
292	$1 Western Cattle in Storm	1,750.00	625.00	45,000.00	(4)		56,900
293	$2 Mississippi River Bridge						
	at St. Louis	2,650.00	875.00	90,000.00	(4)		56,200
	Pan-American Exposition Issue, 1901, May 1, Wmkd. 191						
294	1¢ Great Lakes Steamer	22.50	4.00	300.00	(6)	3,500.00	91,401,500
294a	Center inverted	11,000.00	3,000.00	48,500.00	(3)		
295	2¢ An Early Locomotive	22.50	1.10	300.00	(6)	3,000.00	209,759,700
295a	Center inverted	50,000.00	12,500.00				
296	4¢ Closed Coach Automobile	110.00	20.00	3,000.00	(6)	4,250.00	5,737,100
296a	Center inverted	14,000.00	—	75,000.00	(4)		
297	5¢ Bridge at Niagara Falls	125.00	20.00	3,250.00	(6)	4,500.00	7,201,300
298	8¢ Sault Ste. Marie Canal Locks	150.00	75.00	5,500.00	(6)		4,921,700
299	10¢ American Line Steamship	225.00	35.00	8,250.00	(6)		5,043,700

Upside Down

An upside down stamp is made during the stamp production process and is usually created by human error or equipment malfunction. Of the six stamps in the Pan American series (#294-299), three exist with inverted centers. All three stamps have the frames inverted in relation to the picture.

The 1-cent denomination pictures the one-funneled side-wheeler ship, City of Alpena, *then owned by the Detroit & Cleveland Navigation Company. It is estimated that 700 of the frame errors are in collectors' hands. The 2-cent shows a New York Central and Hudson River Railroad train. According to the Smithsonian Institution, 155 unused and three used examples of this invert exist.*

The 4-cent features a battery-powered type of electric automobile used as a bus by the B & O Railroad to carry passengers. Estimates are that 106 of this inverted center are in circulation.

82C 283 285 286

7 288 289

0 291 292

300   301   302   303   304

305   306   307   308   309   310

311   312   313   319

	Issue of 1902-03, Perf. 12, Wmkd. 191	Un	U	PB/LP	#	FDC	Q
300	1¢ Franklin, 1903	10.00	.05	185.00	(6)		
301	2¢ Washington, 1903	12.50	.05	200.00	(6)	2,750.00	
302	3¢ Jackson, 1903	50.00	3.00	1,000.00	(6)		
303	4¢ Grant, 1903	50.00	1.00	1,000.00	(6)		
304	5¢ Lincoln, 1903	55.00	1.00	1,150.00	(6)		
305	6¢ Garfield, 1903	60.00	2.25	1,150.00	(6)		
306	8¢ Martha Washington, 1902	35.00	2.00	750.00	(6)		
307	10¢ Webster, 1903	65.00	1.50	1,300.00	(6)		
308	13¢ Benjamin Harrison, 1902	35.00	8.50	700.00	(6)		
309	15¢ Clay, 1903	140.00	6.00	4,000.00	(6)		
310	50¢ Jefferson, 1903	450.00	25.00	8,500.00	(6)		
311	$1 David G. Farragut, 1903	800.00	60.00	18,500.00	(6)		
312	$2 Madison, 1903	1,050.00	190.00	27,500.00	(6)		
313	$5 Marshall, 1903	2,750.00	625.00	70,000.00	(6)		

For listings of 312 and 313 with Perf. 10, see Nos. 479 and 480.

	Issues of 1906-08, Imperf.						
314	1¢ blue green Franklin (300),-06	30.00	21.00	300.00	(6)		
314A	4¢ brown Grant (303), 1908	17,500.00	9,000.00				
315	5¢ blue Lincoln (304), 1908	575.00	275.00	5,750.00	(6)		

No. 314A was issued imperforate, but all copies were privately perforated with large oblong perforations at the sides. (Schermack type III).

	Coil Stamps, Perf. 12 Horizontally						
316	1¢ blue green pair						
	Franklin (300), 1908	22,500.00		55,000.00			
317	5¢ blue pair Lincoln (304),-08	4,500.00		6,750.00			
	Perf. 12 Vertically						
318	1¢ blue green pair Franklin						
	(300), 1908	3,500.00	—	5,250.00			
	Issue of 1903, Perf. 12, Shield-shaped Background						
319	2¢ Washington, Nov. 12	6.00	.05	110.00	(6)		
	Issue of 1906, Nos. 320-322; Washington (319), Imperf.						
320	2¢ carmine, Oct 2	30.00	21.00	325.00	(6)		
	Issue of 1908, Coil Stamps, Perf. 12, Horizontally						
321	2¢ carmine pair	35,000.00	—				
	Perf. 12 Vertically						
322	2¢ carmine pair	4,750.00	—	7,000.00			
	Issue of 1904, Perf. 12, Louisiana Purchase Exposition Issue, Apr. 30						
323	1¢ Robert R. Livingston	27.50	5.00	200.00	(4)	3,500.00	79,779,200
324	2¢ Thomas Jefferson	25.00	1.50	200.00	(4)	3,250.00	192,732,400
325	3¢ James Monroe	85.00	35.00	650.00	(4)	3,750.00	4,542,600
326	5¢ William McKinley	110.00	25.00	800.00	(4)	4,750.00	6,926,700

	1904 continued	Un	U	PB/LP	#	FDC	Q
327	10¢ Map of Louisiana Purchase	200.00	35.00	2,000.00	(4)	*7,000.00*	4,011,200
	Issue of 1907, Perf. 12, Jamestown Exposition Issue						
328	1¢ Captain John Smith	20.00	4.00	325.00	(6)	*3,500.00*	77,728,794
329	2¢ Founding of Jamestown	27.50	3.00	450.00	(6)	*2,750.00*	149,497,994
330	5¢ Pocahontas	125.00	30.00	3,250.00	(6)		7,980,594
	Regular Issues of 1908-09, Perf. 12, Wmkd. 191						
331	1¢ Franklin, 1908	8.00	.05	90.00	(6)		
331a	Booklet pane of 6	150.00	*35.00*				
332	2¢ Washington, 1908	7.50	.05	80.00	(6)		
332a	Booklet pane of 6	120.00	*35.00*				
333	3¢ Washington, type I, 1908	30.00	3.00	350.00	(6)		
	Nos. 334-342; Washington (333)						
334	4¢ orange brown, 1908	32.50	1.00	375.00	(6)		
335	5¢ blue, 1908	40.00	2.00	625.00	(6)		
336	6¢ red orange, 1908	50.00	4.50	900.00	(6)		
337	8¢ olive green, 1908	32.50	2.50	475.00	(6)		
338	10¢ yellow, 1909	65.00	1.50	1,000.00	(6)		
339	13¢ blue green, 1909	35.00	22.50	475.00	(6)		
340	15¢ pale ultramarine, 1909	60.00	5.75	750.00	(6)		
341	50¢ violet, 1909	300.00	15.00	*7,500.00*	(6)		
342	$1 violet brown, 1909	450.00	85.00	*12,500.00*	(6)		
	Imperf.						
343	1¢ green Franklin (331), 1908	8.00	3.50	90.00	(6)		
344	2¢ car. Washington (332), 1908	11.00	3.00	160.00	(6)		
	Nos. 345-347; Washington (333)						
345	3¢ deep violet, type I, 1909	22.50	13.50	300.00	(6)		
346	4¢ orange brown, 1909	40.00	20.00	450.00	(6)		
347	5¢ blue, 1909	60.00	35.00	700.00	(6)		
	Coil Stamps of 1908-10						
	Nos. 350-351, 354-356: Washington (333), Perf. 12 Horizontally						
348	1¢ green Franklin (331), 1908	22.50	13.00	175.00			
349	2¢ car. Washington (332), 1909	45.00	6.00	225.00			
350	4¢ orange brown, 1910	110.00	65.00	750.00			
351	5¢ blue, 1909	130.00	80.00	800.00			
	1909, Perf. 12 Vertically						
352	1¢ green Franklin (331), 1909	55.00	18.50	275.00			
353	2¢ car. Washington (332), 1909	45.00	6.00	275.00			
354	4¢ orange brown, 1909	120.00	50.00	130.00			
355	5¢ blue, 1909	130.00	70.00	1,250.00			
356	10¢ yellow, 1909	1,300.00	375.00	7,500.00			
	Issues of 1909, Bluish Paper, Perf. 12						
	Nos. 359-366: Washington (333)						
357	1¢ green Franklin (331)	110.00	100.00	1,300.00	(6)		
358	2¢ car. Washington (332)	100.00	75.00	1,250.00	(6)		

328

329

330

367

368

370

371

	1909 continued	Un	U	PB/LP	#	FDC	Q
359	3¢ deep violet, type I	1,550.00	1,100.00	*16,500.00*	(6)		
360	4¢ orange brown	*14,000.00*	—	*60,000.00*	(3)		
361	5¢ blue	3,500.00	4,000.00	*35,000.00*	(6)		
362	6¢ red orange	1,000.00	600.00	*11,000.00*	(6)		
363	8¢ olive green	*14,000.00*	—	*55,000.00*	(3)		
364	10¢ yellow	1,050.00	650.00	*12,000.00*	(6)		
365	13¢ blue green	2,100.00	1,100.00	*18,500.00*	(6)		
366	15¢ pale ultramarine	950.00	650.00	*10,000.00*	(6)		
	Lincoln Memorial Issue, Feb. 12						
367	2¢ Lincoln, Perf. 12	7.50	2.75	175.00	(6)	*2,500.00*	148,387,191
368	2¢ Lincoln, Imperf.	35.00	30.00	350.00	(6)	*1,900.00*	1,273,900
369	2¢ Lincoln, Perf. 12, Bluish Paper	275.00	175.00	*4,750.00*	(6)		637,000
	Alaska-Yukon Exposition Issue						
370	2¢ William Seward, Perf. 12	12.00	2.25	300.00	(6)	*1,800.00*	152,887,311
371	2¢ William Seward, Imperf.	50.00	35.00	450.00	(6)		525,400
	Hudson-Fulton Celebration Issue, Sep. 25						
372	2¢ Half Moon and Clermont, Perf. 12	16.00	4.75	350.00	(6)	*950.00*	72,634,631
373	2¢ Half Moon and Clermont, Imperf.	60.00	35.00	525.00	(6)	*2,350.00*	216,480
	Issues of 1910-13, Perf. 12, Wmkd. 190						
	Nos. 376-382: Washington (333)						
374	1¢ green Franklin (331), 1910	7.50	.06	95.00	(6)		
374a	Booklet pane of 6	135.00	*30.00*				
375	2¢ car. Washington (332), 1910	7.00	.05	85.00	(6)		
375a	Booklet pane of 6	110.00	*25.00*				
376	3¢ deep violet, type I, 1911	17.50	1.50	185.00	(6)		
377	4¢ brown, 1911	25.00	.50	250.00	(6)		
378	5¢ blue, 1911	25.00	.50	285.00	(6)		
379	6¢ red orange, 1911	35.00	.75	550.00	(6)		
380	8¢ olive green, 1911	115.00	13.50	2,000.00	(6)		
381	10¢ yellow, 1911	110.00	4.00	1,500.00	(6)		
382	15¢ pale ultramarine, 1911	250.00	15.00	3,000.00	(6)		
	Imperf.						
383	1¢ green Franklin (331), 1911	4.00	3.00	75.00	(6)		
384	2¢ car. Washington (332), 1911	6.00	2.00	225.00	(6)		
	Coil Stamps, Perf. 12 Horizontally						
385	1¢ green Franklin (331), 1910	25.00	12.00	200.00			
386	2¢ car. Washington (332), 1910	37.50	11.00	*325.00*			
	Perf. 12 Vertically						
387	1¢ green Franklin (331), 1910	75.00	22.50	325.00			
388	2¢ car. Washington (332), 1910	550.00	75.00	3,750.00			
389	3¢ dp. vio. Washington,						
	type I (333), 1911	*13,000.00*	*4,750.00*	—			
	Perf. 8½ Horizontally						
390	1¢ green Franklin (331), 1910	4.50	3.25	*27.50*			

	1910-13 continued	Un	U	PB/LP	#	FDC	Q
391	2¢ car. Washington (332), 1910	32.50	8.50	175.00			
	Perf. 8½ Vertically, Nos. 394-396; Washington (333)						
392	1¢ green Franklin (331), 1910	20.00	15.00	110.00			
393	2¢ car. Washington (332), 1910	40.00	6.00	200.00			
394	3¢ deep violet, type I, 1911	50.00	27.50	300.00			
395	4¢ brown, 1912	50.00	27.50	300.00			
396	5¢ blue, 1913	50.00	27.50	300.00			
	Panama Pacific Exposition Issue, 1913, Perf. 12						
397	1¢ Balboa	17.50	1.75	200.00	(6)	3,500.00	167,398,463
398	2¢ Locks, Panama Canal	20.00	.50	350.00	(6)		251,856,543
399	5¢ Golden Gate	80.00	11.00	2,750.00	(6)	4,500.00	14,544, 363
400	10¢ Discovery						
	of San Francisco Bay	165.00	25.00	3,500.00	(6)		8,484,182
400A	10¢ orange (400)	250.00	18.50	11,000.00	(6)		
	1914-15, Perf. 10						
401	1¢ green Balboa (397), 1914	27.50	6.50	400.00	(6)		167,398,463
402	2¢ carmine Canal Locks (398),-15	85.00	1.50	2,000.00	(6)		251,856,543
403	5¢ blue Golden Gate (399),-15	190.00	17.50	4,750.00	(6)		14,544,363
404	10¢ orange Discovery of						
	San Francisco Bay (400), 1915	1,400.00	70.00	17,000.00	(6)		8,484,182
	Issues of 1912-14						
	Nos. 405-413: Washington (333), Perf. 12						
405	1¢ green, 1912	7.00	.06	115.00	(6)		
405b	Booklet pane of 6	65.00	7.50				
406	2¢ carmine, type I, 1912	6.00	.05	140.00	(6)		
406a	Booklet pane of 6	70.00	17.50				
407	7¢ black, 1914	100.00	7.00	1,350.00	(6)		
408	1¢ green, Imperf., 1912	1.50	.60	25.00	(6)		
409	2¢ carmine, type I, Imperf., 1912	1.65	.60	50.00	(6)		
	Coil Stamps, Perf. 8½ Horizontally						
410	1¢ green, 1912	6.25	3.50	35.00			
411	2¢ carmine, type I, 1912	7.75	3.75	42.50			
	Perf. 8½ Vertically						
412	1¢ green, 1912	21.00	5.00	90.00			
413	2¢ carmine, type I, 1912	35.00	.60	175.00			
	Perf. 12, Nos. 415-421; Franklin (414)						
414	8¢ Franklin, 1912	35.00	1.50	525.00	(6)		
415	9¢ salmon red, 1914	47.50	15.00	800.00	(6)		
416	10¢ orange yellow, 1912	35.00	.30	625.00	(6)		
417	12¢ claret brown, 1914	40.00	4.50	550.00	(6)		
418	15¢ gray, 1912	75.00	3.50	825.00	(6)		
419	20¢ ultramarine, 1914	175.00	16.00	2,350.00	(6)		
420	30¢ orange red, 1914	120.00	16.00	1,850.00	(6)		

1910-1915

397 398 399 400

405 406 414 420

1912-1916

	1912-14 continued	Un	U	PB/LP	#	FDC	Q
421	50¢ violet, 1914	500.00	16.00	9,000.00	(6)		
	Nos. 422-423: Franklin (414), Perf. 12						
422	50¢ violet, Feb. 12, 1912	250.00	16.50	6,000.00	(6)		
423	$1 violet brown, Feb. 12, 1912						
	Wmkd. 191	600.00	70.00	*12,500.00*	(6)		
	Issues of 1914-15, Perf. 10, Wmkd. 190						
	Nos. 424-430: Washington (333)						
424	1¢ green, 1914	2.75	.06	50.00	(6)		
424d	Booklet pane of 6	4.00	.75				
425	2¢ rose red, type I, 1914	2.50	.05	35.00	(6)		
425e	Booklet pane of 6	15.00	*3.00*				
426	3¢ deep violet, type I, 1914	12.50	1.25	150.00	(6)		
427	4¢ brown, 1914	32.50	.40	400.00	(6)		
428	5¢ blue, 1914	27.50	.40	325.00	(6)		
429	6¢ red orange, 1914	37.50	1.25	325.00	(6)		
430	7¢ black, 1914	90.00	4.25	950.00	(6)		
	Nos. 431-440: Franklin (414)						
431	8¢ pale olive green, 1914	35.00	1.50	400.00	(6)		
432	9¢ salmon red, 1914	47.50	8.50	575.00	(6)		
433	10¢ orange yellow, 1914	45.00	.25	575.00	(6)		
434	11¢ dark green, 1915	22.50	7.00	200.00	(6)		
435	12¢ claret brown, 1914	25.00	4.50	275.00	(6)		
437	15¢ gray, 1914	115.00	7.25	900.00	(6)		
438	20¢ ultramarine, 1914	225.00	4.00	2,850.00	(6)		
439	30¢ orange red, 1914	275.00	14.00	4,000.00	(6)		
440	50¢ violet, 1914	800.00	17.50	11,000.00	(6)		
	Coil Stamps, Perf. 10, 1914						
441	1¢ green	1.00	.90	7.50			
442	2¢ carmine, type I	10.00	7.50	55.00			
443	1¢ green	22.50	6.00	110.00			
444	2¢ carmine, type I	32.50	1.50	175.00			
445	3¢ violet, type I	225.00	110.00	1,100.00			
446	4¢ brown	140.00	35.00	650.00			
447	5¢ blue	40.00	22.50	200.00			
	Coil Stamps, Washington (333), 1915-16, Perf. 10 Horizontally						
448	1¢ green, 1915	6.50	3.00	40.00			
449	2¢ red, type I, 1915	1,500.00	140.00	7,000.00			
450	2¢ carmine, type III, 1916	11.00	3.00	75.00			
	1914-16, Perf. 10 Vertically						
452	1¢ green, 1914	10.00	1.75	72.50			
453	2¢ red, type I, 1914	110.00	4.50	625.00			

1914-1917

		Un	U	PB/LP	#	FDC	Q
	Coil Stamps, 1914-16 Issues, continued						
454	2¢ carmine, type II, 1915	115.00	13.50	700.00			
455	2¢ carmine, type III, 1915	10.00	1.00	70.00			
456	3¢ violet, type I, 1916	300.00	95.00	1,300.00			
457	4¢ brown	30.00	18.00	70.00			
458	5¢ blue	30.00	18.00	185.00			
	Issue of 1914 Washington (333), Imperf., Coil						
459	2¢ carmine, type I, June 30	450.00	*600.00*	2,500.00			
	Issues of 1915, Perf. 10, Wmkd. 191						
460	$1 violet black Franklin						
	(414), Feb. 8	975.00	95.00	*13,500.00*	(6)		
	Perf. 11						
461	2¢ pale carmine red, type I.						
	Washington (333), June 17	100.00	85.00	1,100.00	(6)		
	Privately perforated copies of No. 409 have been made to resemble No. 461.						
	From 1916 all postage stamps except Nos. 519 and 832b are on unwatermarked paper.						
	Issues of 1916-17, Perf. 10						
	Nos. 462-469: Washington (333)						
462	1¢ green, 1916	8.50	.20	150.00	(6)		
462a	Booklet pane of 6	12.00	*1.00*				
463	2¢ carmine, type I, 1916	4.25	.10	100.00	(6)		
463a	Booklet pane of 6	75.00	*15.00*				
464	3¢ violet, type I, 1916	80.00	11.00	1,400.00	(6)		
465	4¢ orange brown, 1916	40.00	1.75	750.00	(6)		
466	5¢ blue, 1916	75.00	1.75	1,000.00	(6)		
467	5¢ car. (error in plate of 2¢), 1917	750.00	525.00	125.00	(6)		
468	6¢ red orange, 1916	95.00	7.50	1,150.00	(6)		
469	7¢ black, 1916	125.00	13.00	1,500.00	(6)		
470	8¢ olive green, 1916	50.00	6.50	600.00	(6)		
471	9¢ salmon red, 1916	57.50	16.00	650.00	(6)		
472	10¢ orange yellow, 1916	110.00	1.00	1,500.00	(6)		
473	11¢ dark green, 1916	30.00	17.50	325.00	(6)		
474	12¢ claret brown, 1916	50.00	5.00	600.00	(6)		
475	15¢ gray, 1916	175.00	12.00	2,500.00	(6)		
476	20¢ light ultramarine, 1916	250.00	12.50	3,500.00	(6)		
477	50¢ light violet, 1917	1,500.00	75.00	*25,000.00*	(6)		
478	$1 violet black, 1916	950.00	20.00	*13,500.00*	(6)		
	Issues of 1917, Perf. 10, Mar. 22						
479	$2 dark blue Madison (312), 1917	500.00	45.00	6,500.00	(6)		
480	$5 light green Marshall (313), 1917	400.00	47.50	5,250.00	(6)		

1916-1922

		Un	U	PB/LP	#	FDC	Q
	Issues of 1916-17, Washington (333), Imperf.						
481	1¢ green, 1916	1.00	.75	15.00	(6)		
482	2¢ carmine, type I, 1916	1.25	1.25	27.50	(6)		
483	3¢ violet, type I, 1917	15.00	8.50	200.00	(6)		
484	3¢ violet, type II, 1917	11.00	4.00	150.00	(6)		
485	5¢ carmine (2¢ error), 1917	13,000		250.00	(6)		
	Coil Stamps, Washington (333), 1916-19, Perf. 10 Horizontally						
486	1¢ green, 1918	1.00	.15	4.50			
487	2¢ carmine, type II, 1919	18.00	2.50	150.00			
488	2¢ carmine, type III, 1917	3.00	1.50	22.50			
489	3¢ violet, type I, 1917	5.50	1.00	35.00			
	1916-22, Perf. 10 Vertically						
490	1¢ green, 1916	.75	.15	4.75			
491	2¢ carmine, type II, 1916	*1,450.00*	200.00	7,000.00			
492	2¢ carmine, type III, 1916	9.00	.15	55.00			
493	3¢ violet, type I, 1917	21.00	3.00	150.00			
494	3¢ violet, type II,1918	11.50	.60	85.00			
495	4¢ orange brown, 1917	12.50	3.50	85.00			
496	5¢ blue, 1919	4.50	.60	30.00			
497	10¢ or. yel. Franklin (414), 1912	26.50	8.50	150.00		*1,350.00*	
	Issues of 1917-19, Perf. 11						
	Nos. 498-507: Washington (333)						
498	1¢ green, 1917	.25	.05	15.00	(6)		
498e	Booklet pane of 6	1.75	*.35*				
499	2¢ rose, type I, 1917	.25	.05	14.00	(6)		
499e	Booklet pane of 6	2.00	*.50*				
500	2¢ deep rose, type Ia, 1917	275.00	120.00	2,500.00	(6)		
501	3¢ light violet, type I, 1917	17.50	.10	190.00	(6)		
501b	Booklet pane of 6	75.00	*15.00*				
502	3¢ dark violet, type II, 1917	20.00	.25	225.00	(6)		
502b	Booklet pane of 6, 1918	50.00	*10.00*				
503	4¢ brown, 1917	13.00	.20	175.00	(6)		
504	5¢ blue, 1917	10.00	.08	140.00	(6)		
505	5¢ rose (error in plate of 2¢),-17	550.00	400.00	35.00	(6)		
506	6¢ red orange, 1917	15.00	.30	210.00	(6)		
507	7¢ black, 1917	32.50	1.50	375.00	(6)		
	Nos. 508-518: Franklin (414)						
508	8¢ olive bistre, 1917	13.50	.70	250.00	(6)		
509	9¢ salmon red, 1917	17.50	2.75	225.00	(6)		

1917-1920

	1917-19 continued	Un	U	PB/LB	#	FDC		Q
510	10¢ orange yellow, 1917	20.00	.10	275.00	(6)			
511	11¢ light green, 1917	10.00	3.75	135.00	(6)			
512	12¢ claret brown, 1917	10.50	.45	140.00	(6)			
513	13¢ apple green, 1919	12.00	7.00	150.00	(6)			
514	15¢ gray, 1917	47.50	1.00	700.00	(6)			
515	20¢ light ultramarine, 1917	60.00	.30	800.00	(6)			
516	30¢ orange red, 1917	45.00	.95	650.00	(6)			
517	50¢ red violet, 1917	90.00	.65	1,500.00	(6)			
518	$1 violet brown, 1917	75.00	1.75	1,200.00	(6)			
	Issue of 1917, Perf. 11, Wmkd. 191							
519	2¢ carmine Washington							
	(332), Oct. 10	250.00	225.00	2,500.00	(6)			
	Privately perforated copies of No. 344 have been made to resemble No. 519.							
	Issues of 1918, Unwmkd., Perf. 11							
523	$2 orange red and black							
	Franklin (547), Aug. 19	1,200.00	175.00	*21,000.00*	(8)			
524	$5 deep green and black							
	Franklin (547), Aug. 19	475.00	27.50	*8,000.00*	(8)			
	Issues of 1918-20, Washington (333)							
	Perf. 11							
525	1¢ gray green, 1918	225.00	.60	30.00	(6)			
526	2¢ carmine, type IV, 1920	30.00	4.00	250.00	(6)	*825.00*		
527	2¢ carmine, type V, 1920	17.50	1.00	150.00	(6)			
528	2¢ carmine, type Va, 1920	8.00	.15	70.00	(6)			
528A	2¢ carmine, type VI, 1920	50.00	1.00	375.00	(6)			
528B	2¢ carmine, type VII, 1920	20.00	.12	160.00	(6)			
529	3¢ violet, type III, 1918	2.25	.10	50.00	(6)			
530	3¢ purple, type IV, 1918	.70	.06	12.00	(6)			
	Imperf.							
531	1¢ green, 1919	10.00	8.00	100.00	(6)			
532	2¢ car. rose, type IV, 1919	40.00	27.50	350.00	(6)			
533	2¢ carmine, type V, 1919	250.00	70.00	2,250.00	(6)			
534	2¢ carmine, type Va, 1919	13.50	9.00	130.00	(6)			
534A	2¢ carmine, type VI, 1919	40.00	27.50	400.00	(6)			
534B	2¢ carmine, type VII, 1919	1,700.00	425.00	*13,500.00*	(6)			
535	3¢ violet, type IV, 1918	9.00	6.50	85.00	(6)			
	Issues of 1919							
	Perf. 12½							
536	1¢ gray green Washington							
	(333), Aug. 15	15.00	13.50	200.00	(6)			

	1919 continued	Un	U	PB/LP	#	FDC	Q
	Perf. 11						
537	3¢ Allied Victory, Mar. 3	12.50	4.25	160.00	(6)	*700.00*	99,585,200
	Nos. 538-546: Washington (333), 1919, Perf. 11x10						
538	1¢ green	10.00	9.00	100.00	(4)		
539	2¢ carmine rose, type II	2,150.00	675.00	*15,000.00*	(4)		
540	2¢ carmine rose, type III	11.00	9.00	110.00	(4)		
541	3¢ violet, type II	37.50	35.00	450.00	(4)		
	1920, Perf. 10x11						
542	1¢ green, May 26	6.50	1.00	135.00	(6)	*525.00*	
	1921, Perf. 10						
543	1¢ green	.50	.06	20.00	(4)		
	1921, Perf. 11						
544	1¢ green, 19x22½mm	*6,500.00*	*1,500.00*				
545	1¢ green, 19½—20mmx22mm	150.00	90.00	1,100.00	(4)		
546	2¢ carmine rose, type III	100.00	70.00	900.00	(4)		
	Issues of 1920, Perf. 11						
547	$2 Franklin	450.00	35.00	9,000.00	(8)		
	Pilgrims 300th Anniv. Issue, Dec. 21						
548	1¢ Mayflower	6.50	3.00	70.00	(6)	*700.00*	137,978,207
549	2¢ Pilgrims Landing	9.50	2.25	100.00	(6)	*625.00*	196,037,327
550	5¢ Signing of Compact	60.00	18.50	800.00	(6)		11,321,607
	Issues of 1922-25, Perf. 11						
551	½¢ Nathan Hale, 1925	.15	.07	7.00	(6)	*25.00*	
552	1¢ Franklin (19x22mm), 1923	2.50	.05	30.00	(6)	*37.50*	
552a	Booklet pane of 6	5.50	.50				
553	1½¢ Harding, 1925	4.00	.20	50.00	(6)	*40.00*	
554	2¢ Washington, 1923	2.00	.05	30.00	(6)	*50.00*	
554c	Booklet pane of 6	7.00	*1.00*				
555	3¢ Lincoln, 1923	22.50	1.25	275.00	(6)	*42.50*	
556	4¢ Martha Washington, 1923	22.50	.20	275.00	(6)	*55.00*	
557	5¢ Theodore Roosevelt, 1922	22.50	.08	300.00	(6)	*125.00*	
558	6¢ Garfield, 1922	42.50	.85	550.00	(6)	*225.00*	
559	7¢ McKinley, 1923	10.00	.75	100.00	(6)	*110.00*	
560	8¢ Grant, 1923	55.00	.85	900.00	(6)	*110.00*	
561	9¢ Jefferson, 1923	17.00	1.25	225.00	(6)	*110.00*	
562	10¢ Monroe, 1923	23.50	.10	375.00	(6)	*110.00*	
563	11¢ Rutherford B. Hayes, 1922	2.25	.25	45.00	(6)	*600.00*	
564	12¢ Grover Cleveland, 1923	9.00	.08	100.00	(6)	*150.00*	
565	14¢ American Indian, 1923	6.00	.85	75.00	(6)	*350.00*	
566	15¢ Statue of Liberty, 1922	24.00	.06	300.00	(6)	*350.00*	
567	20¢ Golden Gate, 1923	27.50	.06	325.00	(6)	*400.00*	
568	25¢ Niagara Falls, 1922	27.50	.50	325.00	(6)	*675.00*	
569	30¢ Buffalo, 1923	45.00	.35	525.00	(6)	*700.00*	

537   547   548   549   550

551   552   553   554   555

556   557   558   559   560

561   562   563   564   565   566

567   568   569

570　　　　571　　　　572　　　　573

610　　　　611

	1922-25 continued	Un	U	PB/LP	#	FDC	Q
570	50¢ Arlington Amphitheater, 1922	80.00	.12	1,200.00	(6)	*1,000.00*	
571	$1 Lincoln Memorial, 1923	60.00	.45	600.00	(6)	4,250.00	
572	$2 U.S. Capitol, 1923	175.00	9.50	2,000.00	(6)	*8,500.00*	
573	$5 Head of Freedom,						
	Capitol Dome, 1923	425.00	15.00	6,500.00	(8)	*11,000.00*	
	Issues of 1923-25, Imperf.						
575	1¢ green Franklin (552), 1923	11.00	3.50	135.00	(6)		
576	1½¢ yel. brown Harding (553),-25	2.50	1.75	37.50	(6)	*50.00*	
577	2¢ carmine Washington (554)	3.00	2.00	40.00	(6)		

For listings of other perforated stamps of issues 551-573 see:

Nos. 578 and 579	Perf. 11x10
Nos. 581 to 591	Perf. 10
Nos. 594 and 595	Perf. 11
Nos. 622 and 623	Perf. 11
Nos. 632 to 642, 653, 692 to 696	Perf. 11x10½
Nos. 697 to 701	Perf. 10½x11

	Perf. 11x10						
578	1¢ green Franklin (552)	80.00	65.00	750.00	(4)		
579	2¢ carmine Washington (554)	57.50	50.00	450.00	(4)		

	Issues of 1923-26, Perf. 10	Un	U	PB/LP	#	FDC	Q
581	1¢ green Franklin (552), 1923	7.50	.65	125.00	(4)	2,000.00	
582	1½¢ brown Harding (553), 1925	5.00	.60	45.00	(4)	52.50	
583	2¢ carmine Washington (554), 1924	2.50	.05	30.00	(4)		
583a	Booklet pane of 6	75.00	25.00				
584	3¢ violet Lincoln (555), 1925	27.50	1.75	300.00	(4)	62.50	
585	4¢ yellow brown						
	M. Washington (556)	17.00	.40	200.00	(4)		
586	5¢ blue T. Roosevelt (557), 1925	16.00	.18	185.00	(4)	62.50	
587	6¢ red orange Garfield (558), 1925	9.00	.40	80.00	(4)	77.50	
588	7¢ black McKinley (559), 1926	11.50	5.00	120.00	(4)	75.00	
589	8¢ olive green Grant (560), 1926	30.00	3.00	325.00	(4)	80.00	
590	9¢ rose Jefferson (561), 1926	5.50	2.25	50.00	(4)	85.00	
591	10¢ orange Monroe (562), 1925	65.00	.10	700.00	(4)	110.00	
	Perf. 11						
594	1¢ green Franklin,						
	19¾x22¼mm (552)	7,000.00	1,850.00				
595	2¢ carmine Washington,						
	19¾x22¼mm (554)	200.00	150.00	1,750.00	(4)		
596	1¢ green Franklin,						
	19¼x22¾mm (552)	—	13,500.00				
	Coil Stamps 1923-29, Perf. 10 Vertically						
597	1¢ green Franklin (552), 1923	.35	.06	2.25		450.00	
598	1½¢ brown Harding (553), 1925	.75	.10	5.25		60.00	
599	2¢ carmine Washington,						
	type I (554), 1929	.30	.05	2.00		750.00	
599A	2¢ carmine Washington,						
	type II (554), 1929	140.00	10.00	800.00			
600	3¢ violet Lincoln (555)	8.00	.08	35.00		80.00	
601	4¢ yellow brown						
	M. Washington (556), 1923	4.00	.40	27.50			
602	5¢ dark blue						
	Theodore Roosevelt (557), 1924	1.50	.18	9.00		85.00	
603	10¢ orange Monroe (562), 1924	4.00	.08	27.50		105.00	
	Coil Stamps 1923-25 Perf. 10 Horizontally						
604	1¢ yel. grn. Franklin (552), 1924	.25	.08	3.00		95.00	
605	1½¢ yel. brn. Harding (553), 1925	.30	.15	2.75		60.00	
606	2¢ carmine Washington (554), 1923	.30	.12	2.00		90.00	
	Harding Memorial Issue, 1923, Flat Plate Printing (19¼x22¼mm)						
610	2¢ Harding, Perf. 11, Sept. 1	.85	.10	32.50	(6)	40.00	1,459,487,085
611	2¢ Harding Imperf., Nov. 15	15.00	6.00	170.00	(6)	100.00	770,000
	Rotary Press Printing (19¼x22¾mm)						
612	2¢ black, Perf. 10 (610), Sept. 12	25.00	2.50	375.00	(4)	110.00	99,950,300
613	2¢ black Perf. 11 (610)	—	13,500.00				

		Un	U	PB/LP	#	FDC	Q
	Huguenot-Walloon 300th Anniv. Issue, 1924, May 1						
614	1¢ Ship *New Netherland*	5.50	5.00	55.00	(6)	35.00	51,378,023
615	2¢ Landing at Fort Orange	9.00	3.50	100.00	(6)	45.00	77,753,423
616	5¢ Huguenot Monument, Florida	55.00	22.50	500.00	(6)	90.00	5,659,023
	Lexington-Concord Issue, 1925, Apr. 4						
617	1¢ Washington at Cambridge	5.50	5.50	50.00	(6)	35.00	15,615,000
618	2¢ Birth of Liberty	10.00	7.50	110.00	(6)	45.00	26,596,600
619	5¢ Statue of Minute Man	50.00	20.00	425.00	(6)	60.00	5,348,800
	Norse-American Issue, 1925, May 18						
620	2¢ Sloop *Restaurationen*	9.00	5.00	300.00	(8)	32.50	9,104,983
621	5¢ Viking Ship	30.00	22.50	950.00	(8)	55.00	1,900,983
	Issues of 1925-26						
622	13¢ Benjamin Harrison, 1926	20.00	.65	225.00	(6)	35.00	
623	17¢ Woodrow Wilson, 1925	27.50	.35	275.00	(6)	35.00	
	Issues of 1926						
627	2¢ Independence,						
	150th Anniv., May 10	4.25	.60	60.00	(6)	17.50	307,731,900
628	5¢ Ericsson Memorial, May 29	11.00	5.00	120.00	(6)	30.00	20,280,500
629	2¢ Battle of White Plains, Oct. 18	2.75	2.25	60.00	(6)	7.00	40,639,485

The First Shot

It was April 19, 1775, when British soldiers, under the command of Major Pitcairn, fired on a group of Americans at Lexington, Massachusetts. This gave birth to the fight for independence that became known throughout the world as the American Revolution. The Lexington-Concord series of commemorative stamps (#617-619) honors the 150th anniversary of the "shot heard round the world."

The American colonies knew that the British army was approaching, and the volunteer army of "Minutemen" was prepared to go into action. On April 18, 1775, Paul Revere, an employee of the British Post Office, received the signal from the belfry of Old North Church and made his famous ride to warn the countryside. On the morning of the 19th, Captain Parker gathered his men on the Lexington common to await the redcoats. Major Pitcairn rode into Lexington at the head of a column of six companies of infantry. The British major ordered the American volunteers to lay down their weapons.

The Minutemen stood their ground and the British fired. Eight Americans died that morning with many more wounded. The British went on to Concord, but the Americans attacked them continuously. The Colonial soldiers shot at the British troops from behind trees and farm houses. Confused by the constant harassment, the British retreated to the safety of Boston, where a large force gave them protection. The first day, the start of a seven-year struggle for independence, is eloquently commemorated by these stamps.

615   616

618   619

621   622   623

629

631

633

643

644

645

646

647

648

649

650

	1926 continued	Un	U	PB/LP	#	FDC	Q
	International Philatelic Exhibition Issue, Oct. 18, Souvenir Sheet						
630	2¢ car. rose, sheet of 25 with						
	selvage inscription (629)	525.00	425.00			1,500.00	107,398
	Imperf.						
631	1½¢ Harding Aug. 27, 18½	2.50	2.10	80.00	(4)	40.00	
	Issues of 1926-27, Perf. 11x10½						
632	1¢ green Franklin (552), 1927	.15	.05	2.50	(4)	60.00	
632a	Booklet pane of 6, 1927	2.50	.25				
633	1½¢ Harding, 1927	2.75	.08	100.00	(4)	60.00	
634	2¢ carmine Washington, type I						
	(554) 1956	.15	.05	1.20	(4)	62.50	
634d	Booklet pane of 6, 1927	1.00	.15				
634A	2¢ carmine Washington, type II						
	(554) 1926	375.00	22.50	2,500.00	(4)		
635	3¢ violet Lincoln (555), 1927	.55	.05	7.50	(4)	52.50	
636	4¢ yellow brown						
	M. Washington (556), 1927	4.25	.08	125.00	(4)	60.00	
637	5¢ dark blue T. Roosevelt (557),-27	3.50	.05	25.00	(4)	60.00	
638	6¢ red orange Garfield (558), 1927	3.50	.05	25.00	(4)	72.50	
639	7¢ black McKinley (559), 1927	3.50	.08	25.00	(4)	75.00	
640	8¢ olive green, Grant (560), 1927	3.50	.05	25.00	(4)	77.50	
641	9¢ orange red Jefferson						
	(561), 1927	3.50	.05	25.00	(4)	95.00	
642	10¢ orange Monroe (562), 1927	5.75	.05	40.00	(4)	100.00	
	Issues of 1927, Perf. 11						
643	2¢ Vermont 150th Anniversary,						
	Aug. 3	1.65	1.65	50.00	(6)	6.00	39,974,900
644	2¢ Burgoyne Campaign, Aug. 3	5.50	3.75	70.00	(6)	20.00	25,628,450
	Issues of 1928						
645	2¢ Valley Forge, May 26	1.25	.65	50.00	(6)	6.00	101,330,328
	Perf. 11x10½						
646	2¢ Battle of Monmouth, Oct. 20	1.50	1.50	55.00	(4)	22.50	9,779,896
647	2¢ carmine , Aug. 13	7.00	6.00	180.00	(4)	22.50	5,519,897
648	5¢ Hawaii 150th Anniv., Aug. 13	21.00	20.00	350.00	(4)	40.00	1,459,897
	Aeronautics Conference Issue, Dec. 12, Perf.11						
649	2¢ Wright Airplane	1.50	1.40	21.00	(6)	12.00	51,342,273
650	5¢ Globe and Airplane	8.50	5.00	100.00	(6)	18.00	10,319,700
	Issues of 1929						
651	2¢ George Rogers Clark, Feb. 25	.85	.80	17.50	(6)	7.00	16,684,674
	Perf. 11x10½						
653	½¢ olive brown Nathan Hale (551)	.05	.05	1.00	(4)	30.00	
	Electric Light Jubilee Issue, Perf. 11						
654	2¢ Edison's First Lamp, June 5	1.00	1.00	40.00	(6)	11.00	31,679,200
	Perf. 11x10½						
655	2¢ carmine rose (654), June 11	.90	.25	65.00	(4)	85.00	210,119,474

	1929 continued	Un	U	PB/LP	#	FDC	Q
	Coil Stamp, Perf. 10 Vertically						
656	2¢ carmine rose (654), June 11	20.00	2.00	85.00		100.00	133,530,000
	Perf. 11						
657	2¢ Sullivan Expedition, June 17	1.00	.90	40.00	(6)	5.50	51,451,880
	Regular Issue of 1929						
	Perf. 11x10½, 658-668 Overprinted Kans.						
658	1¢ green Franklin	2.50	1.65	35.00	(4)	27.50	13,390,000
659	1½¢ brown Harding (553)	3.50	3.00	45.00	(4)	27.50	8,240,000
660	2¢ carmine Washington (554)	3.50	.65	45.00	(4)	27.50	87,410,000
661	3¢ violet Lincoln (555)	18.50	12.00	185.00	(4)	30.00	2,540,000
662	4¢ yellow brown						
	M. Washington (556)	18.50	7.50	185.00	(4)	32.50	2,290,000
663	5¢ deep blue T. Roosevelt (557)	14.00	9.00	170.00	(4)	35.00	2,700,000
664	6¢ red orange Garfield (558)	28.50	17.50	475.00	(4)	42.50	1,450,000
665	7¢ black McKinley (559)	30.00	22.50	425.00	(4)	42.50	1,320,000
666	8¢ olive green Grant (560)	85.00	72.50	850.00	(4)	80.00	1,530,000
667	9¢ light rose Jefferson (561)	14.00	11.00	225.00	(4)	72.50	1,130,000
668	10¢ orange yellow Monroe (562)	23.50	11.00	400.00	(4)	85.00	2,860,000
	669-679 Overprinted Nebr.						
669	1¢ green Franklin	2.50	2.00	35.00	(4)	27.50	8,220,000
670	1½¢ brown Harding (553)	3.25	2.25	40.00	(4)	25.00	8,990,000
671	2¢ carmine Washington (554)	2.25	.85	30.00	(4)	25.00	73,220,000
672	3¢ violet Lincoln (555)	12.50	8.75	200.00	(4)	32.50	2,110,000
673	4¢ yellow brown						
	M. Washington (556)	18.50	11.00	225.00	(4)	37.50	1,600,000
674	5¢ deep blue T. Roosevelt (557)	18.00	13.50	250.00	(4)	37.50	1,860,000
675	6¢ red orange Garfield (558)	40.00	19.00	525.00	(4)	55.00	980,000
676	7¢ black McKinley (559)	22.50	15.00	275.00	(4)	57.50	850,000
677	8¢ olive green Grant (560)	30.00	22.50	375.00	(4)	60.00	1,480,000
678	9¢ light rose Jefferson (561)	35.00	25.00	425.00	(4)	62.50	530,000
679	10¢ orange yellow Monroe (562)	110.00	17.50	1,000.00	(4)	70.00	1,890,000
	Warning: Excellent forgeries of the Kansas and Nebraska overprints exist.						
	Perf. 11						
680	2¢ Battle of Fallen Timbers,						
	Sept. 14	1.00	1.00	40.00	(6)	5.50	29,338,274
681	2¢ Ohio River Canal, Oct. 19	.80	.80	32.50	(6)	5.00	32,680,900
	Issues of 1930						
682	2¢ Mass. Bay Colony, Apr. 8	.80	.60	45.00	(6)	4.25	74,000,774
683	2¢ Carolina-Charleston, Apr. 10	1.75	1.60	70.00	(6)	4.50	25,215,574
	Perf. 11x10½						
684	1½¢ Warren G. Harding	.25	.05	1.50	(4)	5.50	
685	4¢ William H. Taft	.50	.06	9.00	(4)	10.00	

1926-1930

656 (Coil Pair)　　657　　658　　669　　680

681　　682　　683　　684　　685

1930-1932

688   689

690   702   703

704   705   706   707   708   709

710   711   712

713   714   715   716   717

	1930 continued	Un	U	PB/LP	#	FDC	Q
	Coil Stamps, Perf. 10 Vertically						
686	1½¢ brown Harding (684)	1.60	.07	6.00		7.50	
687	4¢ brown Taft (685)	2.75	.50	11.00		20.00	
	Perf. 11						
688	2¢ Braddock's Field, July 9	1.40	1.40	60.00	(6)	6.00	25,609,470
689	2¢ Von Steuben, Sept. 17	.80	.75	35.00	(6)	6.00	66,487,000
	Issues of 1931						
690	2¢ Pulaski, Jan. 16	.25	.18	25.00	(6)	5.00	96,559,400
	Perf. 11x10½						
692	11¢ light blue Hayes (563)	3.00	.10	19.00	(4)	80.00	
693	12¢ brown violet Cleveland (564)	6.50	.06	35.00	(4)	80.00	
694	13¢ yellow green Harrison (622)	2.75	.10	21.50	(4)	85.00	
695	14¢ dark blue Indian (565)	4.00	.30	25.00	(4)	85.00	
696	15¢ gray Statue of Liberty (566)	10.00	.06	60.00	(4)	95.00	
	Perf. 10½x11						
697	17¢ black Wilson (623)	5.25	.25	30.00	(4)	325.00	
698	20¢ car. rose Golden Gate (567)	13.00	.05	65.00	(4)	160.00	
699	25¢ blue green Niagara						
	Falls (568)	11.00	.08	60.00	(4)	350.00	
700	30¢ brown Buffalo (569)	18.50	.07	95.00	(4)	275.00	
701	50¢ lilac Amphitheater (570)	55.00	.07	300.00	(4)	400.00	
	Perf. 11						
702	2¢ Red Cross, May 21	.15	.12	2.50	(4)	4.00	99,074,600
703	2¢ Yorktown, Oct. 12	.40	.35	4.00	(4)	5.00	25,006,400
	Issues of 1932. Perf. 11x10½, Washington Bicentennial Issue , Jan. 1						
704	½¢ Portrait by Charles W. Peale	.08	.05	4.50	(4)	5.00	87,969,700
705	1¢ Bust by Jean Antoine Houdon	.13	.05	5.00	(4)	5.50	1,265,555,100
706	1½¢ Portrait by Charles W. Peale	.55	.08	22.50	(4)	5.50	304,926,800
707	2¢ Portrait by Gilbert Stuart	.10	.05	2.00	(4)	5.50	4,222,198,300
708	3¢ Portrait by Charles W. Peale	.60	.06	18.00	(4)	5.75	456,198,500
709	4¢ Portrait by Charles P. Polk	.30	.06	7.00	(4)	5.75	151,201,300
710	5¢ Portrait by Charles W. Peale	2.25	.10	24.00	(4)	6.00	170,565,100
711	6¢ Portrait by John Trumbull	5.00	.06	80.00	(4)	6.75	111,739,400
712	7¢ Portrait by John Trumbull	.35	.20	7.50	(4)	6.75	83,257,400
713	8¢ Portrait by Charles B.J.F.						
	Saint Memin	5.00	.90	90.00	(4)	6.75	96,506,100
714	9¢ Portrait by W. Williams	4.25	.25	55.00	(4)	7.75	75,709,200
715	10¢ Portrait by Gilbert Stuart	16.50	.10	150.00	(4)	10.00	147,216,000
	Perf. 11						
716	2¢ Olympic Games, Jan. 25	.50	.25	17.50	(6)	7.00	51,102,800
	Perf. 11x10½						
717	2¢ Arbor Day, Apr. 22	.18	.08	12.50	(4)	4.50	100,869,300

	1932 continued	Un	U	PB/LP	#	FDC	Q
	10th Olympic Games Issue, June 15						
718	3¢ Runner at Starting Mark	2.00	.06	25.00	(4)	7.00	168,885,300
719	5¢ Myron's Discobolus	3.25	.30	40.00	(4)	9.00	52,376,100
720	3¢ Washington, June 16	.15	.05	1.50	(4)	10.00	
720b	Booklet pane of 6	22.50	5.00				
	Coil Stamps, Perf. 10 Vertically						
721	3¢ deep violet (720), June 24	3.00	.08	14.00		20.00	
	Perf. 10 Horizontally						
722	3¢ deep violet (720), Oct. 12	1.85	.45	10.00		20.00	
	Perf. 10 Vertically						
723	6¢ red orange Garfield						
	(558), Aug. 18	12.50	.25	75.00		20.00	
	Perf. 11						
724	3¢ William Penn, Oct. 24	.35	.25	20.00	(6)	3.50	49,949,000
725	3¢ Daniel Webster, Oct. 24	.50	.40	32.50	(6)	3.50	49,538,500
	Issues of 1933						
726	3¢ Georgia 200th Anniv. Feb. 12	.35	.25	22.50	(6)	3.50	61,719,200
	Perf. 10½x11						
727	3¢ Peace of 1783, Apr. 19	.15	.10	7.00	(4)	4.00	73,382,400
	Century of Progress Issue, May 25						
728	1¢ Restoration of Ft. Dearborn	.12	.06	3.00	(4)	3.25	348,266,800
729	3¢ Fed. Building at Chicago 1933	.18	.05	4.00	(4)	3.25	480,239,300
	American Philatelic Society Issue, Souvenir Sheets, Aug. 25, Without Gum, Imperf.						
730	1¢ deep yellow green						
	sheet of 25 (728)	45.00	40.00			150.00	456,704
730a	Single stamp	1.00	.50			3.25	11,417,600

APS

President Franklin D. Roosevelt was an ardent stamp collector and a member of the American Philatelic Society (APS). Knowing this, Postmaster General James Farley authorized the printing of two sheets of imperforated stamps commemorating the Century of Progress exhibition (#730-731a), which contained a tribute to APS in the margin of the sheet.

The APS has grown to become the largest stamp organization in the world with more than 52,000 members residing in every state and many foreign countries. Among the services offered to members are sales circuits where collectors can select stamps from booklets sent to their home. The material is placed in the booklets by members who use this method to sell off their duplicate stamps. The group also has the largest philatelic library in the U.S. where members may borrow books by mail or in person.

The society also offers stamp insurance, and publishes a monthly journal,
The American Philatelist.

18

 719

 720

 723

 724

 725

 26

 727

 728

 729

UNDER AUTHORITY OF JAMES A. FARLEY, POSTMASTER GENERAL AT A CENTURY OF PROGRESS

PRINTED BY THE TREASURY DEPARTMENT, BUREAU OF ENGRAVING AND PRINTING

IN COMPLIMENT TO THE AMERICAN PHILATELIC SOCIETY FOR ITS CONVENTION AND EXHIBITION

CHICAGO, ILLINOIS, AUGUST 1933. PLATE NO. 21159

731

732

733

734

736

737

	1933 continued	Un	U	PB/LP	#	FDC	Q
731	3¢ deep violet, sheet of 25 (729)	40.00	37.50			150.00	441,172
731a	Single stamp	.85	.50			3.25	11,029,300
	Perf. 10½x11						
732	3¢ NRA, Aug. 15	.14	.05	2.00	(4)	3.50	1,978,707,300
	Perf. 11						
733	3¢ Byrd's Antarctic Expedition,						
	Oct. 9	.85	.85	27.50	(6)	7.00	5,735,944
734	5¢ Tadeusz Kosciuszko, Oct. 13	.85	.40	55.00	(6)	6.25	45,137,700
	Issues of 1934, National Stamp Exhibition Issue, Souvenir Sheet,						
	Feb. 10, Without Gum, Imperf.						
735	3¢ dk. blue sheet of 6 (733)	25.00	22.50			67.50	811,404
735a	Single stamp	3.00	2.50			6.75	4,868,424
	Perf. 11						
736	3¢ Maryland 300th Anniversary,						
	Mar. 23	.20	.20	15.00	(6)	2.00	46,258,300
	Mothers of America Issue, May 2, Perf. 11x10½						
737	3¢ Whistler's Mother	.15	.06	1.75	(4)	2.00	193,239,100
	Perf. 11						
738	3¢ deep violet (737)	.20	.20	7.25	(6)	2.00	15,432,200
739	3¢ Wisconsin 300th Anniversary,						
	July 7	.20	.12	7.00	(6)	2.00	64,525,400
	National Parks Issue						
740	1¢ El Capitan, Yosemite, Calif.	.10	.06	1.50	(6)	2.25	84,896,350
741	2¢ Grand Canyon, Arizona	.15	.06	2.00	(6)	2.25	74,400,200

"Chicken Downs Eagle"

The United States was in the midst of the worst depression in its history when Franklin D. Roosevelt took office in 1932. The National Recovery Administration (#732) was designed to encourage industrial growth and to help combat unemployment. The administration was given the power to make agreements dealing with hours of work, rates of pay and fixing of prices. Employees were given the right to organize and bargain collectively. Firms were asked to display the Blue Eagle as a symbol of NRA participation.

The stamp design represents the forward stride of four figures symbolizing all classes of our population marching towards recovery. A farmer, a businessman, a laborer and a woman worker are depicted together "In a Common Determination." The original design was taken from a painting showing President Roosevelt as one of a group emerging from the clouds of the depression. A poster was made using the same theme and the Bureau of Engraving and Printing then copied the four figures for the stamp.

A New York poultry firm brought suit against the administration stating that the NRA was unconstitutional. On May 27, 1935, the Supreme Court ruled for the private company. A lowly chicken brought down the Blue Eagle.

	1934 continued	Un	U	PB/LP	#	FDC	Q
742	3¢ Mt. Rainier and Mirror Lake,						
	Washington	.20	.06	3.50	(6)	2.50	95,089,000
743	4¢ Mesa Verde, Colorado	.55	.50	12.00	(6)	3.25	19,178,650
744	5¢ Old Faithful, Yellowstone						
	Wyoming	1.10	.90	14.50	(6)	3.25	30,980,100
745	6¢ Crater Lake, Oregon	2.00	1.25	30.00	(6)	4.00	16,923,350
746	7¢ Great Head, Acadia Park,						
	Maine	1.00	1.00	20.00	(6)	4.00	15,988,250
747	8¢ Great White Throne,						
	Zion Park, Utah	2.85	2.50	32.50	(6)	4.25	15,288,700
748	9¢ Mt. Rockwell and Two Medicine						
	Lake, Glacier National Park,						
	Montana	3.00	.90	30.00	(6)	4.50	17,472,600
749	10¢ Great Smoky Mountains,						
	North Carolina	5.00	1.35	52.50	(6)	9.00	18,874,300
	American Philatelic Society Issue, Souvenir Sheet, Imperf.						
750	3¢ deep violet sheet of six						
	(742), Aug. 28	45.00	35.00			65.00	511,391
750a	Single Stamp	5.00	4.50			7.00	3,068,346
	Trans-Mississippi Philatelic Issue						
751	1¢ green sheet of six (740), Oct. 10	18.50	15.00			45.00	793,551
751a	Single stamp	2.00	1.75			4.50	4,761,306
	Special Printing (Nos. 752 to 771 inclusive), Issued March 15, 1935, Without Gum						
	Issues of 1935, Perf. 10½x11						
752	3¢ violet Peace of 1783 (727)						
	Issues in sheets of 400, Mar. 15	.20	.15	16.00	(4)	13.00	3,274,556
	Perf. 11						
753	3¢ blue Byrd's Antarctic						
	Expedition (733)	.60	.60	25.00	(6)	15.00	2,040,760
	Imperf.						
754	3¢ dp. vio. Whistler's Mother (737)	1.00	.60	35.00	(6)	15.00	2,389,288
755	3¢ deep violet Wisconsin						
	300th Anniversary (739)	1.00	.60	35.00	(6)	15.00	2,294,948
756	1¢ green Yosemite (740)	.30	.20	6.50	(6)	15.00	3,217,636
757	2¢ red Grand Canyon (741)	.40	.35	7.50	(6)	15.00	2,746,640
758	3¢ dp. vio. Mt. Rainier (742)	.75	.70	22.50	(6)	16.00	2,168,088
759	4¢ brown Mesa Verde (743)	2.00	2.00	27.50	(6)	16.00	1,822,684
760	5¢ blue Yellowstone (744)	2.75	3.00	35.00	(6)	16.00	1,724,576
761	6¢ dk. blue Crater Lake (745)	4.00	2.75	47.50	(6)	16.50	1,647,696
762	7¢ black Acadia (746)	3.00	2.50	45.00	(6)	16.50	1,682,948
763	8¢ sage green Zion (747)	3.50	2.75	60.00	(6)	17.00	1,638,644
764	9¢ red orange Glacier Nat'l Park						
	(748)	3.75	2.75	60.00	(6)	18.00	1,625,224
765	10¢ gray black Smoky Mts. (749)	6.25	5.50	72.50	(6)	20.00	1,644,900

742 743 745

744

746 748

747 749

1935-1936

772

773

774

775

776

777

778

	1935 continued	Un	U	PB/LP	#	FDC	Q
766	1¢ yellow green (728)	50.00	50.00				98,712
	Pane of 25						
766a	Single stamp	1.00	.50			11.00	2,467,800
767	3¢ violet (729)	45.00	40.00				85,914
	Pane of 25						
767a	Single stamp	.85	.50			11.00	2,147,850
768	3¢ dark blue (733)	30.00	25.00				
	Pane of 6						
768a	Single stamp	3.25	2.75			13.00	1,,603,200
769	1¢ green (740)	15.00	12.00				279,960
	Pane of 6						
769a	Single stamp	1.75	1.75			8.00	1,679,760
770	3¢ deep violet (742)	35.00	25.00				215,920
	Pane of 6						
770a	Single stamp	3.75	3.75			10.00	1,295,520
771	16¢ dark blue Seal of U.S. (CE2),						
	issued in sheets of 200	4.00	3.50	85.00	(6)	25.00	1,370,560
	Perf. 11x10½						
772	3¢ Connecticut 300th Anniv.,						
	Apr. 26	.15	.06	2.00	(4)	11.00	70,726,800
773	3¢ California-Pacific Exposition,						
	May 29	.12	.06	2.00	(4)	11.00	100,839,600
	Perf. 11						
774	3¢ Boulder Dam, Sep. 30	.12	.06	2.75	(6)	15.00	73,610,650
	Perf. 11x10½						
775	3¢ Michigan 100th Anniv., Nov. 1	.12	.06	2.00	(4)	11.00	75,823,900
	Issues of 1936						
776	3¢ Texas 100th Anniv., Mar. 2	.12	.06	2.00	(4)	12.00	124,324,500
	Perf.10½x11						
777	3¢ Rhode Island 300th Anniv.,						
	May 4	.15	.06	2.00	(4)	10.00	67,127,650
	Third International Philatelic Exhibition Issue, Souvenir Sheet, Imperf.						
778	Violet, sheet of 4 different stamps						
	(772, 773, 775 and 776), May 9	3.50	3.50			17.50	2,809,039
	Perf. 11x10½						
782	3¢ Arkansas 100th Anniv., June 15	.12	.06	2.00	(4)	10.00	72,992,650
783	3¢ Oregon Territory, July 14	.12	.06	2.00	(4)	10.00	74,407,450
784	3¢ Susan B. Anthony, Aug. 26	.10	.05	.75	(4)	21.00	269,522,200

1936-1937

	Issues of 1936-37	Un	U	PB/LP	#	FDC	Q
	Army Issue						
785	1¢ George Washington						
	and Nathanael Greene, 1936	.10	.06	1.00	(4)	6.00	105,196,150
786	2¢ Andrew Jackson and						
	Winfield Scott, 1937	.15	.06	1.10	(4)	6.00	93,848,500
787	3¢ Generals Sherman,						
	Grant and Sheridan, 1937	.20	.08	1.50	(4)	6.00	87,741,150
788	4¢ Generals Robert E. Lee						
	and "Stonewall" Jackson, 1937	.65	.15	13.00	(4)	6.75	35,794,150
789	5¢ U.S. Military Academy,						
	West Point, 1937	1.00	.15	15.00	(4)	8.00	36,839,250
	Navy Issue						
790	1¢ John Paul Jones						
	and John Barry, 1936	.10	.06	1.00	(4)	6.00	104,773,450
791	2¢ Stephen Decatur						
	and Thomas MacDonough, 1937	.15	.06	1.10	(4)	6.00	92,054,550
792	3¢ Admirals David G. Farragut						
	and David D. Porter, 1937	.20	.08	1.50	(4)	6.00	93,291,650
793	4¢ Admirals William T. Sampson,						
	George Dewey and Winfield						
	S. Schley, 1937	.65	.15	13.00	(4)	6.75	34,552,950
794	5¢ Seal of U.S. Naval Academy						
	and Naval Cadets, 1937	1.00	.15	15.00	(4)	8.00	36,819,050
	Issues of 1937						
795	3¢ Northwest Ordinance						
	150th Anniversary, July 13	.12	.06	2.00	(4)	8.50	84,825,250
	Perf. 11						
796	5¢ Virginia Dare, Aug. 18	.35	.25	11.00	(6)	9.50	25,040,400
	Society of Philatelic Americans, Souvenir Sheet, Imperf.						
797	10¢ blue green (749), Aug. 26	1.25	.85			8.00	5,277,445
	Perf. 11x10½						
798	3¢ Constitution 150th Anniv.,						
	Sept. 17	.15	.07	1.65	(4)	8.50	99,882,300
	Territorial Issues, Perf. 10½x11						
799	3¢ Hawaii, Oct. 18	.15	.07	2.00	(4)	9.50	78,454,450
	Perf. 11x10½						
800	3¢ Alaska, Nov. 12	.15	.07	2.00	(4)	9.50	77,004,200
801	3¢ Puerto Rico, Nov. 25	.15	.07	1.75	(4)	9.50	81,292,450
802	3¢ Virgin Islands, Dec. 15	.15	.07	2.00	(4)	9.50	76,474,550

785

786

787

788

789

790

791

792

793

794

795

796

798

799

800

801

802

1938

803   804   805   806

807   808   809   810   811   812

813   814   815   816   817

818   819   820   821   822   823

824   825   826   827   828   829

830   831   832   833   834

	Un	U	PB/LP	#	FDC	Q
Presidential Issue, 1938						
803 ½¢ Benjamin Franklin	.05	.05	.40	(4)	1.25	
804 1¢ George Washington	.06	.05	.25	(4)	2.00	
804b Booklet pane of 6	1.75	.20				
805 1½¢ Martha Washington	.06	.05	.30	(4)	2.00	
806 2¢ John Adams	.06	.05	.35	(4)	2.00	
806b Booklet pane of 6	4.25	.50				
807 3¢ Thomas Jefferson	.10	.05	.50	(4)	2.00	
807a Booklet pane of 6	8.50	.50				
808 4¢ James Madison	.45	.05	2.00	(4)	2.00	
809 4½¢ White House	.20	.06	1.60	(4)	2.50	
810 5¢ James Monroe	.40	.05	1.80	(4)	2.25	
811 6¢ John Q. Adams	.45	.05	2.00	(4)	2.25	
812 7¢ Andrew Jackson	.50	.05	2.00	(4)	2.50	
813 8¢ Martin Van Buren	.65	.05	2.75	(4)	2.50	
814 9¢ William H. Harrison	.70	.05	3.00	(4)	2.65	
815 10¢ John Tyler	.50	.05	2.20	(4)	2.75	
816 11¢ James K. Polk	1.00	.08	4.50	(4)	2.75	
817 12¢ Zachary Taylor	1.65	.06	6.75	(4)	3.00	
818 13¢ Millard Fillmore	1.75	.08	7.25	(4)	3.00	
819 14¢ Franklin Pierce	1.75	.10	7.25	(4)	3.25	
820 15¢ James Buchanan	.60	.05	2.60	(4)	3.25	
821 16¢ Abraham Lincoln	1.75	.35	7.25	(4)	3.50	
822 17¢ Andrew Johnson	1.50	.12	7.00	(4)	3.75	
823 18¢ Ulysses S. Grant	3.00	.08	13.00	(4)	4.25	
824 19¢ Rutherford B. Hayes	1.85	.50	9.00	(4)	4.25	
825 20¢ James A. Garfield	1.20	.05	5.75	(4)	4.50	
826 21¢ Chester A. Arthur	2.25	.10	10.50	(4)	5.00	
827 22¢ Grover Cleveland	2.25	.50	12.50	(4)	5.25	
828 24¢ Benjamin Harrison	7.00	.25	30.00	(4)	5.25	
829 25¢ William McKinley	1.40	.05	6.25	(4)	6.50	
830 30¢ Theodore Roosevelt	9.00	.05	38.50	(4)	10.00	
831 50¢ William Howard Taft	13.50	.06	57.50	(4)	20.00	
Perf. 11						
832 $1 Woodrow Wilson	15.00	.10	62.50	(4)	55.00	
832b Wmkd. USIR	350.00	90.00				
833 $2 Warren G. Harding	37.50	6.00	200.00	(4)	110.00	
834 $5 Calvin Coolidge	140.00	5.50	650.00	(4)	175.00	

This series was in use for approximately 16 years when the Liberty Series began replacing it. Various shades of these stamps are in existence due to the numerous reprintings.

		Un	U	PB/LP	#	FDC	Q
	Issues of 1938, Perf. 11x10½						
835	3¢ Constitution Ratification,						
	June 21	.25	.08	5.50	(4)	9.00	73,043,650
	Perf. 11						
836	3¢ Swedish-Finnish 300th Anniv.,						
	June 27	.25	.10	6.00	(6)	8.50	58,564,368
	Perf. 11x10½						
837	3¢ Northwest Territory, July 15	.25	.08	15.00	(4)	8.50	65,939,500
838	3¢ Iowa Territory 100th Anniv.,						
	Aug. 24	.25	.08	9.00	(4)	8.50	47,064,300
	Issues of 1939, Coil Stamps, Perf. 10 Vertically						
839	1¢ green Washington (804)	.25	.06	1.50		7.00	
840	1½¢ bistre brown						
	M. Washington (805)	.30	.06	1.50		7.00	
841	2¢ rose car. Adams (806)	.30	.05	1.75		7.00	
842	3¢ deep violet Jefferson (807)	.75	.05	3.00		8.00	
843	4¢ red violet Madison (808)	9.00	.35	35.00		9.00	
844	4½¢ dk. gray White House (809)	.60	.45	4.00		9.00	
845	5¢ bright blue Monroe (810)	6.50	.35	30.00		10.00	
846	6¢ red orange J.Q. Adams (811)	1.40	.20	8.75		15.00	
847	10¢ brown red Tyler (815)	15.00	.40	60.00		20.00	
	Perf. 10 Horizontally						
848	1¢ green Washington (804)	1.00	.12	3.75		7.00	
849	1½¢ bistre brown						
	M. Washington (805)	1.50	.40	4.75		8.00	
850	2¢ rose car. Adams (806)	3.50	.50	8.50		10.00	
851	3¢ deep violet Jefferson (807)	2.75	.45	7.50		12.50	
	Perf. 10½x11						
852	3¢ Golden Gate Exposition,						
	Feb. 18	.12	.06	1.75	(4)	7.50	114,439,600
853	3¢ New York World's Fair, Apr. 1	.15	.06	2.00	(4)	10.00	101,699,550
	Perf. 11						
854	3¢ Washington's Inauguration,						
	Apr. 30	.35	.10	4.25	(6)	7.50	72,764,550
	Perf. 11x10½						
855	3¢ Baseball Anniversary						
	100th, June 12	.35	.08	4.00	(4)	20.00	81,269,600
	Perf. 11						
856	3¢ Panama Canal, Aug. 15	.30	.08	6.00	(6)	7.50	67,813,350
	Perf. 10½x11						
857	3¢ 300th Anniv. of Printing,						
	Sept. 25	.15	.08	1.65	(4)	7.50	71,394,750
	Perf. 11x10½						
858	3¢ 50th Anniv. of Statehood,						
	Nov. 2	.15	.08	1.65	(4)	7.00	66,835,000

35

836

837

838

52

853

854

55

856

857

860

861

862

863

865

866

867

868

870

871

872

873

875

876

877

878

		Un	U	PB/LP	#	FDC	Q
	Famous Americans Issue, 1940, Perf. 10½x11						
	Authors						
859	1¢ Washington Irving	.08	.06	1.10	(4)	2.00	56,348,320
860	2¢ James Fenimore Cooper	.10	.08	1.25	(4)	2.00	53,177,110
861	3¢ Ralph Waldo Emerson	.12	.06	2.00	(4)	2.00	53,260,270
862	5¢ Louisa May Alcott	.35	.30	12.00	(4)	5.00	22,104,950
863	10¢ Samuel L. Clemens						
	(Mark Twain)	2.50	2.35	55.00	(4)	8.25	13,201,270
	Poets						
864	1¢ Henry W. Longfellow	.12	.08	1.75	(4)	2.00	51,603,580
865	2¢ John Greenleaf Whittier	.10	.08	1.75	(4)	2.00	52,100,510
866	3¢ James Russell Lowell	.18	.06	3.50	(4)	2.00	51,666,580
867	5¢ Walt Whitman	.35	.25	12.00	(4)	4.50	22,207,780
868	10¢ James Whitcomb Riley	3.50	3.00	55.00	(4)	8.25	11,835,530
	Educators						
869	1¢ Horace Mann	.09	.08	1.75	(4)	2.00	52,471,160
870	2¢ Mark Hopkins	.10	.06	1.40	(4)	2.00	52,366,440
871	3¢ Charles W. Eliot	.30	.06	3.25	(4)	2.00	51,636,270
872	5¢ Frances E. Willard	.50	.35	13.00	(4)	4.75	20,729,030
873	10¢ Booker T. Washington	2.50	2.25	35.00	(4)	8.25	14,125,580
	Scientists						
874	1¢ John James Audubon	.08	.06	1.00	(4)	2.00	59,409,000
875	2¢ Dr. Crawford W. Long	.10	.06	1.20	(4)	2.00	57,888,600
876	3¢ Luther Burbank	.10	.06	1.75	(4)	2.00	58,273,180
877	5¢ Dr. Walter Reed	.30	.25	9.50	(4)	4.50	23,779,000
878	10¢ Jane Addams	2.00	2.00	35.00	(4)	8.25	15,112,580
	Composers						
879	1¢ Stephen Collins Foster	.08	.06	1.25	(4)	2.00	57,322,790
880	2¢ John Philip Sousa	.10	.06	1.25	(4)	2.00	58,281,580
881	3¢ Victor Herbert	.15	.06	1.75	(4)	2.00	56,398,790
882	5¢ Edward MacDowell	.60	.30	14.00	(4)	4.50	21,147,000
883	10¢ Ethelbert Nevin	5.50	2.25	50.00	(4)	7.75	13,328,000

	1940 continued	Un	U	PB/LP	#	FDC	Q
	Artists						
884	1¢ Gilbert Charles Stuart	.08	.06	1.10	(4)	2.00	54,389,510
885	2¢ James A. McNeill Whistler	.10	.06	1.10	(4)	2.00	53,636,580
886	3¢ Augustus Saint-Gaudens	.10	.06	1.25	(4)	2.00	55,313,230
887	5¢ Daniel Chester French	.40	.22	12.50	(4)	4.00	21,720,580
888	10¢ Frederic Remington	2.75	2.25	45.00	(4)	7.75	13,600,580
	Inventors						
889	1¢ Eli Whitney	.12	.08	2.50	(4)	2.00	47,599,580
890	2¢ Samuel F. B. Morse	.10	.06	1.30	(4)	2.00	53,766,510
891	3¢ Cyrus Hall McCormick	.20	.06	2.50	(4)	2.00	54,193,580
892	5¢ Elias Howe	1.50	.40	22.50	(4)	5.00	20,264,580
893	10¢ Alexander Graham Bell	15.50	3.25	120.00	(4)	13.50	13,726,580
	Issues of 1940, Perf. 11x10½						
894	3¢ Pony Express, Apr. 3	.50	.15	6.50	(4)	6.75	46,497,400
	Perf. 10½x11						
895	3¢ Pan American Union, Apr. 14	.40	.12	5.50	(4)	5.25	47,700,000
	Perf. 11x10½						
896	3¢ Idaho Statehood,						
	50th Anniversary, July 3	.20	.08	3.50	(4)	5.25	50,618,150
	Perf. 10½x11						
897	3¢ Wyoming Statehood,						
	50th Anniversary, July 10	.20	.08	2.75	(4)	5.25	50,034,400
	Perf. 11x10½						
898	3¢ Coronado Expedition, Sept. 7	.20	.08	2.75	(4)	5.25	60,943,700
	National Defense Issue, Oct. 16						
899	1¢ Statue of Liberty	.05	.05	.70	(4)	5.00	
900	2¢ Anti-aircraft Gun	.06	.05	.70	(4)	5.00	
901	3¢ Torch of Enlightenment	.12	.05	1.40	(4)	5.00	
	Perf. 10½x11						
902	3¢ Thirteenth Amendment,						
	Oct. 20	.25	.15	6.50	(4)	6.00	44,389,550
	Issue of 1941, Perf. 11x10½						
903	3¢ Vermont Statehood, Mar. 4	.22	.10	2.50	(4)	5.50	54,574,550
	Issues of 1942						
904	3¢ Kentucky Statehood, June 1	.15	.12	2.25	(4)	5.00	63,558,400
905	3¢ Win the War, July 4	.10	.05	.60	(4)	4.75	

1940-1942

884   885   886   887   888

889   890   891   892   893

894   896

895   897

898   899   900   901

902

903   904   905

1942-1944

906

907

908

909

910

911

912

913

914

915

916

917

918

919

920

921

922

923

	1942 continued	Un	U	PB/LP	#	FDC	Q
906	5¢ Chinese Resistance, July 7	.40	.30	25.00	(4)	7.00	21,272,800
	Issues of 1943						
907	2¢ Allied Nations, Jan. 14	.08	.05	.50	(4)	4.25	1,671,564,200
908	1¢ Four Freedoms, Feb. 12	.06	.05	1.00	(4)	4.25	1,227,334,200
	Overrun Countries Issue, 1943-44, Perf. 12						
909	5¢ Poland, June 22	.35	.20			5.75	19,999,646
910	5¢ Czechoslovakia, July 12	.30	.15			5.50	19,999,646
911	5¢ Norway, July 27	.25	.12			5.00	19,999,646
912	5¢ Luxembourg, Aug. 10	.25	.12			5.00	19,999,646
913	5¢ Netherlands, Aug. 24	.25	.12			5.00	19,999,646
914	5¢ Belgium, Sept. 14	.25	.12			5.00	19,999,646
915	5¢ France, Sept. 28	.25	.10			5.00	19,999,646
916	5¢ Greece, Oct. 12	.85	.60			5.00	14,999,646
917	5¢ Yugoslavia, Oct. 26	.50	.40			5.00	14,999,646
918	5¢ Albania, Nov. 9	.50	.40			5.00	14,999,646
919	5¢ Austria, Nov. 23	.30	.25			5.00	14,999,646
920	5¢ Denmark, Dec. 7	.50	.50			5.00	14,999,646
921	5¢ Korea, Nov. 2, 1944	.28	.25			6.50	14,999,646
	Inscribed "KORPA"	22.50	17.50				
	Issues of 1944, Perf. 11x10½						
922	3¢ Transcontinental Railroad,						
	May 10	.20	.15	2.50	(4)	6.75	61,303,000
923	3¢ Steamship, May 22	.15	.15	2.50	(4)	4.50	61,001,450

A Wartime Oddity

Poland, one of the many countries overrun by Germany during the second World War, was honored by the United States as part of a series of stamps issued during 1943-44 (#909).

During the war, Germany established a Prisoner of War camp at Woldenberg for captured Polish officers. Some of the 5,908 officers who were imprisoned set up an internal post office so that mail could be sent from barracks to barracks. Incoming mail was brought to one location and sorted for delivery. This was done with the cooperation of the German authorities.

In order to help pay the postmen, numerous postage stamps were issued. On November 8 to 11, 1942, the stamp collectors in the prison camp held a philatelic exhibition for their own amusement and for that of their fellow officers. A set of 27 stamp design essays was offered for sale for five marks. Since engraving tools were not available, the pictures were made by use of woodcuts. Some of the designs were later utilized for stamps to be used by the Woldenberg mail system.

One of these essays by Second Lieutenant Zygmunt Pazda commemorates the discovery of America and pictures an American ship with the American flag flying from its bow. This is the only stamp made in Nazi Germany during World War II that illustrates the flag of its war-time enemy, the United States.

	1944 continued	Un	U	PB/LP	#	FDC	Q
924	3¢ Telegraph, May 24	.12	.10	1.60	(4)	4.00	60,605,000
925	3¢ Philippines, Sept. 27	.12	.12	3.00	(4)	4.00	50,129,350
926	3¢ 50th Anniversary of						
	Motion Picture, Oct. 31	.12	.10	2.00	(4)	4.00	53,479,400
	Issues of 1945						
927	3¢ Florida Statehood, Mar. 3	.10	.08	1.00	(4)	4.00	61,617,350
928	5¢ United Nations Conference,						
	Apr. 25	.12	.08	.70	(4)	4.00	75,500,000
	Perf. 10½x11						
929	3¢ Iwo Jima (Marines), July 11	.10	.05	.50	(4)	6.00	137,321,000
	Issues of 1945-46, Perf. 11x10½						
	Franklin D. Roosevelt Issue						
930	1¢ F.D.R. and home at Hyde Park	.05	.05	.30	(4)	3.00	128,140,000
931	2¢ Roosevelt and "Little						
	White House," Ga.	.08	.08	.40	(4)	3.00	67,255,000
932	3¢ Roosevelt and White House	.10	.08	.65	(4)	3.00	133,870,000
933	5¢ F.D.R., Globe and						
	Four Freedoms, 1946	.12	.08	.75	(4)	3.00	76,455,400
934	3¢ U.S. Army in Paris, Sept. 28	.10	.05	.60	(4)	4.00	128,357,750
935	3¢ U.S. Navy, Oct. 27	.10	.05	.60	(4)	4.00	135,863,000
936	3¢ U.S. Coast Guard, Nov. 10	.10	.05	.60	(4)	4.00	111,616,700
937	3¢ Alfred E. Smith, Nov. 26	.10	.05	.50	(4)	3.00	308,587,700
938	3¢ Texas Statehood, Dec. 29	.10	.05	.50	(4)	3.00	170,640,000
	Issues of 1946						
939	3¢ Merchant Marine, Feb. 26	.10	.05	.50	(4)	3.00	135,927,000

America's Smallest Post Office

The U.S. Army post office in Roedelheim, a suburb of Frankfurt, Germany, measures 7 feet by 7 feet. There are two employees, both active duty soldiers. Incoming mail arrives at 10 a.m., and the 100 people served by the facility pick up their mail from 80 post office boxes since there is no carrier route delivery. The hours of operation are 11:30 a.m. to 12:15 p.m. Outgoing mail is forwarded to another post office for cancellation.

The smallest post office in the continental U.S. is located in Ochopee, Florida 33943. This office measures 8 feet 4 inches by 7 feet 3 inches, and has been publicized as the nation's smallest post office. Forty families call at the post office for their mail. The only employee, other than the postmaster, is an independent contractor who serves 160 roadside mail boxes on a 123-mile route.

The Florida post office, located in the Everglades area, has no air conditioning, no water fountain and no rest room. The postmaster, Evelyn Shealy, is proud of her building and will be glad to give visitors a tour of the facility.

924

925

926

927

928

929

930

931

932

933

934

935

940

941

942

943

944

945

946

947

948

949

	1946 continued	Un	U	PB/LP	#	FDC	Q
940	3¢ Veterans of World War II, May 9	.10	.05	.55	(4)	3.00	260,339,100
941	3¢ Tennessee Statehood, June 1	.10	.05	.50	(4)	3.00	132,274,500
942	3¢ Iowa Statehood, Aug. 3	.10	.05	.50	(4)	3.00	132,430,000
943	3¢ Smithsonian Institution, Aug. 10	.10	.05	.50	(4)	3.00	139,209,500
944	3¢ Kearny Expedition, Oct. 16	.10	.05	.50	(4)	3.00	114,684,450
	Issues of 1947, Perf. 10½x11						
945	3¢ Thomas A. Edison, Feb. 11	.10	.05	.50	(4)	3.00	156,540,510
	Perf. 11x10½						
946	3¢ Joseph Pulitzer, Apr. 10	.10	.05	.50	(4)	3.00	120,452,600
947	3¢ 100th Anniv. of the						
	Postage Stamp, May 17	.10	.05	.50	(4)	3.00	127,104,300
	Imperf.						
948	Souvenir sheet of two, May 19	1.75	1.00			3.50	10,299,600
948a	5¢ blue, single stamp (1)	.35	.30				
948b	10¢ brn. org., single stamp (2)	.50	.30				
	Issued in sheets of two with marginal inscription commemorating the 100th anniversary of U.S. postage stamps and the Centenary International Philatelic Exhibition, held in New York in 1947.						
	Perf. 11x10½						
949	3¢ Doctors, June 9	.10	.05	.50	(4)	2.00	132,902,000
950	3¢ Utah, July 24	.10	.05	.50	(4)	2.00	131,968,000
951	3¢ U.S. Frigate Constitution,						
	Oct. 21	.10	.05	.50	(4)	2.00	131,488,000
	Perf. 10½x11						
952	3¢ Everglades Nat'l Park, Dec. 5	.10	.05	.50	(4)	2.00	122,362,000

Henry Knox
(Great Americans Series)

During the winter of 1775-76, General George Washington sent 25-year-old Colonel Henry Knox to Fort Ticonderoga near the Canadian border with a difficult request for even a seasoned veteran of the military—to bring back a large store of cannon captured by Ethan Allen from the British. Using oxen, horses and the sheer power of his personality, the young soldier retrieved a remarkable 55 pieces of artillery totaling 120,000 pounds and transported it 300 miles over snow and ice to Boston, where it was successfully used to drive the British from the besieged city.

Credited with organizing the American artillery, the enterprising Knox continued an active role in nearly every important military engagement throughout the Revolutionary War, becoming Washington's trusted friend and advisor. He accompanied the General at the crossing of the Delaware River on Christmas night in 1776, and at Valley Forge during the cruel winter of 1777.

After the British surrender at Yorktown, Knox was made a major general, the youngest American to hold that rank in the Continental army, and placed in command at West Point. He was appointed America's first secretary of war under the Articles of Confederation in 1785, and retained that post in 1789 as a key member of President Washington's first cabinet.

	Issues of 1948	Un	U	PB/LP	#	FDC	Q
953	3¢ Dr. George Washington Carver,						
	Jan. 5	.10	.05	.50	(4)	2.00	121,548,000
	Perf. 11x10½						
954	3¢ Calif. Gold 100th Anniversary,						
	Jan. 24	.10	.05	.50	(4)	2.00	131,109,500
955	3¢ Mississippi Territory, Apr. 7	.10	.05	.50	(4)	2.00	122,650,500
956	3¢ Four Chaplains, May 28	.10	.05	.50	(4)	2.00	121,953,500
957	3¢ Wisconsin Statehood, May 29	.10	.05	.50	(4)	2.00	115,250,000
958	5¢ Swedish Pioneer, June 4	.15	.10	1.00	(4)	2.00	64,198,500
959	3¢ Progress of Women, July 19	.10	.05	.50	(4)	2.00	117,642,500
	Perf. 10½x11						
960	3¢ William Allen White, July 31	.10	.06	.60	(4)	2.00	77,649,600
	Perf. 11x10½						
961	3¢ U.S.-Canada Friendship,						
	Aug. 2	.10	.05	.50	(4)	2.00	113,474,500
962	3¢ Francis Scott Key, Aug. 9	.10	.05	.50	(4)	2.00	120,868,500
963	3¢ Salute to Youth, Aug. 11	.10	.06	.50	(4)	2.00	77,800,500
964	3¢ Oregon Territory, Aug. 14	.10	.10	.90	(4)	2.00	52,214,000
	Perf. 10½x11						
965	3¢ Harlan Fiske Stone, Aug. 25	.10	.08	1.70	(4)	2.00	53,958,100
966	3¢ Palomar Mt. Obs., Aug. 30	.12	.10	2.50	(4)	2.00	61,120,010
	Perf. 11x10½						
967	3¢ Clara Barton, Sept. 7	.10	.08	.60	(4)	1.50	57,823,000
968	3¢ Poultry Industry, Sept. 9	.12	.08	.80	(4)	1.50	52,975,000
	Perf. 10½x11						
969	3¢ Gold Star Mothers, Sept. 21	.12	.08	.65	(4)	2.00	77,149,000
970	3¢ Fort Kearny, Sept. 22	.12	.08	.65	(4)	2.00	58,332,000
971	3¢ Volunteer Firemen, Oct. 4	.12	.08	.75	(4)	2.00	56,228,000

The Four Chaplains

The Four Chaplains stamp (#956) is a simple tribute to four men of four faiths who were united in one cause, giving spiritual and physical aid to American troops.

The troop transport, U.S.S. Dorchester, *was torpedoed off the coast of Greenland in February 1943. These four men of religion demonstrated their faith by praying with the men, assisting them into lifeboats and giving solace to those who remained on board. They then gave their personal life jackets to four soldiers on the sinking ship. The four chaplains were George L. Fox (Methodist), Alexander D. Goods (Jewish), Clark V. Poling (Reformed Church) and John P. Washington (Catholic).*

When last seen they were still on deck with arms linked, praying, as the ship sank.

953

954

955

956

957

958

959

960

961

962

963

964

965

966

967

972

973

974

975

976

977

978

979

980

981

982

983

984

985

986

	1948 continued	Un	U	PB/LP	#	FDC	Q
972	3¢ Five Indian Tribes, Oct. 15	.12	.08	.75	(4)	1.50	57,832,000
973	3¢ Rough Riders, Oct. 27	.12	.10	1.20	(4)	1.50	53,875,000
974	3¢ Juliette Low, Oct. 29	.12	.08	.65	(4)	1.50	63,834,000
	Perf. 10½x11						
975	3¢ Will Rogers, Nov. 4	.12	.08	1.00	(4)	1.50	67,162,200
976	3¢ Fort Bliss 100th Anniv., Nov. 5	.15	.08	2.00	(4)	1.50	64,561,000
	Perf. 11x10½						
977	3¢ Moina Michael, Nov. 9	.12	.08	.65	(4)	1.50	64,079,500
978	3¢ Gettysburg Address, Nov. 19	.12	.08	.70	(4)	1.50	63,388,000
	Perf. 10½x11						
979	3¢ American Turners, Nov. 20	.12	.08	.65	(4)	1.50	62,285,000
980	3¢ Joel Chandler Harris, Dec. 9	.12	.08	1.00	(4)	1.50	57,492,610
	Issues of 1949, Perf. 11x10½						
981	3¢ Minnesota Territory, Mar. 3	.10	.05	.50	(4)	1.50	99,190,000
982	3¢ Washington & Lee University,						
	Apr. 12	.10	.05	.50	(4)	1.50	104,790,000
983	3¢ Puerto Rico Election, Apr. 27	.10	.05	.50	(4)	1.50	108,805,000
984	3¢ Annapolis 300th Anniv.,						
	May 23	.10	.05	.50	(4)	1.50	107,340,000
985	3¢ Grand Army of the Republic,						
	Aug. 29	.10	.05	.50	(4)	1.50	117,020,000
	Perf. 10½x11						
986	3¢ Edgar Allan Poe, Oct. 7	.10	.05	.60	(4)	1.50	122,633,000
	Issues of 1950, Perf. 11x10½						
987	3¢ American Bankers Association,						
	Jan. 3	.10	.05	.50	(4)	1.50	130,960,000
	Perf. 10½x11						
988	3¢ Samuel Gompers, Jan. 27	.10	.05	.75	(4)	1.50	128,478,000
	National Capital 150th Anniv. Issue, Perf. 10½x11, 11x10½						
989	3¢ Statue of Freedom	.10	.05	.50	(4)	1.50	132,090,000
990	3¢ Executive Mansion	.10	.05	.50	(4)	1.50	130,050,000

	1950 continued	Un	U	PB/LP	#	FDC	Q
991	3¢ Supreme Court Building	.10	.05	.50	(4)	1.50	131,350,000
992	3¢ U.S. Capitol Building	.10	.05	.50	(4)	1.50	129,980,000
	Perf. 11x10½						
993	3¢ Railroad Engineers, Apr. 29	.10	.05	.50	(4)	1.50	122,315,000
994	3¢ Kansas City, Mo., June 3	.10	.05	.50	(4)	1.50	122,170,000
995	3¢ Boy Scouts, June 30	.10	.06	.55	(4)	2.25	131,635,000
996	3¢ Indian Territory, July 4	.10	.05	.50	(4)	1.50	121,860,000
997	3¢ California Statehood, Sept. 9	.10	.05	.50	(4)	1.50	121,120,000
	Issues of 1951						
998	3¢ Confederate Veterans, May 30	.10	.05	.50	(4)	1.50	119,120,000
999	3¢ Nevada 100th Anniv., July 14	.10	.05	.50	(4)	1.50	112,125,000
1000	3¢ Landing of Cadillac, July 24	.10	.05	.50	(4)	1.50	114,140,000
1001	3¢ Colorado Statehood, Aug. 1	.10	.05	.50	(4)	1.50	114,490,000
1002	3¢ American Chemical Society,						
	Sept. 4	.10	.05	.50	(4)	1.50	117,200,000
1003	3¢ Battle of Brooklyn, Dec. 10	.10	.05	.50	(4)	1.50	116,130,000
	Issues of 1952						
1004	3¢ Betsy Ross, Jan. 2	.10	.05	.60	(4)	1.50	116,175,000
1005	3¢ 4-H Club, Jan. 15	.10	.05	.75	(4)	1.50	115,945,000
1006	3¢ B&O Railroad, Feb. 28	.10	.05	.50	(4)	2.00	112,540,000
1007	3¢ American Auto. Assn., Mar. 4	.10	.05	.60	(4)	.85	117,415,000
1008	3¢ NATO, Apr. 4	.10	.05	.55	(4)	.85	2,899,580,000
1009	3¢ Grand Coulee Dam, May 15	.10	.05	.50	(4)	.85	114,540,000

Camels and Rockets

In the late 1800s the military commander of Fort Bliss, Texas, imported some camels from Egypt as replacements for horses. The soldiers tried using the camels for transportation and to carry mail, but found that the creatures were temperamental and would not work with other nearby animals. The 3-cent stamp commemorating the 100th anniversary of Fort Bliss (#976) was issued on November 5, 1948, and has camels in its border design.

Fort Bliss survived and became the first home in the United States for German rocket scientists after World War II. By February 1946, more than 100 scientists were stationed on this Texas army post working on the guided-missile program. Tests were conducted utilizing captured German V-1 rockets, and the nation was on its way to the establishment of our future space program. The Army's growing missile program required more space than was available at the army post, and, in 1950, the missile complex was moved. More than 100 members of the original Werner Von Braun rocket team and 1,000 other employees moved to the Redstone Arsenal in Huntsville, Alabama.

Fort Bliss today is the Army Air Defense Center that trains missilemen, artillerymen and air defense units. A look at the nation's first space stamp reminds the collector of the unusual combination of camels and rockets.

1950-1952

991

992

993

994

995

996

997

998

999

1000

1001

1002

1003

1004

1005

1006

1007

1008

1009

1010

1011

1012

1013

1014

1015

1016

1017

1018

1019

1020

1021

1022

1023

1024

1025

1026

1027

	1952 continued	Un	U	PB/LP	#	FDC	Q
1010	3¢ General Lafayette, June 13	.10	.05	.50	(4)	.85	113,135,000
	Perf. 10½x11						
1011	3¢ Mt. Rushmore Mem., Aug. 11	.10	.05	.60	(4)	.85	116,255,000
	Perf. 11x10½						
1012	3¢ Engineering, Sept. 6	.10	.05	.50	(4)	.85	113,860,000
1013	3¢ Service Women, Sept. 11	.10	.05	.50	(4)	.85	124,260,000
1014	3¢ Gutenberg Bible, Sept. 30	.10	.05	.50	(4)	.85	115,735,000
1015	3¢ Newspaper Boys, Oct. 4	.10	.05	.50	(4)	.85	115,430,000
1016	3¢ Red Cross, Nov. 21	.10	.05	.50	(4)	.85	136,220,000
	Issues of 1953						
1017	3¢ National Guard, Feb. 23	*.10*	.05	.50	(4)	.85	114,894,600
1018	3¢ Ohio Statehood, Mar. 2	.10	.05	.80	(4)	.85	118,706,000
1019	3¢ Washington Territory, Mar. 2	.10	.05	.50	(4)	.85	114,190,000
1020	3¢ Louisiana Purchase, Apr. 30	.10	.05	.50	(4)	.85	113,990,000
1021	5¢ Opening of Japan 100th Anniv.,						
	July 14	.15	.10	1.40	(4)	.85	89,289,600
1022	3¢ American Bar Assn., Aug. 24	.10	.05	.50	(4)	.85	114,865,000
1023	3¢ Sagamore Hill, Sept. 14	.10	.05	.50	(4)	1.00	115,780,000
1024	3¢ Future Farmers, Oct. 13	.10	.05	.50	(4)	.85	115,244,600
1025	3¢ Trucking Industry, Oct. 27	.10	.05	.50	(4)	.85	123,709,600
1026	3¢ General Patton, Nov. 11	.15	.05	.75	(4)	.85	114,798,600
1027	3¢ New York City						
	300th Anniversary, Nov. 20	.15	.05	.75	(4)	.85	115,759,600

The Parcel Post Bank

The trucking industry (#1025) in its early days had many unusual loads, but none so improbable as a load of 80,000 bricks sent through the mail to build a bank in Utah. The freight cost of shipping the bricks from Salt Lake City to Vernal in 1916 was four times as much as the bricks were worth. The contractor ordered the factory to ship the 40 tons of bricks by parcel post in 50-pound packages. There was no restriction on number of packages or weight. The mail route was a combination of railroad and teams of horses which constituted the trucking industry in Utah at that time.

The brick company started mailing the bricks in 50-pound crates, one ton at a time. The railroad brought the packages to Mack, Utah, where freight wagons and teams of horses struggled with the heavy landslide of cartons. The postmaster at Vernal immediately informed his superiors that tons of packages were backing up and that they could not deliver the mail on time. The report of a mountain of undelivered bricks was forwarded to the Postmaster General in Washington.

The postal regulations were rewritten immediately limiting shipments in one day to 200 pounds. The notice stated, "It is not the intent of the U.S. Post Office that buildings should be shipped through the mail."

	1953 continued	Un	U	PB/LP	#	FDC	Q
1028	3¢ Gadsden Purchase, Dec. 30	.10	.05	.50	(4)	.85	116,134,600
	Issues of 1954						
1029	3¢ Columbia University 200th						
	Anniv., Jan. 4	.10	.05	.50	(4)	.85	118,540,000
	Liberty Issue, 1954-61, Perf. 11x10½, 10½x11						
1030	½¢ Benjamin Franklin, 1955	.05	.05	.30	(4)	.85	Unlimited
1031	1¢ George Washington, 1954	.05	.05	.25	(4)	.85	Unlimited
1031A	1¼¢ Palace of the Governors,						
	Santa Fe, 1960	.05	.05	1.75	(4)	.85	Unlimited
1032	1½¢ Mount Vernon, 1956	.08	.05	7.50	(4)	.60	Unlimited
1033	2¢ Thomas Jefferson, 1954	.05	.05	.25	(4)	.60	Unlimited
1034	2½¢ Bunker Hill Monument						
	and Massachusetts flag, 1959	.08	.05	2.00	(4)	.60	Unlimited
1035	3¢ Statue of Liberty, 1954	.08	.05	.40	(4)	.60	Unlimited
1035a	Booklet pane of 6	3.00	.50				
1036	4¢ Abraham Lincoln, 1954	.10	.05	.50	(4)	.60	Unlimited
1036a	Booklet pane of 6	2.00	.50				
1037	4½¢ The Hermitage, 1959	.15	.08	1.75	(4)	.60	Unlimited
1038	5¢ James Monroe, 1954	.17	.05	.75	(4)	.60	Unlimited
1039	6¢ Theodore Roosevelt, 1955	.40	.05	2.00	(4)	.65	Unlimited
1040	7¢ Woodrow Wilson, 1956	.25	.05	1.50	(4)	.70	Unlimited
	Perf. 11						
1041	8¢ Statue of Liberty, 1954	.30	.06	5.00	(4)	.80	Unlimited
1042	8¢ Statue of Liberty, redrawn, 1958	.30	.05	1.75	(4)	.60	Unlimited
	Perf. 11x10½, 10½x11						
1042A	8¢ John J. Pershing, 1961	.25	.05	1.50	(4)	.60	Unlimited
1043	9¢ The Alamo, 1956	.30	.05	1.50	(4)	.90	Unlimited
1044	10¢ Independence Hall, 1956	.35	.05	1.65	(4)	.90	Unlimited
	Perf. 11						
1044A	11¢ Statue of Liberty, 1961	.30	.06	1.50	(4)	.90	Unlimited
	Perf. 11x10½, 10½x11						
1045	12¢ Benjamin Harrison, 1959	.55	.05	2.75	(4)	.90	Unlimited
1046	15¢ John Jay, 1958	.85	.05	3.75	(4)	1.00	Unlimited
1047	20¢ Monticello, 1956	.90	.05	4.50	(4)	1.20	Unlimited
1048	25¢ Paul Revere, 1958	2.75	.05	12.00	(4)	1.30	Unlimited
1049	30¢ Robert E. Lee, 1955	2.00	.08	8.50	(4)	1.50	Unlimited
1050	40¢ John Marshall, 1955	3.75	.10	16.00	(4)	1.75	Unlimited
1051	50¢ Susan B. Anthony, 1955	4.00	.05	17.00	(4)	6.00	Unlimited
1052	$1 Patrick Henry, 1955	12.00	.06	50.00	(4)	11.00	Unlimited
	Perf. 61						
1053	$5 Alexander Hamilton, 1956	120.00	8.00	500.00	(4)	65.00	Unlimited
	Coil Stamps, Perf. 10 Vertically						
1054	1¢ dark green Washington						
	(1031), 1954	.35	.12	2.00		.75	Unlimited

1953-1961

1028

1029

1030

1031

1031A

1032

1033

1034

1035

1036

1037

1038

1039

1040

1041

1042

1042A

1043

1044

1044A

1045

1046

1047

1048

1049

1050

1051

1052

1053

1954-1965

1060

1061

1062

1063

1064

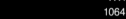

1065

1066

1067

1068

1069

1070

1071

1072

1073

1074

	1954-65 continued	Un	U	PB/LP	#	FDC	Q
	Perf. 10 Horizontally						
1054A	1¼¢ turquoise, Palace of the						
	Governors, Santa Fe (1031A), 1960	.25	.20	3.00		1.00	Unlimited
	Perf. 10 Vertically						
1055	2¢ rose carmine						
	Jefferson (1033), 1954	.10	.05	.75		.75	Unlimited
1056	2½¢ gray blue, Bunker Hill Monument						
	& Massachusetts flag (1034), 1959	.55	.35	7.50		1.20	Unlimited
1057	3¢ deep violet Statue of Liberty						
	(1035), 1954	.15	.05	1.00		.75	Unlimited
1058	4¢ red violet Lincoln (1036), 1958	.15	.05	1.20		.75	Unlimited
	Perf. 10 Horizontally						
1059	4½¢ bl. grn. Hermitage (1037), 1959	3.25	1.20	20.00		1.75	Unlimited
	Perf. 10 Vertically						
1059A	25¢ green P. Revere (1048), 1965	.70	.30	3.25		1.20	Unlimited
	Issues of 1954, Perf. 11x10½						
1060	3¢ Nebraska Territory, May 7	.10	.05	.50	(4)	.75	115,810,000
1061	3¢ Kansas Territory, May 31	.10	.05	.50	(4)	.75	113,603,700
	Perf. 10½x11						
1062	3¢ George Eastman, July 12	.10	.05	.60	(4)	.75	128,002,000
	Perf. 11x10½						
1063	3¢ Lewis and Clark Expedition,						
	July 28	.10	.05	.50	(4)	.75	116,078,150
	Issues of 1955, Perf. 10½x11						
1064	3¢ Pennsylvania Academy of						
	Fine Arts, Jan. 15	.10	.05	.50	(4)	.75	116,139,800
	Perf. 11x10½						
1065	3¢ Land Grant Colleges, Feb. 12	.10	.05	.50	(4)	.75	120,484,800
1066	8¢ Rotary International, Feb. 23	.20	.12	1.50	(4)	.90	53,854,750
1067	3¢ Armed Forces Reserve, May 21	.10	.05	.50	(4)	.75	176,075,000
	Perf. 10½x11						
1068	3¢ New Hampshire, June 21	.10	.05	.50	(4)	.75	125,944,400
	Perf. 11x10½						
1069	3¢ Soo Locks, June 28	.10	.05	.50	(4)	.75	122,284,600
1070	3¢ Atoms for Peace, July 28	.12	.05	.80	(4)	.75	133,638,850
1071	3¢ Fort Ticonderoga, Sept. 18	.10	.05	.50	(4)	.75	118,664,600
	Perf. 10½x11						
1072	3¢ Andrew W. Mellon, Dec. 20	.10	.05	.60	(4)	.75	112,434,000
	Issues of 1956						
1073	3¢ Benjamin Franklin, Jan. 17	.10	.05	.50	(4)	.75	129,384,550
	Perf. 11x10½						
1074	3¢ Booker T. Washington, Apr. 5	.10	.05	.50	(4)	.75	121,184,600
	Fifth International Philatelic Exhibition, Souvenir Sheet, Imperf.						
1075	Sheet of 2, Apr. 28	5.00	4.50			7.50	2,900,731
1075a	3¢ deep violet (1035)	1.35	1.10				

	1956 continued	Un	U	PB/LP	#	FDC	Q
1075b	8¢ dk. vio. bl. & car. (1041)	1.75	1.50				
	Perf. 11x10½						
1076	3¢ New York Coliseum and						
	Columbus Monument, Apr. 30	.10	.05	.50	(4)	.75	119,784,200
	Wildlife Conservation Issue						
1077	3¢ Wild Turkey, May 5	.12	.05	.65	(4)	1.00	123,159,400
1078	3¢ Pronghorn Antelope, June 22	.12	.05	.65	(4)	1.00	123,138,800
1079	3¢ King Salmon, Nov. 9	.12	.05	.65	(4)	1.00	109,275,000
	Perf. 10½x11						
1080	3¢ Pure Food and Drug Laws,						
	June 27	.10	.05	.50	(4)	.80	112,932,200
	Perf. 11x10½						
1081	3¢ Wheatland, Aug. 5	.10	.05	.50	(4)	.80	125,475,000
	Perf. 10½x11						
1082	3¢ Labor Day, Sept. 3	.10	.05	.50	(4)	.80	117,855,000
	Perf. 11x10½						
1083	3¢ Nassau Hall, Sept. 22	.10	.05	.50	(4)	.80	122,100,000
	Perf. 10½x11						
1084	3¢ Devils Tower, Sept. 24	.10	.05	.50	(4)	.80	118,180,000
	Perf. 11x10½						
1085	3¢ Children's Issue, Dec. 15	.10	.05	.50	(4)	.80	100,975,000
	Issues of 1957						
1086	3¢ Alexander Hamilton, Jan. 11	.10	.05	.50	(4)	.80	115,299,450
	Perf. 10½x11						
1087	3¢ Polio, Jan. 15	.10	.05	.50	(4)	.80	186,949,627
	Perf. 11x10½						
1088	3¢ Coast and Geodetic Survey,						
	Feb. 11	.10	.05	.50	(4)	.80	115,235,000
1089	3¢ Architects, Feb. 23	.10	.05	.50	(4)	.80	106,647,500
	Perf. 10½x11						
1090	3¢ Steel Industry, May 22	.10	.05	.50	(4)	.80	112,010,000
	Perf. 11x10½						
1091	3¢ Int'l. Naval Review, June 10	.10	.05	.50	(4)	.80	118,470,000
1092	3¢ Oklahoma Statehood, June 14	.10	.05	.60	(4)	.80	102,230,000
1093	3¢ School Teachers, July 1	.10	.05	.50	(4)	.80	102,410,000

1076

1077

1078

1079

1080

1081

1082

1083

1084

1085

1086

1087

1088

1089

1090

1091

1092

1093

1957-1958

1094

1095

1096

1097

1098

1099

1100

1104

1105

1106

1107

1108

1109

1110

1111

1112

	1957 continued	Un	U	PB/LP	#	FDC	Q
	Perf. 11						
1094	4¢ Flag Issue, July 4	.10	.05	.60	(4)	.80	84,054,400
	Perf. 10½x11						
1095	3¢ Shipbuilding, Aug. 15	.10	.05	.70	(4)	.80	126,266,000
	Perf. 11						
1096	8¢ Champion of Liberty, Aug. 31,						
	Ramon Magsaysay	.22	.15	1.75	(4)	.80	39,489,600
	Perf. 10½x11						
1097	3¢ Lafayette, Sept. 6	.10	.05	.50	(4)	.80	122,990,000
	Perf. 11						
1098	3¢ Wildlife Conservation, Nov. 22	.10	.05	.65	(4)	1.00	174,372,800
	Perf. 10½x11						
1099	3¢ Religious Freedom, Dec. 27	.10	.05	.50	(4)	.80	114,365,000
	Issues of 1958						
1100	3¢ Gardening-Horticulture, Mar. 15	.10	.05	.50	(4)	.80	122,765,200
	Perf. 11x10½						
1104	3¢ Brussels Fair, Apr. 17	.10	.05	.50	(4)	.80	113,660,200
1105	3¢ James Monroe, Apr. 28	.10	.05	.60	(4)	.80	120,196,580
1106	3¢ Minnesota Statehood, May 11	.10	.05	.50	(4)	.80	120,805,200
	Perf. 11						
1107	3¢ Geophysical Year, May 31	.10	.05	.75	(4)	.80	125,815,200
	Perf. 11x10½						
1108	3¢ Gunston Hall, June 12	.10	.05	.50	(4)	.80	108,415,200
	Perf. 10½x11						
1109	3¢ Mackinac Bridge, June 25	.10	.05	.50	(4)	.90	107,195,200
1110	4¢ Champion of Liberty, July 24,						
	Simon Bolivar	.10	.05	.60	(4)	.80	115,745,280
	Perf. 11						
1111	8¢ Champion of Liberty, July 24,						
	Simon Bolivar	.25	.15	5.00	(4)	.80	39,743,640
	Perf. 11x10½						
1112	4¢ Atlantic Cable 100th Anniversary,						
	Aug. 15	.10	.05	.50	(4)	.80	114,570,200

	1958 continued	Un	U	PB/LP	#	FDC	Q
	Lincoln 150th Anniv. Issue, 1958-59, Perf. 10½x11, 11x10½						
1113	1¢ Portrait by George Healy,						
	Feb. 12, 1959	.05	.05	.40	(4)	.80	120,400,200
1114	3¢ Sculptured Head						
	by Gutzon Borglum, Feb. 27, 1959	.10	.06	.60	(4)	.80	91,160,200
1115	4¢ Lincoln and Stephen Douglas						
	Debating, Aug. 27, 1958	.10	.05	.55	(4)	.80	114,860,200
1116	4¢ Statue in Lincoln Memorial						
	by Daniel Chester French,						
	May 30, 1959	.10	.05	.65	(4)	.80	126,500,000
	Issues of 1958, Perf. 10½x11						
1117	4¢ Champion of Liberty, Sept. 19,						
	Lajos Kossuth	.10	.05	.60	(4)	.80	120,561,280
	Perf. 11						
1118	8¢ Champion of Liberty, Sept. 19,						
	Lajos Kossuth	.22	.12	3.50	(4)	.80	44,064,576
	Perf. 10½x11						
1119	4¢ Freedom of Press, Sept. 22	.10	.05	.50	(4)	.80	118,390,200
	Perf. 11x10½						
1120	4¢ Overland Mail, Oct. 10	.10	.05	.50	(4)	.80	125,770,200
	Perf. 10½x11						
1121	4¢ Noah Webster, Oct. 16	.10	.05	.50	(4)	.80	114,114,280
	Perf. 11						
1122	4¢ Forest Conservation, Oct. 27	.10	.05	.60	(4)	.80	156,600,200
	Perf. 11x10½						
1123	4¢ Fort Duquesne, Nov. 25	.10	.05	.50	(4)	.80	124,200,200
	Issues of 1959						
1124	4¢ Oregon Statehood, Feb. 14	.10	.05	.50	(4)	.80	120,740,200
	Perf. 10½x11						
1125	4¢ Champion of Liberty, Feb. 25,						
	José de San Martin	.10	.05	.55	(4)	.80	133,623,280
	Perf. 11						
1126	8¢ Champion of Liberty, Feb. 25,						
	José de San Martin	.20	.12	1.75	(4)	.80	45,569,088
	Perf. 10½x11						
1127	4¢ NATO, Apr. 1	.10	.05	.50	(4)	.80	122,493,280
	Perf. 11x10½						
1128	4¢ Arctic Explorations, Apr. 6	.13	.05	.85	(4)	.80	131,260,200
1129	8¢ World Peace through World						
	Trade, Apr. 20	.20	.12	1.50	(4)	.80	47,125,200
1130	4¢ Nevada Silver, June 8	.10	.05	.50	(4)	.80	123,105,000
	Perf. 11						
1131	4¢ St. Lawrence Seaway, June 26	.10	.05	.50	(4)	.80	126,105,050

1114

1115

1116

1118

1119

1120

1122

1123

1124

1126

1127

1128

1132

1133

1134

135

1136

1137

1138

139

1140

1141

142

1143

1144

145

1147

1148

	1959 continued	Un	U	PB/LP	#	FDC	Q
1132	4¢ 49-Star Flag, July 4	.10	.05	.50	(4)	.80	209,170,000
1133	4¢ Soil Conservation, Aug. 26	.10	.05	.65	(4)	.80	120,835,000
	Perf. 10½x11						
1134	4¢ Petroleum Industry, Aug. 27	.10	.05	.50	(4)	.80	115,715,000
	Perf. 11x10½						
1135	4¢ Dental Health, Sept. 14	.10	.05	.50	(4)	.80	118,445,000
	Perf. 10½x11						
1136	4¢ Champion of Liberty, Sept. 29,						
	Ernst Reuter	.10	.05	.60	(4)	.80	111,685,000
	Perf. 11						
1137	8¢ Champion of Liberty, Sept. 29,						
	Ernst Reuter	.20	.12	1.75	(4)	.80	43,099,200
	Perf. 10½x11						
1138	4¢ Dr. Ephraim McDowell, Dec. 3	.10	.05	.50	(4)	.80	115,444,000
	Issues of 1960, Perf. 11, American Credo						
1139	4¢ Quotation from Washington's						
	Farewell Address, 1960	.18	.05	1.00	(4)	.80	126,470,000
1140	4¢ B. Franklin Quotation, 1960	.18	.05	1.00	(4)	.80	124,560,000
1141	4¢ T. Jefferson Quotation, 1960	.18	.05	1.00	(4)	1.00	115,455,000
1142	4¢ Francis Scott Key Quotation, 1960	.18	.05	1.00	(4)	1.00	122,060,000
1143	4¢ Lincoln Quotation, 1960	.18	.05	1.00	(4)	1.00	120,540,000
1144	4¢ Patrick Henry Quotation, 1961	.18	.05	1.00	(4)	1.00	113,075,000
1145	4¢ Boy Scout Jubilee, Feb. 8	.10	.05	.50	(4)	1.25	139,325,000
	Perf. 10½x11						
1146	4¢ Olympic Winter Games, Feb. 18	.10	.05	.50	(4)	.80	124,445,000
1147	4¢ Champion of Liberty, Mar. 7,						
	Masaryk	.10	.05	.60	(4)	.80	113,792,000
	Perf. 11						
1148	8¢ Champion of Liberty, Masaryk	.20	.12	1.75	(4)	.80	44,215,200

B or Benj.?

The second in the series of the American "Credo" stamps (#1140) bears the statement of Benjamin Franklin, "Fear to do ill, and you need fear nought else." The entire series was printed in a style and type used on colonial currency, and the Franklin stamp carries a symbol of an eagle within an olive wreath.

The original press release dated January 2, 1960, shows the familiar signature of Franklin with his typical "Benj." abbreviation for the first name. However, when the stamp was issued on March 31, 1960, the signature was changed to "B" in keeping with the rest of the series.

Some catalogs may still show the press release photograph of the stamp, which is in error.

	1960 continued	Un	U	PB/LP	#	FDC	Q
	Perf. 11x10½						
1149	4¢ World Refugee Year, Apr. 7	.10	.05	.50	(4)	.80	113,195,000
	Perf. 11						
1150	4¢ Water Conservation, Apr. 18	.10	.05	.65	(4)	.80	121,805,000
	Perf. 10½x11						
1151	4¢ SEATO, May 31	.10	.05	.50	(4)	.80	115,353,000
	Perf. 11x10½						
1152	4¢ American Woman, June 2	.10	.05	.50	(4)	.80	111,080,000
	Perf. 11						
1153 ·	4¢ 50-Star Flag, July 4	.10	.05	.50	(4)	.80	153,025,000
	Perf. 11x10½						
1154	4¢ Pony Express 100th Anniv., July 19	.10	.05	.50	(4)	.80	119,665,000
	Perf. 10½x11						
1155	4¢ Employ the Handicapped, Aug. 28	.10	.05	.50	(4)	.80	117,855,000
1156	4¢ World Forestry Congress, Aug. 29	.10	.05	.50	(4)	.80	118,185,000
	Perf. 11						
1157	4¢ Mexican Independence, Sept. 16	.10	.05	.50	(4)	.80	112,260,000
1158	4¢ U.S.-Japan Treaty, Sept. 28	.10	.05	.50	(4)	.80	125,010,000
	Perf. 10½x11						
1159	4¢ Champion of Liberty, Oct. 8, I.J. Paderewski	.10	.05	.55	(4)	.80	119,798,000
	Perf. 11						
1160	8¢ Champion of Liberty, I.J. Paderewski	.20	.12	1.75	(4)	.80	42,696,000
	Perf. 10½x11						
1161	4¢ Sen. Taft Memorial, Oct. 10	.10	.05	.50	(4)	.80	106,610,000
	Perf. 11x10½						
1162	4¢ Wheels of Freedom, Oct. 15	.10	.05	.50	(4)	.80	109,695,000
	Perf. 11						
1163	4¢ Boy's Clubs of America, Oct. 18	.10	.05	.50	(4)	.80	123,690,000
1164	4¢ Automated P.O., Oct. 20	.10	.05	.50	(4)	.80	123,970,000
	Perf. 10½ x 11						
1165	4¢ Champion of Liberty, Oct. 26, Baron Gustaf Mannerheim	.10	.05	.55	(4)	.80	124,796,000
	Perf. 11						
1166	8¢ Champion of Liberty, Baron Gustaf Mannerheim	.20	.12	1.75	(4)	.80	42,076,800

1960

1149

1150

1151

1152

1153

1154

1155

1156

1157

1158

1159

1160

1161

1162

1163

1164

1165

1166

135

1960-1965

1167

1168

1169

1170

1171

1172

1173

1174

1175

1176

1177

1178

1179

1180

1181

1182

1183

1184

	1960-61 continued	Un	U	PB/LP	#	FDC	Q
1167	4¢ Camp Fire Girls, Nov. 4	.10	.05	.50	(4)	.80	116,210,000
	Perf. 10½x11						
1168	4¢ Champion of Liberty, Nov. 2,						
	Giuseppe Garibaldi	.10	.05	.55	(4)	.80	126,252,000
	Perf. 11						
1169	8¢ Champion of Liberty,						
	Giuseppe Garibaldi	.20	.12	1.75	(4)	.80	42,746,400
	Perf. 10½x11						
1170	4¢ Sen. George Memorial, Nov. 5	.10	.05	.50	(4)	.80	124,117,000
1171	4¢ Andrew Carnegie, Nov. 25	.10	.05	.50	(4)	.80	119,840,000
1172	4¢ John Foster Dulles Memorial,						
	Dec. 6	.10	.05	.55	(4)	.80	117,187,000
	Perf. 11x10½						
1173	4¢ Echo I—Communications for						
	Peace, Dec. 15	.35	.12	2.25	(4)	1.40	124,390,000
	Issues of 1961, Perf. 10½x11						
1174	4¢ Champion of Liberty, Jan. 26,						
	Mahatma Gandhi	.10	.05	.55	(4)	.80	112,966,000
	Perf. 11						
1175	8¢ Champion of Liberty,						
	Mahatma Gandhi	.20	.12	2.00	(4)	.80	41,644,200
1176	4¢ Range Conservation, Feb. 2	.10	.05	.65	(4)	.75	110,850,000
	Perf. 10½x11						
1177	4¢ Horace Greeley, Feb. 3	.10	.05	.55	(4)	.75	98,616,000
	Civil War 100th Anniv. Issue, 1961-1965, Perf. 11x10½						
1178	4¢ Fort Sumter Centenary, 1961	.18	.05	1.10	(4)	1.25	101,125,000
1179	4¢ Shiloh Centenary, 1962	.15	.05	1.00	(4)	1.25	124,865,000
	Perf. 11						
1180	5¢ Gettysburg Centenary, 1963	.15	.05	1.00	(4)	1.25	79,905,000
1181	5¢ Wilderness Centenary, 1964	.15	.05	1.00	(4)	1.25	125,410,000
1182	5¢ Appomattox Centenary, 1965	.15	.05	1.10	(4)	1.25	112,845,000
	Issues of 1961						
1183	4¢ Kansas Statehood, May 10	.10	.05	.55	(4)	.75	106,210,000
	Perf. 11x10½						
1184	4¢ Sen. George W. Norris, July 11	.10	.05	.55	(4)	.75	110,810,000

	1961 continued	Un	U	PB/LP	#	FDC	Q
1185	4¢ Naval Aviation, Aug. 20	.10	.05	.55	(4)	.90	116,995,000
	Perf. 10½x11						
1186	4¢ Workmen's Comp., Sept. 4	.10	.05	.55	(4)	.75	121,015,000
	Perf. 11						
1187	4¢ Frederic Remington, Oct. 4	.12	.05	1.00	(4)	.75	111,600,000
	Perf. 10½x11						
1188	4¢ Republic of China, Oct. 10	.10	.05	.55	(4)	.75	110,620,000
1189	4¢ Naismith-Basketball, Nov. 6	.10	.05	.55	(4)	1.00	109,110,000
	Perf. 11						
1190	4¢ Nursing, Dec. 28	.10	.05	.70	(4)	.75	145,350,000
	Issues of 1962						
1191	4¢ New Mexico Statehood, Jan. 6	.10	.05	.55	(4)	.75	112,870,000
1192	4¢ Arizona Statehood, Feb. 14	.10	.05	.75	(4)	.75	121,820,000
1193	4¢ Project Mercury, Feb. 20	.10	.10	.75	(4)	1.50	289,240,000
1194	4¢ Malaria Eradication, Mar. 30	.10	.05	.55	(4)	.75	120,155,000
	Perf. 10½x11						
1195	4¢ Charles Evans Hughes, Apr. 11	.10	.05	.55	(4)	.75	124,595,000
	Perf. 11						
1196	4¢ Seattle World's Fair, Apr. 25	.10	.05	.70	(4)	.75	147,310,000
1197	4¢ Louisiana Statehood, Apr. 30	.10	.05	.55	(4)	.75	118,690,000
	Perf. 11x10½						
1198	4¢ Homestead Act, May 20	.10	.05	.55	(4)	.75	122,730,000
1199	4¢ Girl Scout Jubilee, July 24	.10	.05	.55	(4)	.90	126,515,000
1200	4¢ Sen. Brien McMahon, July 28	.10	.05	.75	(4)	.75	130,960,000
1201	4¢ Apprenticeship, Aug. 31	.10	.05	.55	(4)	.75	120,055,000

Dead Letters Come to Life

The Dead Letter office of the Post Office Department played an important role immediately after the Civil War by reuniting loved ones with photographs of dead and missing servicemen.

Tens of thousands of photographs were taken from undelivered mail addressed to men who were lost in battle. The letters had no return address and ended up in the Property Branch Section of the government agency. Someone in the vast bureaucracy of the government gathered all the pictures and placed them on huge pieces of cardboard and in open books for viewing by the relatives of servicemen. A room in the Dead Letter Office was set aside for viewing by mothers and fathers, wives, and sweethearts of sons and husbands who did not return home. Many times the photograph, plus the notation "Deceased" on the envelope, would be the only knowledge that the loved one would never return.

The five value set of stamps (#1178-1182) marked the 100th anniversary of the Civil War and brought back the memory of the struggle and the bitter aftermath of the photographs hanging on a wall in a government office in Washington.

1961-1962

1185

1186

1187

1188

1189

1190

1191

1192

1193

1194

1195

1196

1197

1198

1199

1200

1201

1202

1203

1204

1205

1206

1207

1208

1209

1213

1230

1231

1232

1233

1234

1235

1236

1237

	1962 continued	Un	U	PB/LP	#	FDC	Q
	Perf. 11						
1202	4¢ Sam Rayburn, Sept. 16	.10	.05	.55	(4)	.75	120,715,000
1203	4¢ Dag Hammarskjöld, Oct. 23	.10	.05	.70	(4)	.75	121,440,000
1204	4¢ Dag Hammarskjöld Special						
	Printing: black, brown and yellow						
	(yellow inverted), Nov. 16	.12	.08	4.50	(4)	6.00	40,270,000
1205	4¢ Christmas Issue, Nov. 1	.10	.05	.50	(4)	.75	861,970,000
1206	4¢ Higher Education, Nov. 14	.10	.05	.55	(4)	.75	120,035,000
1207	4¢ Winslow Homer, Dec. 15	.15	.05	1.00	(4)	.75	117,870,000
	Flag Issue of 1963						
1208	5¢ Flag over White House, Jan. 9	.12	.05	.55	(4)	.75	
	Regular Issue of 1962-66, Perf. 11x10½						
1209	1¢ Andrew Jackson, March 22	.05	.05	.25	(4)	.75	
1213	5¢ George Washington, Nov. 23	.12	.05	.75	(4)	.75	
1213a	Booklet pane of 5 (Your Mailman)	2.00	.75				
	Coil Stamps, Perf. 10 Vertically						
1225	1¢ green Jackson (1209), May 31	.20	.05	.85		.75	
1229	5¢ dk. blue gray Washington (1213),						
	Nov. 23	1.75	.05	4.75		.75	
	Issues of 1963, Perf. 11						
1230	5¢ Carolina Charter, Apr. 6	.12	.05	.60	(4)	.75	129,945,000
1231	5¢ Food for Peace—Freedom from						
	Hunger, June 4	.12	.05	.60	(4)	.75	135,620,000
1232	5¢ W. Virginia Statehood, June 20	.12	.05	.60	(4)	.75	137,540,000
1233	5¢ Emancipation Proclamation,						
	Aug. 16	.12	.05	.60	(4)	.75	132,435,000
1234	5¢ Alliance for Progress, Aug. 17	.12	.05	.60	(4)	.75	135,520,000
	Perf. 10½x11						
1235	5¢ Cordell Hull, Oct. 5	.12	.05	.60	(4)	.75	131,420,000
	Perf. 11x10½						
1236	5¢ Eleanor Roosevelt, Oct. 11	.12	.05	.60	(4)	.75	133,170,000
	Perf. 11						
1237	5¢ Science, Oct. 14	.12	.05	.60	(4)	.75	130,195,000

	1963 continued	Un	U	PB/LP	#	FDC	Q
1238	5¢ City Mail Delivery, Oct. 26	.12	.05	.60	(4)	.75	128,450,000
1239	5¢ Red Cross 100th Anniv., Oct. 29	.12	.05	.60	(4)	.75	118,665,000
1240	5¢ Christmas Issue, Nov. 1	.12	.05	.60	(4)	.75	1,291,250,000
1241	5¢ John James Audubon, Dec. 7	.12	.05	.60	(4)	.75	175,175,000
	Issues of 1964, Perf. 10½x11						
1242	5¢ Sam Houston, Jan. 10	.12	.05	.60	(4)	.75	125,995,000
	Perf. 11						
1243	5¢ Charles M. Russell, Mar. 9	.15	.05	.75	(4)	.75	128,925,000
	Perf. 11x10½						
1244	5¢ New York World's Fair, Apr. 22	.12	.05	.60	(4)	.75	145,700,000
	Perf. 11						
1245	5¢ John Muir, Apr. 29	.12	.05	.60	(4)	.75	120,310,000
	Perf. 11x10½						
1246	5¢ Kennedy Memorial, May 29	.12	.05	.60	(4)	.75	511,750,000
	Perf. 10½x11						
1247	5¢ New Jersey 300th Anniv., June 15	.12	.05	.60	(4)	.75	123,845,000
	Perf. 11						
1248	5¢ Nevada Statehood, July 22	.12	.05	.60	(4)	.75	122,825,000
1249	5¢ Register and Vote, Aug. 1	.12	.05	.60	(4)	.75	453,090,000
	Perf. 10½x11						
1250	5¢ Shakespeare, Aug. 14	.12	.05	.60	(4)	.75	123,245,000
1251	5¢ Doctors Mayo, Sept. 11	.12	.05	.60	(4)	.75	123,355,000
	Perf. 11						
1252	5¢ American Music, Oct. 15,	.12	.05	.60	(4)	.75	126,970,000
1253	5¢ Homemakers, Oct. 26, Perf. 11	.12	.05	.60	(4)	.75	121,250,000

John James Audubon
(Great Americans Series)

"I am growing old too fast," complained America's foremost naturalist in a journal one evening when he was but in his late forties, "...may God grant me life to see the last plate of my mammoth work finished." To the man who preferred to "fish, hunt and collect curiosities in the field," over every business venture he ever tried, time was everything.

Broke and without his family, Audubon persisted in the exhaustive, illustrated inventory of North America's birds with a near maniacal obsession that took virtually the last half of his lifetime, but brought him instant fame with its publication in 1827. Birds of America was a four-volume set of 435 illustrations, each volume's "elephant folio" measuring about 40" by 30". In it were meticulous color figures of 1,065 birds—illustrated natural size with rare artistic talent and, despite his lack of formal training, acute scientific observation . With this outstanding volume of work the master naturalist had accomplished the near impossible, yet he saw to the completion of the two-volume Quadrapeds of North America during the last years of his life. The Audubon Society was founded in his honor.

1238

1239

1240

1241

1242

1243

1244

1245

1246

1247

1248

1249

1250

1251

1252

1253

1254 1255
1256 1257

1258

1259

1260

1261

1262

1263

1264

1265

1266

1267

1268

1269

1270

1271

1272

	1964 continued	Un	U	PB/LP	#	FDC	Q
	Christmas Issue, Nov. 9						
1254	5¢ Holly, Perf. 11	.75	.05	4.00	(4)	.75	351,940,000
1255	5¢ Mistletoe, Perf. 11	.75	.05	4.00	(4)	.75	351,940,000
1256	5¢ Poinsettia, Perf. 11	.75	.05	4.00	(4)	.75	351,940,000
1257	5¢ Sprig of Conifer, Perf. 11	.75	.05	4.00	(4)	.75	351,940,000
	Block of four, #1254-1257	3.50	1.25			3.00	
	Perf. 10½x11						
1258	5¢ Verrazano-Narrows Bridge,						
	Nov. 21	.12	.05	.60	(4)	.75	120,005,000
	Perf. 11						
1259	5¢ Fine Arts, Dec. 2	.12	.05	.75	(4)	.75	125,800,000
	Perf. 10½x11						
1260	5¢ Amateur Radio, Dec. 15	.12	.05	.75	(4)	.75	122,230,000
	Issues of 1965, Perf. 11						
1261	5¢ Battle of New Orleans, Jan. 8	.12	.05	.75	(4)	.75	115,695,000
1262	5¢ Physical Fitness-Sokol, Feb. 15	.12	.05	.75	(4)	.75	115,095,000
1263	5¢ Crusade Against Cancer, Apr. 1	.12	.05	.75	(4)	.75	119,560,000
	Perf. 10½x11						
1264	5¢ Churchill Memorial, May 13	.12	.05	.75	(4)	.75	125,180,000
	Perf. 11						
1265	5¢ Magna Carta, June 15	.12	.05	.75	(4)	.75	120,135,000
1266	5¢ Intl. Cooperation Year, June 26	.12	.05	.75	(4)	.75	115,405,000
1267	5¢ Salvation Army, July 2	.12	.05	.75	(4)	.75	115,855,000
	Perf. 10½x11						
1268	5¢ Dante Alighieri, July 17	.12	.05	.75	(4)	.75	115,340,000
1269	5¢ Herbert Hoover, Aug. 10	.12	.05	.75	(4)	.75	114,840,000
	Perf. 11						
1270	5¢ Robert Fulton, Aug. 19	.12	.05	.75	(4)	.75	116,140,000
1271	5¢ Settlement of Florida, Aug. 28	.12	.05	1.00	(4)	.75	116,900,000
1272	5¢ Traffic Safety, Sept. 3	.12	.05	1.00	(4)	.75	114,085,000

UN and USA

Since March 28, 1951, the United Nations has issued its own stamps in denominations that conform to that of the U S. Postal Service. Mail posted with U.N. stamps must be posted within the U.N. Building in New York City. Post cards and stamped envelopes are required to meet the specifications of the USPS as to size and quality of paper.

The USPS collects money from the U.N. as reimbursement for handling all mail entering and leaving the U.N. Building. United Nations mail addressed outside of the U.S. is introduced into the international mail stream by the U.S. Postal Service. Revenue from United Nations stamps bought for philatelic purposes is retained by the U.N. for its own use.

In addition, the U.S. also publicizes the goals of the U.N. through its own stamps such as the International Cooperation Year issue (#1266).

	1965 continued	Un	U	PB/LP	#	FDC	Q
1273	5¢ John Singleton Copley, Sept. 17	.15	.05	1.25	(4)	.75	114,880,000
1274	11¢ International Telecommunication Union,						
	Oct. 6	.50	.25	12.00	(4)	.75	26,995,000
1275	5¢ Adlai E. Stevenson, Oct. 23	.12	.05	.75	(4)	.75	128,495,000
1276	5¢ Christmas Issue, Nov. 2	.12	.05	.60	(4)	.75	1,139,930,000
	Issues of 1965-78, Prominent Americans, Perf. 11x10, 10½x11						
1278	1¢ Thomas Jefferson, 1968	.05	.05	.20	(4)	.35	
1278a	Booklet pane of 8, 1968	1.00	.25				
1278b	Booklet pane of 4, 1971	.75	.20				
1279	1¼¢ Albert Gallatin, 1967	.10	.05	25.00	(4)	.35	
1280	2¢ Frank Lloyd Wright, 1966	.05	.05	.30	(4)	.35	
1280a	Booklet pane of 5 + label, 1968	1.20	.40				
1280c	Booklet pane of 6, 1971	1.00	.35				
1281	3¢ Francis Parkman, 1967	.06	.05	.40	(4)	.35	
1282	4¢ Abraham Lincoln, 1965	.08	.05	.40	(4)	.35	
1283	5¢ George Washington, 1966	.10	.05	.50	(4)	.45	
1283B	5¢ Washington redrawn, 1967	.12	.05	1.00	(4)	.45	
1284	6¢ Franklin D. Roosevelt, 1966	.18	.05	.80	(4)	.45	
1284b	Booklet pane of 8, 1967	1.50	.50				
1284c	Booklet pane of 5 + label, 1968	1.25	.50				
1285	8¢ Albert Einstein, 1966	.25	.05	1.25	(4)	.50	
1286	10¢ Andrew Jackson, 1967	.25	.05	1.75	(4)	.60	
1286A	12¢ Henry Ford, 1968	.30	.05	1.30	(4)	.50	
1287	13¢ John F. Kennedy, 1967	.30	.05	1.65	(4)	.65	
1288	15¢ Oliver Wendell Holmes, 1968	.30	.06	1.50	(4)	.60	
	Perf. 10, 1978						
1288B	15¢ dk. rose claret Holmes (1288),						
	Booklet pane of 8	.30	.05			.65	
1288c	Booklet pane of 8, 1978	2.40	1.25				
1289	20¢ George C. Marshall, 1967	.55	.06	2.50	(4)	.80	
1290	25¢ Frederick Douglass, 1967	.60	.05	2.75	(4)	1.00	
1291	30¢ John Dewey, 1968	.75	.08	3.50	(4)	1.20	
1292	40¢ Thomas Paine, 1968	.95	.10	4.25	(4)	1.60	
1293	50¢ Lucy Stone, 1968	1.10	.05	5.00	(4)	3.25	
1294	$1 Eugene O'Neill, 1967	2.40	.08	10.50	(4)	7.50	
1295	$5 John Bassett Moore, 1966	12.50	2.00	50.00	(4)	60.00	
	Coil Stamps, Issues of 1966-78, Perf. 10 Horizontally						
1297	3¢ violet Parkman (1281), 1975	.12	.05	.60		.75	
1298	6¢ gray brown F.D.R. (1284), 1967	.30	.05	3.00		.75	
	Perf. 10 Vertically						
1299	1¢ green Jefferson (1278), 1968	.06	.05	.35		.75	
1303	4¢ black Lincoln (1282), 1966	.15	.05	2.25		.75	
1304	5¢ blue Washington (1283), 1966	.15	.05	.90		.75	
1305	6¢ Franklin D. Roosevelt, 1968	.20	.05	1.25		.75	

UNITED STATES POSTAGE 5 CENTS

273

INTERNATIONAL TELECOMMUNICATION UNION
1865 — 1965
11 CENTS UNITED STATES POSTAGE

1274

STEVENSON

U.S. 5 CENTS

1275

5¢ U.S. POSTAGE

CHRISTMAS

1276

UNITED STATES 1¢

278

1¼¢ UNITED STATES
GALLATIN

1279

FRANK LLOYD WRIGHT
2¢ U.S. POSTAGE

1280

FRANCIS PARKMAN
AMERICAN HISTORIAN
U.S. POSTAGE 3¢

1281

LINCOLN
4¢ UNITED STATES

1282

WASHINGTON 5¢

283

UNITED STATES WASHINGTON 5¢

1283B

6¢
FRANKLIN D. ROOSEVELT
U.S. POSTAGE

1284

United States 8¢
EINSTEIN

1285

10¢ ANDREW JACKSON
UNITED STATES

1286

UNITED STATES 12 CENTS

286A

JOHN F. KENNEDY
13¢ UNITED STATES

1287

15¢ U.S. POSTAGE
OLIVER WENDELL HOLMES

1288

STATESMAN SOLDIER
GEORGE MARSHALL
UNITED STATES 20¢

1289

FREDERICK DOUGLASS
25¢ U.S. POSTAGE

1290

JOHN DEWEY
UNITED STATES
30 CENTS

291

Thomas Paine
U.S. 40¢

1292

LUCY STONE
50¢

1293

EUGENE O'NEILL
ONE DOLLAR
PLAYWRIGHT
UNITED STATES

1294

JOHN BASSETT MOORE
FIVE DOLLARS U.S.

1295

U.S. POSTAGE
6¢

1306

1307

1308

1309

1310

1312

1313

1314

1311

1315

1316

1317

1318

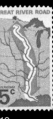

1319

		Un	U	PB/LP	#	FDC	Q
	Coil Stamps, Issues of 1966-78, continued						
1305E	15¢ rose claret Holmes (1288), 1978	.30	.05	1.65		.75	
1305C	$1 dull purple Eugene O'Neill						
	(1294), 1973	2.25	.20	6.50		3.00	
	Issues of 1966, Perf. 11						
1306	5¢ Migratory Bird Treaty, Mar. 16	.12	.05	.75	(4)	.75	116,835,000
1307	5¢ Humane Treatment of Animals,						
	Apr. 9	.12	.05	.90	(4)	.75	117,470,000
1308	5¢ Indiana Statehood, Apr. 16	.12	.05	.75	(4)	.75	123,770,000
1309	5¢ American Circus, May 2	.12	.05	.90	(4)	.75	131,270,000
	Sixth International Philatelic Exhibition Issues						
1310	5¢ Stamped Cover, May 21	.12	.05	.90	(4)	.75	122,285,000
	Imperf.						
1311	5¢ Souvenir Sheet, May 23	.30	.15			.75	14,680,000
	Issued in sheets of one stamp with marginal inscription commemorating the Sixth International Philatelic Exhibition (SIPEX), held in Washington, D.C. from May 21-30.						
	Perf. 11						
1312	5¢ Bill of Rights, July 1	.12	.05	.75	(4)	.75	114,160,000
	Perf. 10½x11						
1313	5¢ Polish Millennium, July 30	.12	.05	.90	(4)	.75	128,475,000
	Perf. 11						
1314	5¢ National Park Service, Aug. 25	.12	.05	.75	(4)	.75	119,535,000
1315	5¢ Marine Corps Reserve, Aug. 29	.12	.05	1.00	(4)	.75	125,110,000
1316	5¢ General Federation of Women's						
	Clubs, Sept. 12	.12	.05	1.00	(4)	.75	114,853,200
1317	5¢ Johnny Appleseed, Sept. 24	.12	.05	1.00	(4)	.75	124,290,000
1318	5¢ Beautification of America, Oct. 5	.12	.05	1.00	(4)	.75	128,460,000
1319	5¢ Great River Road, Oct. 21	.12	.05	1.00	(4)	.75	127,585,000

A Philatelic World's Fair

SIPEX, the Sixth International Philatelic Exhibition (#1310-11), held in Washington, D.C., in 1966, continued a rich tradition of stamp exhibitions in the United States that started in 1926 when the first show of this magnitude was held in New York City.

Today, in order to obtain approval to hold an international exhibition in the U.S., application must be made to an international body named the Federation Internationale de Philatelie (FIP). The FIP then examines the proposed site of the show and decides whether the organizing committee has the staff resources and the financial ability to hold an exhibition. If everything meets the approval of the Board of Directors of the FIP, patronage is then granted.

FIP-sponsored exhibitions generally are held in each country once every 10 years. AMERIPEX will be held in Chicago in 1986 and an application already has been made for the 1996 exhibition to take place in New York City. Due to the many events scheduled with each exhibition, they have been referred to as "Philatelic World's Fairs."

	1966 continued	Un	U	PB/LP	#	FDC	Q
1320	5¢ Savings Bond—Servicemen,						
	Oct. 26	.12	.05	1.00	(4)	.75	115,875,000
1321	5¢ Christmas Issue, Nov. 1	.12	.05	.75	(4)	.75	1,173,547,420
1322	5¢ Mary Cassatt, Nov. 17	.20	.05	2.75	(4)	.75	114,015,000
	Issues of 1967						
1323	5¢ National Grange, Apr. 17	.12	.05	.90	(4)	.75	121,105,000
1324	5¢ Canada 100th Anniv., May 25	.12	.05	.90	(4)	.75	132,045,000
1325	5¢ Erie Canal, July 4	.12	.05	.90	(4)	.75	118,780,000
1326	5¢ "Peace"—Lions, July 5	.12	.05	.90	(4)	.75	121,985,000
1327	5¢ Henry David Thoreau, July 12	.12	.05	.90	(4)	.75	111,850,000
1328	5¢ Nebraska Statehood, July 29	.12	.05	.90	(4)	.75	117,225,000
1329	5¢ Voice of America, Aug. 1	.12	.05	1.00	(4)	.75	111,515,000
1330	5¢ Davy Crockett, Aug. 17	.12	.05	1.00	(4)	.75	114,270,000
	Space Accomplishments Issue, Sept. 29						
1331	5¢ Space-Walking Astronaut	.90	.25				60,432,500
1332	5¢ Gemini 4 Capsule and Earth	.90	.25				60,432,500
	Block of 4, 2 #1331 & 2 #1332	5.00	5.00	9.50		10.00	
1333	5¢ Urban Planning, Oct. 2	.15	.05	1.25	(4)	.75	110,675,000
1334	5¢ Finnish Independence, Oct. 6	.15	.05	1.25	(4)	.75	110,670,000
	Perf. 12						
1335	5¢ Thomas Eakins, Nov. 2	.18	.05	1.50	(4)	.75	113,825,000
	Perf. 11						
1336	5¢ Christmas Issue, Nov. 6	.12	.05	.60	(4)	.75	1,208,700,000
1337	5¢ Mississippi Statehood, Dec. 11	.15	.05	1.00	(4)	.75	113,330,000
	Issues of 1968-71						
1338	6¢ Flag and White House, 1968	.12	.05	.60	(4)	.75	

Walk In Space

When astronaut Edward H. White performed his first walk in space during the flight of Gemini IV, he carried a whole range of communication equipment.

The 25-foot tether, or "umbilical cord," was coated with actual gold to reflect heat and light. The tether carried oxygen and communication to his space helmet. In addition, White carried a chest pack with an emergency oxygen supply, a modified 35 mm. single lens reflex camera loaded with color film, and a hand-held oxygen-jet gun that was used for propulsion. He went the full length of the tether three times then returned to the space ship, using the gun to halt his motion and prevent his hitting the vehicle. The original plans called for a 10-minute walk in space, but White remained outside the spacecraft for a full 22 minutes.

The pair of stamps (#1331-32) commemorating the space walk conveys part of the excitement of the epic-making journey.

1320

1321

1322

1323

1324

1325

Search for Peace

1326

1327

1328

1329

1330

1331   1332

1333

1334

1335

1336

1337

1338

1339

1340

1341

1342

1343

1344

1345

1346

1347

1348

1349

1350

1351

1352

1353

1354

1355

1968-1971

	1968-71 continued	Un	U	PB/LP	#	FDC	Q
	Perf. 11x10½						
1338D	6¢ dark blue, red & green						
	(1338), 1970	.20	.05	4.25 (20)		.75	
1338F	8¢ multicolored (1338), 1971	.20	.05	4.25 (20)		.75	
	Coil Stamps of 1969-71, Perf. 10 Vertically						
1338A	6¢ dark blue, red & green						
	(1338), 1969	.20	.05	—		.75	
1338G	8¢ multicolored (1338), 1971	.20	.05	—		.75	
	Issues of 1968, Perf. 11						
1339	6¢ Illinois Statehood, Feb. 12	.18	.05	1.00	(4)	.75	141,350,000
1340	6¢ HemisFair '68, Mar. 30	.18	.05	1.00	(4)	.75	144,345,000
1341	$1 Airlift, Apr. 4	6.00	3.00	32.50	(4)	6.50	
1342	6¢ "Youth"—Elks, May 1	.18	.05	1.00	(4)	.75	147,120,000
1343	6¢ Law and Order, May 17	.18	.05	1.00	(4)	.75	130,125,000
1344	6¢ Register and Vote, June 27	.18	.05	1.00	(4)	.75	158,700,000
	Historic Flag Series, July 4						
1345	6¢ Ft. Moultrie Flag (1776)	1.00	.50			4.00	23,153,000
1346	6¢ Ft. McHenry Flag (1795-1818)	1.00	.50			4.00	23,153,000
1347	6¢ Washington's Cruisers Flag						
	(1775)	.60	.50			4.00	23,153,000
1348	6¢ Bennington Flag (1777)	.60	.40			4.00	23,153,000
1349	6¢ Rhode Island Flag (1775)	.60	.45			4.00	23,153,000
1350	6¢ First Stars and Stripes Flag						
	(1777)	.60	.35			4.00	23,153,000
1351	6¢ Bunker Hill Flag (1775)	.60	.35			4.00	23,153,000
1352	6¢ Grand Union Flag (1776)	.60	.35			4.00	23,153,000
1353	6¢ Phila. Light Horse Flag (1775)	.80	.35			4.00	23,153,000
1354	6¢ First Navy Jack (1775)	.80	.40			4.00	23,153,000
	Plate Block, (1345-1354)			18.00 (20)			
	#1345-1354 printed se-tenant in vertical rows of 10.						
	Perf. 12						
1355	6¢ Walt Disney, Sept. 11	.20	.05	1.25	(4)	1.00	153,015,000

	1968 continued	Un	U	PB/LP	#	FDC	Q
	Perf. 11						
1356	6¢ Father Marquette, Sept. 20	.20	.05	1.00	(4)	.75	132,560,000
1357	6¢ Daniel Boone, Sept. 26	.20	.05	1.00	(4)	.75	130,385,000
1358	6¢ Arkansas River, Oct. 1	.20	.05	1.00	(4)	.75	132,265,000
1359	6¢ Leif Erikson, Oct. 9	.20	.05	1.00	(4)	.75	128,710,000
	Perf. 11x10½						
1360	6¢ Cherokee Strip, Oct. 15	.20	.05	1.00	(4)	.75	124,775,000
	Perf. 11						
1361	6¢ John Trumbull, Oct. 18	.25	.05	1.10	(4)	.75	128,295,000
1362	6¢ Waterfowl Conservation, Oct. 24	.25	.05	1.75	(4)	.75	142,245,000
1363	6¢ Christmas Issue, Nov. 1	.20	.05	2.75	(10)	.75	1,410,580,000
1364	6¢ American Indian, Nov. 4	.30	.05	1.35	(4)	.75	125,100,000
	Issues of 1969, Beautification of America, Jan. 16						
1365	6¢ Capitol, Azaleas and Tulips	1.10	.15	8.50	(4)	2.00	48,142,500
1366	6¢ Washington Monument,						
	Potomac River and Daffodils	1.10	.15	8.50	(4)	2.00	48,142,500
1367	6¢ Poppies and Lupines						
	along Highway	1.10	.15	8.50	(4)	2.00	48,142,500
1368	6¢ Blooming Crabapples						
	along Street	1.10	.15	8.50	(4)	2.00	48,142,500
	Block of four, #1365-1368	5.50	3.50			5.00	
1369	6¢ American Legion, Mar. 15	.20	.05	1.10	(4)	.75	148,770,000
1370	6¢ Grandma Moses, May 1	.25	.05	1.35	(4)	.75	139,475,000
1371	6¢ Apollo 8, May 5	.30	.06	1.50	(4)	2.00	187,165,000
1372	6¢ W. C. Handy, May 17	.20	.05	1.00	(4)	.75	125,555,000

Eagles on Stamps

The collecting of stamps based on the pictorial design is known as topical collecting. This aspect of collecting is very popular throughout the world because the stamp collector can specialize in one particular species or collect a whole gamut of subjects.

As our national bird, the bald eagle has appeared on more U.S. stamps than any other form of wildlife. Its first appearance on regular postage stamps was in 1869 (#116) where it appeared on top of a shield grasping an olive branch in its talons. After that, our national bird found a place on postage stamps mainly as a decorative feature, usually in replicas of national or state seals.

The eagle also has appeared on airmail stamps as a symbol of our country. The early stamps pictured either airplanes, parts of planes or the zeppelin. When the stamp designers wanted something different, they rediscovered the eagle and used it to denote airmail in the familiar pose of holding a shield (#C23).

Topical collecting can be specialized to just one bird, such as the eagle, as pictured on The Natural History issue (#1387), or the collector can choose any picture on a stamp. The only limit is your imagination.

1356

1357

1358

1359

1360

1361

1362

1363

1364

1365   1366
1367   1368

1369

1370

1371

1372

1969

1373

1374

1375

1376
1378

1377
1379

1380

1381

1382

1383

1384

1384a

1385

1386

	1969 continued	Un	U	PB/LP	#	FDC	Q
1373	6¢ California Settlement, July 16	.20	.05	1.00	(4)	.75	144,425,000
1374	6¢ John Wesley Powell, Aug. 1	.20	.05	1.00	(4)	.75	135,875,000
1375	6¢ Alabama Statehood, Aug. 2	.20	.05	1.00	(4)	.75	151,110,000
	Botanical Congress Issue						
1376	6¢ Douglas Fir (Northwest)	1.50	.15	10.00	(4)	2.00	39,798,750
1377	6¢ Lady's Slipper (Northeast)	1.50	.15	10.00	(4)	2.00	39,798,750
1378	6¢ Ocotillo (Southwest)	1.50	.15	10.00	(4)	2.00	39,798,750
1379	6¢ Franklinia (Southeast)	1.50	.15	10.00	(4)	2.00	39,798,750
	Block of four, #1376-1379	7.00	5.00			7.00	
	Perf. 10½x11						
1380	6¢ Dartmouth College Case, Sept. 22	.20	.05	1.35	(4)	.75	129,540,000
	Perf. 11						
1381	6¢ Professional Baseball, Sept. 24	.25	.05	1.75	(4)	.75	130,925,000
1382	6¢ Intercollegiate Football, Sept. 26	.25	.05	1.75	(4)	.75	139,055,000
1383	6¢ Dwight D. Eisenhower, Oct. 14	.20	.05	1.00	(4)	.75	150,611,200
	Perf. 11x10½						
1384	6¢ Christmas Issue, Nov. 3	.18	.05	2.25	(10)	.75	1,709,795,000
1384a	Precanceled	.60	.06				
1385	6¢ Hope for Crippled, Nov. 20	.18	.05	1.00	(4)	.75	127,545,000
1386	6¢ William M. Harnett, Dec. 3	.18	.05	1.20	(4)	.75	145,788,800

Antarctic Map Mystery

A 1513 map, researched by an employee of a museum in Istanbul, Turkey, shows the Old World, including Antarctica. What makes this map strange is the fact that this barren continent was not discovered until 1820.

The map, drawn and dated by Piri Reis, has been examined closely by modern scientists who found that the 16th century drawing was absolutely accurate, even judged by today's cartographic standards. Jeff Ertughrul reported in Stamp News *that an examination by mathematicians revealed that the contours on the map were similar to those in satellite photos of the Earth taken from space. In a margin of the map, Reis explained that his map was taken from those previously drawn by Columbus, 20 maps made during the reign of Alexander the Great, eight maps of Arabic origin, and maps by four Portuguese explorers. Since Reis' map also contained the Isthmus of Panama, the Caribbean islands and the known geographical data of the South Atlantic, it is not known which of his predecessors drew the original map of Antarctica.*

Turkey commemorated the map of Antarctica on a stamp in 1983 which pictures a likeness of the Turkish seaman, Piri Reis, and the map which illustrates Antarctica 300 years before it was discovered. The United States featured a map of the island continent on a postage stamp (#1431) commemorating the tenth anniversary of the Antarctic Treaty.

		Un	U	PB/LP	#	FDC	Q
	Issues of 1970, Natural History, May 6						
1387	6¢ American Bald Eagle	.22	.12	1.75	(4)	2.00	50,448,550
1388	6¢ African Elephant Herd	.22	.12	1.75	(4)	2.00	50,448,550
1389	6¢ Tlingit Chief in						
	Haida Ceremonial Canoe	.22	.12	1.75	(4)	2.00	50,448,550
1390	6¢ Brontosaurus, Stegosaurus						
	and Allosaurus from Jurassic						
	Period	.22	.12	1.75	(4)	2.00	50,448,550
	Block of four, #1387-1390	1.00	1.00			3.00	
1391	6¢ Maine Statehood, July 9	.18	.05	1.10	(4)	.75	171,850,000
	Perf. 10½x11						
1392	6¢ Wildlife Conservation, July 20	.18	.05	1.10	(4)	.75	142,205,000
	Issues of 1970-74, Perf. 11x10½, 10½x11, 11						
1393	6¢ Dwight D. Eisenhower, 1970	.12	.05	.60	(4)	.75	
	Booklet pane of 8	1.00	.50				
	Booklet pane of 5 + label	.85	.35				
1393D	7¢ Benjamin Franklin, 1972	.14	.05	1.35	(4)	.75	
1394	8¢ Eisenhower, 1971	.16	.05	1.00	(4)	.75	
1395	8¢ Eisenhower (1393), 1971	.16	.05			.75	
	Booklet pane of 8, 1971	1.50	1.25				
	Booklet pane of 6, 1971	1.00	.75				
	Booklet pane of 4 + 2 labels, 1972	1.00	.50				
	Booklet pane of 7 + label, 1972	1.25	1.00				
1396	8¢ U.S. Postal Service, 1971	.25	.05	5.00	(12)	.75	
1397	14¢ Fiorello H. LaGuardia, 1972	.32	.05	2.35	(4)	.85	
1398	16¢ Ernie Pyle, 1971	.35	.05	2.35	(4)	.75	
1399	18¢ Dr. Elizabeth Blackwell, 1974	.40	.06	2.25	(4)	1.25	
1400	21¢ Amadeo P. Giannini, 1973	.45	.06	2.25	(4)	1.00	
	Coil Stamps, Perf. 10 Vertically						
1401	6¢ dark blue gray Eisenhower						
	(1393), 1970	.20	.05	1.00		.75	
1402	8¢ deep claret Eisenhower						
	(1395), 1971	.22	.05	1.00		.75	
	Issues of 1970, Perf. 11						
1405	6¢ Edgar Lee Masters, Aug. 22	.18	.05	1.00	(4)	.75	137,660,000
1406	6¢ Woman Suffrage, Aug. 26	.18	.05	1.00	(4)	.75	135,125,000
1407	6¢ South Carolina, Sept. 12	.18	.05	1.00	(4)	.75	135,895,000
1408	6¢ Stone Mountain Mem., Sept. 19	.18	.05	1.00	(4)	.75	132,675,000
1409	6¢ Fort Snelling, Oct. 17	.18	.05	1.00	(4)	.75	134,795,000

1970-1974

AMERICAN BALD EAGLE

AFRICAN ELEPHANT HERD

HAIDA CEREMONIAL CANOE

THE AGE OF REPTILES

1387
1389

1388
1390

1391

1392

1393

1393D

1394

1396

1397

1398

1399

1400

EDGAR LEE
MASTERS
AMERICAN POET

UNITED STATES 6¢

1405

WOMAN SUFFRAGE

50TH ANNIVERSARY

1406

SOUTH CAROLINA

1407

Stone Mountain Memorial

1408

GREAT NORTHWEST
1820 FORT SNELLING 1970

1409

1414

1414a

410
412

1411
1413

1419

1420

415
417

1416
1418

1425

421

1422

1423

1424

426

1970-1971

		Un	U	PB/LP	#	FDC	Q
	Perf. 11x10½, Anti-Pollution Issue, Oct. 28						
1410	6¢ Save Our Soil	.45	.13	2.75	(4)	1.40	40,400,000
1411	6¢ Save Our Cities	.45	.13	2.75	(4)	1.40	40,400,000
1412	6¢ Save Our Water	.45	.13	2.75	(4)	1.40	40,400,000
1413	6¢ Save Our Air	.45	.13	2.75	(4)	1.40	40,400,000
	Block of four, #1410-1413	2.50	2.00			4.25	
	Christmas Issue, Nov. 5, Perf. 10½x11						
1414	6¢ Nativity, by Lorenzo Lotto	.20	.05	2.25	(8)	1.40	638,730,000
1414a	Precanceled	.35	.08				358,245,000
	Perf. 11x10½						
1415	6¢ Tin and Cast-Iron Locomotive	.85	.10	8.50	(8)	1.40	122,313,750
1415a	Precanceled	2.00	.15				109,912,500
1416	6¢ Toy Horse on Wheels	.85	.10	8.50	(8)	1.40	122,313,750
1416a	Precanceled	2.00	.15				109,912,500
1417	6¢ Mechanical Tricycle	.85	.10			1.40	122,313,750
1417a	Precanceled	2.00	.15				109,912,500
1418	6¢ Doll Carriage	.85	.10			1.40	122,313,750
1418a	Precanceled	2.00	.15				109,912,500
	Block of 4, #1415-1418	4.50	3.50				
	Block of 4, #1415a-1418a	9.00	6.00				
	Perf. 11						
1419	6¢ United Nations, Nov. 20	.18	.05	1.25	(4)	.75	127,610,000
1420	6¢ Landing of the Pilgrims, Nov. 21	.18	.05	1.25	(4)	.75	129,785,000
	Disabled Veterans and Servicemen Issue, Nov. 24						
1421	6¢ Disabled American Veterans						
	Emblem	.20	.10	3.00	(4)	.75	67,190,000
1422	6¢ U.S. Servicemen	.20	.10	3.00	(4)	.75	67,190,000
	Pair #1421-1422	.50	.65			1.20	
	Issues of 1971						
1423	6¢ American Wool Industry, Jan. 19	.18	.05	1.00	(4)	.75	135,305,000
1424	6¢ Gen. Douglas MacArthur,						
	Jan. 26	.18	.05	1.00	(4)	.75	134,840,000
1425	6¢ Blood Donor, Mar. 12	.18	.05	1.00	(4)	.75	130,975,000
	Perf. 11x10½						
1426	8¢ Missouri 150th Anniv., May 8	.20	.05	3.50	(12)	.75	161,235,000
	Perf. 11, Wildlife Conservation Issue, June 12						
1427	8¢ Trout	.30	.10	1.75	(4)	1.75	43,920,000
1428	8¢ Alligator	.30	.10	1.75	(4)	1.75	43,920,000
1429	8¢ Polar Bear and Cubs	.30	.10	1.75	(4)	1.75	43,920,000
1430	8¢ California Condor	.30	.10	1.75	(4)	1.75	43,920,000
	Block of four #1427-1430	1.30	1.00			3.00	

	1971 continued	Un	U	PB/LP	#	FDC	Q
1431	8¢ Antarctic Treaty, June 23	.25	.05	1.50	(4)	.75	138,700,000
1432	8¢ American Revolution						
	200th Anniversary, July 4	.50	.05	3.25	(4)	.75	138,165,000
1433	8¢ John Sloan, Aug. 2	.20	.05	1.50	(4)	.75	152,125,000
	Decade of Space Achievements Issue, Aug. 2						
1434	8¢ Earth, Sun, Landing Craft						
	on Moon	.20	.10	1.10	(4)		88,147,500
1435	8¢ Lunar Rover and Astronauts	.20	.10	1.75	(4)		88,147,500
	Pair # (1434/1435)	.50	.65			1.75	
1436	8¢ Emily Dickinson, Aug. 28	.18	.05	1.25	(4)	.75	142,845,000
1437	8¢ San Juan, Sept 12	.18	.05	1.25	(4)	.75	148,755,000
	Perf. 10½x11						
1438	8¢ Prevent Drug Abuse, Oct. 5	.18	.05	1.85	(6)	.75	139,080,000
1439	8¢ CARE, Oct. 27	.18	.05	2.10	(8)	.75	130,755,000
	Perf. 11, Historic Preservation Issue, Oct. 29						
1440	8¢ Decatur House,						
	Washington, D.C.	.25	.12	1.85	(4)	1.50	42,552,000
1441	8¢ Whaling Ship						
	Charles W. Morgan	.25	.12	1.85	(4)	1.50	42,552,000
1442	8¢ Cable Car, San Francisco, Calif.	.25	.12	1.85	(4)	1.50	42,552,000
1443	8¢ San Xavier del Bac Mission, Ariz.	.25	.12	1.85	(4)	1.50	42,552,000
	Block of four, # 1440-1443	1.20	1.20			3.00	
	Perf. 10½x11, Christmas Issue, Nov. 10						
1444	8¢ Adoration of the Shepherds,						
	by Giorgione	.18	.05	2.50	(12)	.75	1,074,350,000
1445	8¢ Partridge in a Pear Tree,						
	by Jamie Wyeth	.18	.05	2.50	(12)	.75	979,540,000
	Issues of 1972, Perf. 11						
1446	8¢ Sidney Lanier, Feb. 3	.18	.05	1.00	(4)	.75	137,355,000
	Perf. 10½x11						
1447	8¢ Peace Corps. Feb. 11	.18	.05	1.50	(6)	.75	150,400,000

431

1432

1433

434   1435

1436

1437

438

1439

HISTORIC PRESERVATION

1440
1442

1441
1443

1448
1450

1449
1451

1452

1453

1454

1455

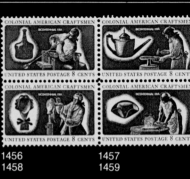

1456
1458

1457
1459

1460

1461

1462

1463

1464
1466

1465
1467

164

	1972 continued	Un	U	PB/LP	#	FDC	Q
	Perf. 11 National Parks 100th Anniversary Issue, Apr. 5						
1448	2¢ Hulk of Ship	.06	.06	1.60	(4)		172,730,000
1449	2¢ Cape Hatteras Lighthouse,	.06	.06	1.60	(4)		172,730,000
1450	2¢ Laughing Gulls on Driftwood,	.06	.06	1.60	(4)		172,730,000
1451	2¢ Laughing Gulls and Dune,	.06	.06	1.60	(4)		172,730,000
	Block of four, # 1448-1451	.25	.30			1.25	
1452	6¢ Wolf Trap Farm, June 26	.16	.08	1.25	(4)	.75	104,090,000
1453	8¢ Yellowstone, Mar. 1	.18	.05	1.00	(4)	.75	164,096,000
1454	15¢ Mt. McKinley, July 28	.35	.22	2.75	(4)	.75	53,920,000

Note: Beginning with this issue, the U.S.P.S. began to offer stamp collectors first day cancellations affixed to 8x10½ inch souvenir pages. The pages are similar to the stamp announcements that have appeared on post office bulletin boards since Scott No. 1132.

		Un	U	PB/LP	#	FDC	Q
1455	8¢ Family Planning, Mar. 18	.16	.05	1.00	(4)	.75	153,025,000
	Perf. 11x10½, American Revolution Bicentennial Issue, Jul. 4,						
	Craftsmen in Colonial America						
1456	8¢ Glassmaker	.30	.08	1.75	(4)	1.00	50,472,500
1457	8¢ Silversmith	.30	.08	1.75	(4)	1.00	50,472,500
1458	8¢ Wigmaker	.30	.08	1.75	(4)	1.00	50,472,500
1459	8¢ Hatter	.30	.08	1.75	(4)	1.00	50,472,500
	Block of four, # 1456-1459	1.25	1.25			2.50	
	Olympic Games Issue, Aug. 17						
1460	6¢ Bicycling and Olympic Rings	.16	.12	2.25	(10)	.75	67,335,000
1461	8¢ Bobsledding	.16	.05	2.25	(10)	.85	179,675,000
1462	15¢ Running	.35	.18	4.50	(10)	1.00	46,340,000
1463	8¢ P.T.A. 75th Anniv., Sept. 15	.16	.05	1.00	(4)	.75	180,155,000
	Perf. 11, Wildlife Conservation Issue, Sep. 20						
1464	8¢ Fur Seals	.25	.08	1.40	(4)	2.00	49,591,200
1465	8¢ Cardinal	.25	.08	1.40	(4)	2.00	49,591,200
1466	8¢ Brown Pelican	.25	.08	1.40	(4)	2.00	49,591,200
1467	8¢ Bighorn Sheep	.25	.08	1.40	(4)	2.00	49,591,200
	Block of 4, # 1464-1467	1.10	.85			3.00	

Note: With this issue the U.S.P.S. introduced the "American Commemorative Series" Stamp Panels. Each panel contains a block of four mint stamps, mounted with text, and background illustrations.

	1972 continued	Un	U	PB/LP	#	FDC	Q
	Perf. 11x10½						
1468	8¢ Mail Order 100th Anniv.,						
	Sept. 27	.16	.05	2.75	(12)	.75	185,490,000
	Perf. 10½x11						
1469	8¢ Osteopathic Medicine, Oct. 9	.16	.05	1.35	(6)	.75	162,335,000
	Perf. 11						
1470	8¢ American Folklore Issue,						
	Oct. 13	.16	.05	1.00	(4)	.75	162,789,950
	Perf. 10½x11, Christmas Issue, Nov. 9						
1471	8¢ Angel form "Mary,						
	Queen of Heaven"	.16	.05	2.75	(12)	.75	1,003,475,000
1472	8¢ Santa Claus	.16	.05	2.75	(12)	.75	1,017,025,000
	Perf. 11						
1473	8¢ Pharmacy, Nov. 11	.16	.05	1.00	(4)	.75	165,895,000
1474	8¢ Stamp Collecting, Nov. 17	.16	.05	1.00	(4)	.75	166,508,000
	Issues of 1973, Perf. 11x10½						
1475	8¢ Love, Jan. 26	.16	.05	1.35	(6)	.75	330,055,000
	This "special stamp for someone special" depicts "Love" by contemporary artist Robert Indiana.						
	Perf. 11						
	American Revolution Bicentennial Issues, Communications in Colonial America						
1476	8¢ Printer and Patriots Examining						
	Pamphlet, Feb. 16	.20	.05	1.35	(4)	.75	166,005,000
1477	8¢ Posting a Broadside, Apr. 13	.20	.05	1.35	(4)	.75	163,050,000
1478	8¢ Postrider, June 22	.20	.05	1.35	(4)	.75	159,005,000
1479	8¢ Drummer, Sept. 28	.20	.05	1.35	(4)	.75	147,295,000
	Boston Tea Party, July 4						
1480	8¢ British Merchantman	.20	.10	1.35	(4)	1.75	49,068,750
1481	8¢ British Three-master	.20	.10	1.35	(4)	1.75	49,068,750
1482	8¢ Boats and Ship's Hull	.20	.10	1.35	(4)	1.75	49,068,750
1483	8¢ Boat and Dock	.20	.10	1.35	(4)	1.75	49,068,750
	Block of four, #1480-1483	.85	.80			3.75	
	American Arts Issue						
1484	8¢ George Gershwin, Feb. 28	.16	.05	2.75	(12)	.75	139,152,000

468

1469

1470

1471

1472

1473

1474

1475

1476

1477

1478

1479

1480
1482

1481
1483

1484

1973

1485
1486
1487

Copernicus
1473-1973

8¢US

1488

Nearly 27 billion
U.S. stamps
are sold yearly
to carry
your letters to
every corner
of the world.

People Serving You

1489

Mail is
picked up
from nearly
a third of a million
local collection
boxes, as well
as your mailbox.

People Serving You

1490

More than
87 billion letters
and packages
are handled
yearly—almost
300 million every
delivery day.

People Serving You

1491

The People
in your
Postal Service
handle and
deliver more
than 500 million
packages yearly.

People Serving You

1492

Thousands of
machines, buildings,
and vehicles
must be operated
and maintained
to keep your
mail moving.

People Serving You

1493

The skill
of sorting mail
manually
is still vital
to delivery of
your mail.

People Serving You

1494

Employees
use modern, high-
speed equipment
to sort and process
huge volumes of
mail in central
locations.

People Serving You

1495

Thirteen billion
pounds of mail are
handled yearly by
postal employees
as they speed
your letters and
packages.

People Serving You

1496

Our customers
include
54 million urban
and 12 million
rural families,
plus 9 million
businesses.

People Serving You

1497

Employees
cover
4 million miles
each delivery day
to bring mail to
your home or
business.

People Serving You

1498

	1973 continued	Un	U	PB/LP #	FDC	Q
1485	8¢ Robinson Jeffers, Aug. 13	.16	.05	2.75 (12)	.75	128,048,000
1486	8¢ Henry Ossawa Tanner, Sept. 10	.16	.05	2.75 (12)	.75	146,008,000
1487	8¢ Willa Cather, Sept. 20	.16	.05	2.75 (12)	.75	139,608,000
1488	8¢ Nicolaus Copernicus, Apr. 23	.16	.05	1.00 (4)	.75	159,475,000
	Perf. 10½x11, Postal Service Employees Issue, Apr. 30					
1489	8¢ Stamp Counter	.20	.12	2.25 (10)	1.10	48,602,000
1490	8¢ Mail Collection	.20	.12	2.25 (10)	1.10	48,602,000
1491	8¢ Letter Facing Conveyor	.20	.12	2.25 (10)	1.10	48,602,000
1492	8¢ Parcel Post Sorting	.20	.12	2.25 (10)	1.10	48,602,000
1493	8¢ Mail Cancelling	.20	.12	2.25 (10)	1.10	48,602,000
1494	8¢ Manual Letter Routing	.20	.12	2.25 (10)	1.10	48,602,000
1495	8¢ Electronic Letter Routing	.20	.12	2.25 (10)	1.10	48,602,000
1496	8¢ Loading Mail on Truck	.20	.12	2.25 (10)	1.10	48,602,000
1497	8¢ Mailman	.20	.12	2.25 (10)	1.10	48,602,000
1498	8¢ Rural Mail Delivery	.20	.12	2.25 (10)	1.10	48,602,000
	Plate Block of 20, #1489-1498			4.50 (20)	6.00	

Cats

The Guinness Book reported that cats were used for a mail service in Liege, Belgium in 1879. Bundles of letters were tied to approximately 37 cats to carry the mail to villages within an 18 mile radius of the Liege city center. The cats proved to be thoroughly undisciplined, and the experiment was short-lived. In spite of this, cats are a very popular subject for topical collectors who collect stamps based on the subjects' designs.

When Charles Lindbergh made a flight around the country in 1927, he was said to have been accompanied by a black cat. Since the famous pilot was very conscious of weight aboard his plane, it is unlikely that he ever took a cat on board. However, this did not stop Spain, who issued a stamp commemorating the first solo crossing of the Atlantic Ocean with a stamp picturing Lindbergh, the Statue of Liberty, "The Spirit of St. Louis" plane, and a black cat looking on.

There is a United States issue with a cat in the scene of the 100th anniversary of mail order commemorative stamp (#1468). The scene depicts an event in the life of a rural family, going to the post office to pick up mail order merchandise. A close look at the stamp reveals a black cat atop a bag of flour staring at a nearby dog.

	1973 continued	Un	U	PB/LP #	FDC	Q
	Perf. 11					
1499	8¢ Harry S. Truman, May 8	.16	.05	1.00 (4)	.75	157,052,800
	Electronics Progress Issue, July 10					
1500	6¢ Marconi's Spark Coil and Gap	.12	.10	1.25 (4)	.75	53,005,000
1501	8¢ Transistor and					
	Printed Circuit Board	.16	.05	1.00 (4)	.75	159,775,000
1502	15¢ Microphone, Speaker,					
	Vacuum Tube, TV Camera	.30	.20	3.00 (4)	.80	39,005,000
1503	8¢ Lyndon B. Johnson, Aug. 27	.16	.05	2.50 (12)	.75	152,624,000
	Issues of 1973-74, Rural America Issue					
1504	8¢ Angus and Longhorn Cattle,					
	by F.C. Murphy, Oct. 5, 1973	.16	.05	1.00 (4)	.75	145,840,000
1505	10¢ Chautauqua centenary,					
	Aug. 6, 1974	.20	.05	1.00 (4)	.75	151,335,000
1506	10¢ Kansas hard winter wheat					
	centenary, Aug. 16, 1974	.20	.05	1.00 (4)	.75	141,085,000
	Perf. 10½x11, Christmas Issue, Nov. 7, 1973					
1507	8¢ Madonna and Child by Raphael	.16	.05	2.10 (12)	.75	885,160,000
1508	8¢ Christmas Tree in Needlepoint	.16	.05	2.10 (12)	.75	939,835,000
	Issue of 1973-74, Perf. 11x10½					
1509	10¢ 50-Star and 13-Star Flags, 1973	.20	.05	5.50 (20)	.75	
1510	10¢ Jefferson Memorial					
	and Signature, 1973	.20	.05	1.00 (4)	.75	
1510b	Booklet pane of 5 + label, 1973	1.00	.30			
1510c	Booklet pane of 8, 1973	1.60	.30			
1510d	Booklet pane of 6, 1974	1.20	.30			
1511	10¢ Mail Transport; "ZIP", 1974	.20	.05	2.25 (8)	.75	
1512-1517 not assigned						
	Coil Stamps, Perf. 10 Vertically					
1518	6.3¢ Bells, Oct. 1, 1974	.13	.07	.35	.75	
1519	10¢ red & blue Flags (1509), 1973	.25	.05	—	.75	
1520	10¢ blue Jefferson Memorial					
	(1510),-73	.20	.05	.50	.75	

Harry S. Truman

U.S. Postage 8 cents

499

Progress in Electronics

1500

Progress in Electronics

1501

Progress in Electronics

502

Lyndon B. Johnson

United States

8 cents

1503

RURAL AMERICA

1504

505

RURAL AMERICA

1506

Christmas

Raphael
National Gallery
of Art

1507

We hold these Truths...

IT ALL DEPENDS ON

ZIP CODE

6³c

U.S. Postage

1974

1525

1526

1527

1528

1529

1525	1526	1527	1528

1530   1531   1532   1533
1534   1535   1536   1537

	Issues of 1974, Perf. 11	Un	U	PB/LP #	FDC	Q
1525	10¢ V.F.W. Emblem, Mar. 11	.20	.05	1.25 (4)	.75	143,930,000
	Perf. 10½x11					
1526	10¢ Robert Frost, Mar. 26	.20	.05	1.00 (4)	.75	145,235,000
	Perf. 11					
1527	10¢ Cosmic Jumper and Smiling					
	Sage, by Peter Max, Apr. 18	.20	.05	2.60 (12)	.75	135,052,000
	Perf. 11x10½					
1528	10¢ Horses Rounding Turn, May 4	.20	.05	2.60 (12)	.75	156,750,000
	Perf. 11					
1529	10¢ Skylab II, May 14	.20	.05	1.00 (4)	1.25	164,670,000
	Centenary of UPU Issue, June 6					
1530	10¢ Michelangelo, by Raphael	.20	.18	3.40 (16)	1.10	23,769,600
1531	10¢ "Five Feminine Virtues,"					
	by Hokusai	.20	.18	3.40 (16)	1.10	23,769,600
1532	10¢ Old Scraps,					
	by John Frederick Peto	.20	.18	3.40 (16)	1.10	23,769,600
1533	10¢ The Lovely Reader,					
	by Jean Liotard	.20	.18	3.40 (16)	1.10	23,769,600
1534	10¢ Lady Writing Letter, by Terborch	.20	.18	3.40 (16)	1.10	23,769,600
1535	10¢ Inkwell and Quill,					
	by Jean Chardin	.20	.18	3.40 (16)	1.10	23,769,600
1536	10¢ Mrs. John Douglas,					
	by Thomas Gainsborough	.20	.18	3.40 (16)	1.10	23,769,600
1537	10¢ Don Antonio Noriega, by Goya	.20	.18	3.40 (16)	1.10	23,769,600
	Block or strip of 8, #1530-37	1.60	2.00		4.25	

Animals In Space

Skylab (#1529) was the United States' first space station and clearly deserves a place in our history books. However, before our government permitted human beings to venture into Earth's outer atmosphere, experiments were carried out with various animals.

Suborbital space flights were made during the early 1950s from Holloman Air Force Base in New Mexico. Aerobee rockets carried monkeys and mice to the then-astounding height of 40 miles in order to study the effects of weightlessness. Additional "passengers" in later years included frogs, flies, leeches, spiders, rats and the famous monkeys Sam, Ham and Goliath.

Space topical collectors have special covers that picture many of the animals carried into space. These covers contain a cachet and are cancelled on the day of the flights. The cachet is a design that appears on an envelope and can be printed, hand-drawn, or rubber stamped. It relates to the event or anniversary occurring on the date of cancellation or to the subject matter of the stamp. The envelopes are usually inexpensive and are a visible record of history.

	1974 continued	Un	U	PB*LP	#	FDC	Q
	Mineral Heritage Issue, June 13						
1538	10¢ Petrified Wood	.20	.10	1.50	(4)	1.50	41,803,200
1539	10¢ Tourmaline	.20	.10	1.50	(4)	1.50	41,803,200
1540	10¢ Amethyst	.20	.10	1.50	(4)	1.50	41,803,200
1541	10¢ Rhodochrosite	.20	.10	1.50	(4)	1.50	41,803,200
	Block of 4, #1538-1541	.80	.80			3.00	
1542	10¢ Fort Harrod, June 15	.20	.05	1.20	(4)	.75	156,265,000
	American Revolution Bicentennial, First Continental Congress, July 4						
1543	10¢ Carpenter's Hall	.20	.10	1.20	(4)	1.10	48,896,250
1544	10¢ "We ask but for Peace,						
	Liberty and Safety"	.20	.10	1.20	(4)	1.10	48,896,250
1545	10¢ "Deriving their Just Powers"	.20	.10	1.30	(4)	1.10	48,896,250
1546	10¢ Independence Hall	.20	.10	1.20	(4)	1.10	48,896,250
	Block of four, #1543-1546	.80	.80			3.00	
1547	10¢ Molecules and Drops of						
	Gasoline and Oil, Sept. 22	.20	.05	1.00	(4)	.75	148,850,000
1548	10¢ The Headless Horsemen,						
	Oct. 10	.20	.05	1.00	(4)	.75	157,270,000
1549	10¢ Little Girl, Oct. 12	.20	.05	1.00	(4)	.75	150,245,000
	Christmas Issues, 1974						
1550	10¢ Angel, Oct. 23	.20	.05	2.25 (10)		.75	835,180,000
1551	10¢ Sleigh Ride, by Currier and						
	Ives, Oct. 23	.20	.05	2.60 (12)		.75	882,520,000
1552	10¢ Weather Vane; precanceled,						
	Nov. 15, Imperf. Self-adhesive	.20	.08	5.50 (20)		.75	213,155,000

1974

1538

1539

1540

1541

1542

1543
1545

1544
1546

1547

1548

1549

1550

1551

1552

Benjamin West
American artist
10 cents U.S. postage

1553

Paul Laurence
Dunbar
American poet
10 cents U.S. postage

1554

MOVIEMAKER   US 10¢
D.W. GRIFFITH

1555

PIONEER ★ JUPITER
US 10¢

1556

MARINER 10 ★ VENUS/MERCURY
US 10¢

1557

UNITED STATES
collective bargaining
out of conflict . . . accord
10¢

1558

Contributors To The Cause
U.S. 8¢
Sybil Ludington ✪ Youthful Heroine

YOUTHFUL HEROINE
On the dark night of April 26, 1777,
16-year-old Sybil Ludington rode
her horse "Star" alone through the
Connecticut countryside rallying
her father's militia to repel a
raid by the British on Danbury.

1559

Contributors To The Cause
U.S. 10¢
Salem Poor ✪ Gallant Soldier

GALLANT SOLDIER
The conspicuously courageous
actions of black foot soldier
Salem Poor at the Battle of
Bunker Hill on June 17, 1775,
earned him citations for his
bravery and leadership ability.

1560

Contributors To The Cause
U.S. 10¢
Haym Salomon ✪ Financial Hero

FINANCIAL HERO
Businessman and broker Haym
Salomon was responsible for
raising most of the money
needed to finance the American
Revolution and later to save
the new nation from collapse.

1561

Contributors To The Cause
U.S. 18¢
Peter Francisco ✪ Fighter Extraordinary

FIGHTER EXTRAORDINARY
Peter Francisco's strength
and bravery made him a
legend around campfires.
He fought with distinction
at Brandywine, Yorktown
and Guilford Court House.

1562

Lexington & Concord 1775 by Sandham
US Bicentennial 10cents

1563

Bunker Hill 1775 by Trumbull
US Bicentennial 10c

1564

1975

		Un	U	PB*LP #	FDC	Q
	Issues of 1975					
	American Art Issue, Perf. 10½x11, 11					
1553	10¢ Benjamin West, Self-portrait,					
	Feb. 10	.20	.05	2.20 (10)	.75	156,995,000
1554	10¢ Paul Laurence Dunbar, May 1	.20	.05	2.20 (10)	.75	146,365,000
1555	10¢ D. W. Griffith, May 27	.20	.05	1.00 (4)	.75	148,805,000
	Space Issue, Perf. 11					
1556	10¢ Pioneer 10, Feb. 28	.20	.05	1.00 (4)	1.25	173,685,000
1557	10¢ Mariner 10, Apr. 4	.20	.05	1.00 (4)	1.25	158,600,000
1558	10¢ "Labor and Management",					
	Mar. 13	.20	.05	1.80 (8)	.75	153,355,000
	American Bicentennial Issues, Contributors to the Cause, Mar. 25, Perf. 11x10½					
1559	8¢ Sybil Ludington	.16	.13	2.00 (10)	.75	63,205,000
1560	10¢ Salem Poor	.20	.05	2.50 (10)	.75	157,865,000
1561	10¢ Haym Salomon	.20	.05	2.50 (10)	.75	166,810,000
1562	18¢ Peter Francisco	.36	.20	5.00 (10)	.75	44,825,000
	Perf. 11					
1563	10¢ "Birth of Liberty",					
	by Henry Sandham, April 19	.20	.05	2.60 (12)	.75	144,028,000
	Perf. 11x10½					
1564	10¢ Battle of Bunker Hill,					
	by John Trumbull, June 17	.20	.05	2.60 (12)	.75	139,928,000

Adam and Eve

Dr. Stephen Hector Taylor-Smith was a dental surgeon and stamp collector who believed rockets could be used for mail delivery. He devoted many years to rocket mail experiments from various locations in India which were inaccessible to regular communication channels.

His first test rocket firing took place on September 30, 1934, from a ship heading for Saugor Island, located 84 miles off the coast of Calcutta. Unfortunately, the rocket with 173 covers aboard exploded in mid-air scattering the envelopes over the sea. All but three of the covers were salvaged and are considered "collector's items" today. Undaunted, Smith conducted several more tests on the island itself, including some shore-to-ship, which also failed to hit their target.

Dr. Smith also was the first person who had live animals flown in a rocket. On June 29, 1935, two young birds, named Adam and Eve, were carried by rocket across the Indian Damoodar River. In addition to the two birds, the rocket also contained 189 "Rocketgrams" which read, "World's First Rocket Livestock Dispatch."

As we glance at today's space stamps (#1556-57), one can only marvel at the foresight of rocket experiments carried on 50 years ago.

1975

1975 continued	Un	U	PB/LP #	FDC	Q
Military Uniforms, July 4, Perf. 11					
1565 10¢ Soldier with Flintlock Musket,					
Uniform Button	.20	.08	2.60 (12)	.90	44,963,750
1566 10¢ Sailor with Grappling Hook,					
First Navy Jack, 1775	.20	.08		.90	44,963,750
1567 10¢ Marine with Musket,					
Full-rigged Ship	.20	.08	2.60 (12)	.90	44,963,750
1568 10¢ Militiaman with Musket,					
Powder Horn	.20	.08		.90	44,963,750
Block of 4, #1565-1568	.80	.70		2.40	
Apollo-Soyuz Space Issue, July 15, Perf. 11x10½					
1569 10¢ Apollo and Soyuz after					
Docking, and Earth	.20	.10	2.60 (12)	1.00	80,931,600
1570 10¢ Spacecraft before Docking,					
Earth and Project Emblem	.20	.10	3.40 (16)	1.00	80,931,600
Pair, #1569-1570	.40	.25		2.75	
1571 10¢ Worldwide Equality for Women,					
Aug. 26	.20	.05	1.40 (6)	.75	145,640,000
Postal Service Bicentennial Issue, Sep. 3					
1572 10¢ Stagecoach and Trailer Truck	.20	.08	2.60 (12)	.75	42,163,750
1573 10¢ Old and New Locomotives	.20	.08	2.60 (12)	.75	42,163,750
1574 10¢ Early Mail Plane and Jet	.20	.08		.75	42,163,750
1575 10¢ Satellite for Transmission					
of Mailgrams	.20	.08		.75	42,163,750
Block of 4, #1572-1575	.80	.80		2.40	
Perf. 11					
1576 10¢ World Peace, Sept. 29	.20	.05	1.00 (4)	.75	146,615,000
Banking and Commerce Issue, Oct. 6					
1577 10¢ Engine Turning, Indian Head					
Penny and Morgan Silver Dollar	.20	.08	1.00 (4)	.75	73,098,000
1578 10¢ Seated Liberty, Quarter,					
$20 Gold (Double Eagle),					
Engine Turning	.20	.08	1.00 (4)	.75	73,098,000
Pair, #1577-1578	.40	.20		1.00	

CONTINENTAL ARMY

CONTINENTAL NAVY

CONTINENTAL MARINES

AMERICAN MILITIA

APOLLO SOYUZ 1975

APOLLO SOYUZ SPACE TEST PROJECT

1569
1570

1565 1566
1567 1568

INTERNATIONAL WOMEN'S YEAR

1571

US 10¢ 200 Years of Postal Service

US 10¢ 200 Years of Postal Service

US 10¢ 200 Years of Postal Service

US 10¢ 200 Years of Postal Service

1572 1573
1574 1575

World Peace through LAW

1576

BANKING COMMERCE

1577 1578

Ghirlandaio: National Gallery
Christmas US postage

.579

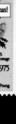

Merry Christmas!

US Postage

1975

Early Card by Louis Prang

1580

1582b

1581
1584

1582
1585

COLLECT
STAMPS
FOR
THE
FUN
OF IT

591
593

1592
1594

1595a

1596
1597

1618
1599

	1975 continued	Un	U	PB/LP	#	FDC	Q
	Christmas Issue, Oct. 14, Perf. 11						
1579	(10¢) Madonna by						
	Domenico Ghirlandaio	.20	.05	2.60	(12)	.75	739,430,000
1580	(10¢) Christmas Card,						
	by Louis Prang, 1878	.20	.05	2.60	(12)	.75	878,690,000
	Issues of 1975-81, Americana, Perf. 11x10½						
1581	1¢ Inkwell & Quill, 1977	.05	.05	.25	(4)	.40	
1582	2¢ Speaker's Stand, 1977	.05	.05	.25	(4)	.40	
1584	3¢ Early Ballot Box, 1977	.06	.05	.30	(4)	.40	
1585	4¢ Books, Bookmark, Eyeglasses,	.08	.05	.40	(4)	.40	
	Size: 17½x20½mm., 1977						
1590	9¢ Capitol Dome (1591), 1977						
	(from booklet pane-see #1623a	.75	.20			1.00	
1590a	Perf. 10	25.00	6.00				
	Size: 18½x22½mm.						
1591	9¢ Capitol Dome, 1975	.18	.05	.90	(4)	.60	
1592	10¢ Contemplation of Justice, 1977	.20	.05	1.00	(4)	.60	
1593	11¢ Printing Press, 1975	.22	.05	1.10	(4)	.60	
1594	12¢ Torch, 1981	.24	.05	1.15	(4)	.60	
1595	13¢ Liberty Bell, 1975	.26	.05			.60	
1595a	Booklet pane of 6	1.60	.50				
1595b	Booklet pane of 7 + label	1.80	.50				
1595c	Booklet pane of 8	2.10	.50				
1595d	Booklet pane of 5 + label, 1976	1.30	.50				
1596	13¢ Eagle and Shield, 1975	.26	.05	3.38	(12)	.60	
	Perf. 11						
1597	15¢ Fort McHenry Flag, 1978	.30	.05	2.10	(6)	.65	
	Perf. 11x10½						
1598	15¢ Fort McHenry Flag (1597), 1978	.30	.05			.65	
1598a	Booklet pane of 8	2.50	.60				
1599	16¢ Head of Liberty, 1978	.32	.05	2.25	(4)	.65	
1603	24¢ Old North Church, 1975	.48	.09	2.75	(4)	.75	
1604	28¢ Fort Nisqually, 1978	.56	.08	3.25	(4)	1.20	
1605	29¢ Sandy Hook Lighthouse, 1978	.58	.08	3.25	(4)	1.10	
1606	30¢ One-room Schoolhouse, 1979	.60	.08	3.00	(4)	1.10	
	No. 1590 is on white paper. No. 1591 on gray paper. Nos. 1590 and 1590a, 1595, 1598 issued only in booklets. Additional American Series, see No. 1813.						
1608	50¢ Whale Oil Lamp, 1979	1.00	.25	5.00	(4)	1.25	
1610	$1 Candle and Rushlight Holder,						
	1979	2.00	.25	9.00	(4)	3.00	
1611	$2 Kerosene Table Lamp, 1978	4.00	.50	18.00	(4)	4.75	
1612	$5 Railroad Lantern, 1979	10.00	2.00	45.00	(4)	10.00	

	1975-1981 continued	Un	U	PB/LP #	FDC	Q
	Coil Stamps, Perf. 10 Vertically					
1613	3.1¢ Guitar, 1979	.20	.05	.40	.40	
1614	7.7¢ Saxhorns, 1976	.20	.08	.40	.60	
1615	7.9¢ Drum, 1976	.20	.08	.40	.60	
1615C	8.4¢ Piano, 1978	.25	.08	.50	.60	
1616	9¢ Capitol Dome (1591), 1976	.22	.05	.44	.60	
1617	10¢ Contemplation of Justice					
	(1592), 1977	.20	.05	.40	.60	
1618	13¢ Liberty Bell (1595), 1975	.26	.05	1.00	.65	
1618C	15¢ Fort McHenry Flag (1597),					
	1978	.40	.05	—	.65	
1619	16¢ Head of Liberty (1599), 1978	.32	.05	1.50	.60	
	Perf. 11x10½					
1622	13¢ Flag over Independence					
	Hall, 1975	.26	.05		.65	
1623	13¢ Flag over Capitol, 1977	.26	.05		1.00	
1623a	Booklet pane of 8	2.50	.60			
1623b	Perf. 10	1.50	1.00			
1623c	Booklet pane of 8, Perf. 10					
	(1# 1590a & 7# 1623b)	37.50	—			
	Nos. 1623, 1623b issued only in booklets					
	(Se-tenant pair, #1590 and #1623)				.75	
	Coil Stamp. Perf. 10 Vertically					
1625	13¢ Flag over Independence Hall					
	(1622), 1975	.30	.05		.65	
	Issues of 1976					
1629	13¢ Drummer Boy	.26	.08		.65	
1630	13¢ Old Drummer	.26	.08		.65	
1631	13¢ Fifer ·	.26	.08		.65	
	Strip of 3, # 1629/1631	.78	.60	3.40 (12)	1.75	218,585,000
1632	13¢ Interphil	.26	.05	1.30 (4)	.65	157,825,000
	American Bicentennial, State Flags Issue, Feb. 23, 1976					
1633	13¢ Delaware	.45	.30		1.75	8,720,100
1634	13¢ Pennsylvania	.45	.30		1.75	8,720,100
1635	13¢ New Jersey	.45	.30		1.75	8,720,100
1636	13¢ Georgia	.45	.30		1.75	8,720,100
1637	13¢ Connecticut	.45	.30		1.75	8,720,100
1638	13¢ Massachusetts	.45	.30		1.75	8,720,100

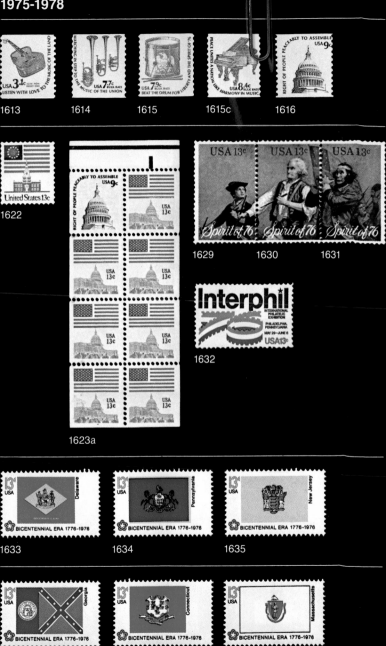

1613

1614

1615

1615c

1616

1622

1623a

1629

1630

1631

1632

1633

1634

1635

1639

1640

1641

1642

1643

1644

1645

1646

1647

1648

1649

1650

1651

1652

1653

1654

1655

1656

	1976 continued	Un	U	PB/LP	#	FDC	Q
1639	13¢ Maryland	.45	.30			1.75	8,720,100
1640	13¢ South Carolina	.45	.30			1.75	8,720,100
1641	13¢ New Hampshire	.45	.30			1.75	8,720,100
1642	13¢ Virginia	.45	.30			1.75	8,720,100
1643	13¢ New York	.45	.30			1.75	8,720,100
1644	13¢ North Carolina	.45	.30			1.75	8,720,100
1645	13¢ Rhode Island	.45	.30			1.75	8,720,100
1646	13¢ Vermont	.45	.30			1.75	8,720,100
1647	13¢ Kentucky	.45	.30			1.75	8,720,100
1648	13¢ Tennessee	.45	.30			1.75	8,720,100
1649	13¢ Ohio	.45	.30			1.75	8,720,100
1650	13¢ Louisiana	.45	.30			1.75	8,720,100
1651	13¢ Indiana	.45	.30			1.75	8,720,100
1652	13¢ Mississippi	.45	.30			1.75	8,720,100
1653	13¢ Illinois	.45	.30			1.75	8,720,100
1654	13¢ Alabama	.45	.30			1.75	8,720,100
1655	13¢ Maine	.45	.30			1.75	8,720,100
1656	13¢ Missouri	.45	.30			1.75	8,720,100

Abraham Baldwin
(Great Americans Series)

"Take care, hold the wagon back; there is more danger of its running too fast than of its going too slow." Such was the tempered wisdom of a man considered by many to be the "father" of the American state university system. The son of a Connecticut blacksmith, Abraham Baldwin first practiced the ministry after graduation from Yale in 1772, then joined the Revolutionary army as a chaplain. During the war, he studied law, emerging with a new profession and a new home in Savannah, Georgia.

Believing that a popular government can succeed only when its citizens are educated, Baldwin wrote the charter for Franklin College in 1785, the oldest college at the University of Georgia, thereby creating the first document of its kind to establish a state university in the United States. The charter became a blueprint for the development of the University of Georgia and a model for the development of higher education across the country.

Later serving in both houses of Congress, Baldwin represented Georgia at the federal constitutional convention at Philadelphia in 1787, where he was credited with the compromise that saved the convention by establishing proportional representation by the states in Congress. When the U.S. Constitution was completed, Baldwin was one of its signers.

The epitaph of this prophetic statesman might well have read, "Serene, benign, good-humored, moderate though firm amid the violence of party strife, he died probably without an enemy."

	1976 continued	Un	U	PB/LP	#	FDC	Q
1657	13¢ Arkansas	.45	.30			1.75	8,720,100
1658	13¢ Michigan	.45	.30			1.75	8,720,100
1659	13¢ Florida	.45	.30			1.75	8,720,100
1660	13¢ Texas	.45	.30			1.75	8,720,100
1661	13¢ Iowa	.45	.30			1.75	8,720,100
1662	13¢ Wisconsin	.45	.30			1.75	8,720,100
1663	13¢ California	.45	.30			1.75	8,720,100
1664	13¢ Minnesota	.45	.30			1.75	8,720,100
1665	13¢ Oregon	.45	.30			1.75	8,720,100
1666	13¢ Kansas	.45	.30			1.75	8,720,100
1667	13¢ West Virginia	.45	.30			1.75	8,720,100
1668	13¢ Nevada	.45	.30			1.75	8,720,100
1669	13¢ Nebraska	.45	.30			1.75	8,720,100
1670	13¢ Colorado	.45	.30			1.75	8,720,100
1671	13¢ North Dakota	.45	.30			1.75	8,720,100
1672	13¢ South Dakota	.45	.30			1.75	8,720,100
1673	13¢ Montana	.45	.30			1.75	8,720,100
1674	13¢ Washington	.45	.30			1.75	8,720,100

Upside Down Flags

According to some Tennessee residents, the postage stamp picturing their state flag (#1648) illustrates the flag upside down. The U.S. Postal Service states that the stamp design is correct and based on the official Tennessee statutes. This is the story behind the stamp design.

The Postal Service designer of the stamp went to the original Tennessee statutes to get the official, legal description of the flag. The first Tennessee flag, the 1905 official description and the stamp design were all the same.

After the stamps were issued on February 23, 1976, the Tennessee state archivist researched a 1905 drawing (which was not part of the official written statute) and declared that the stamp and all the current flags flying over Tennessee were wrong. A historical society came up with an actual flag made after the adoption of the 1905 statute. The society's flag was different than the stamp, the archivist's drawing and all the current flags. If all that weren't confusing enough, the same man who made the original drawing also sewed the first Tennessee flag, and the two are different.

The General Assembly of the State of Tennessee passed a resolution after the stamp was issued stating that the flag illustrated on the postage stamps was wrong and that all the offending stamps should be recalled. No one, however, suggested that all the current state flags be replaced even though they too are in conflict with the statute, the 1905 drawing and the first flag.

1976

1657

1658

1659

1660

1661

1662

1663

1664

1665

1666

1667

1668

1669

1670

1671

1672

1673

1674

1976

1675

1676

1677

1678

1679

1680

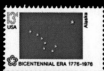

1681

1682

1683

1684

1685

The Surrender of Lord Cornwallis at Yorktown
From a Painting by John Trumbull

1686

	1976 continued	Un	U	PB/LP #	FDC	Q
1675	13¢ Idaho	.45	.30		1.75	8,720,100
1676	13¢ Wyoming	.45	.30		1.75	8,720,100
1677	13¢ Utah	.45	.30		1.75	8,720,100
1678	13¢ Oklahoma	.45	.30		1.75	8,720,100
1679	13¢ New Mexico	.45	.30		1.75	8,720,100
1680	13¢ Arizona	.45	.30		1.75	8,720,100
1681	13¢ Alaska	.45	.30		1.75	8,720,100
1682	13¢ Hawaii	.45	.30		1.75	8,720,100
	Pane of 50, #1633-1682	—		25.00 (50)	32.50	
1683	13¢ Bell's Telephone Patent					
	Application, Mar. 10	.26	.05	1.30 (4)	.65	159,915,000
1684	13¢ Ford-Pullman Monoplane					
	and Laird Swallow Biplane, Mar. 19	.26	.05	2.90 (10)	.65	156,960,000
1685	13¢ Various Flasks, Separatory					
	Funnel, Computer Tape, Apr. 6	.26	.05	3.40 (12)	.65	158,470,000
	American Bicentennial Issues, Souvenir Sheets, May 29					
	Sheets of 5 Stamps Each					
1686	13¢ Surrender of Cornwallis at					
	Yorktown, by John Trumbull	4.50	—		6.00	1,990,000
	a. 13¢ Two American Officers	.65	.40			1,990,000
	b. 13¢ Gen. Benjamin Lincoln	.65	.40			1,990,000
	c. 13¢ George Washington	.65	.40			1,990,000
	d. 13¢ John Trumbull, Col. Cobb,					
	von Steuben,					
	Lafayette, Thomas Nelson	.65	.40			1,990,000
	e. 13¢ Alexander Hamilton, John					
	Laurens, Walter Stewart	.65	.40			1,990,000

Philatelic Exhibition Sheets

The American Bicentennial Souvenir Sheets (#1686-89) were issued to commemorate the 200th anniversary of the United States. They also played a secondary role, that of honoring INTERPHIL, the Seventh International Philatelic Exhibition to be held in the U.S.

An interesting, inexpensive collection can be built around the stamps, souvenir cards and sheets issued at various stamp shows. The first appearance of a philatelic exhibition item was in Austria in 1881. The design of the stamp labels were based on the first issue of Austria's stamps, with the value removed and the year inserted in its place.

The first U.S. philatelic exhibition item was issued in 1887 when the Chicago Philatelic Society printed a menu card commemorating its show. There have been thousands of other philatelic souvenirs printed after these early items to coincide with stamp shows. Some were distributed free prior to the show and others were sold at a nominal amount to help finance the event.

A collection of stamp souvenir sheets and stamps relating to shows can be acquired with a great deal of patience and a small expenditure of money.

	1976 continued	Un	U	PB/LP	#	FDC	Q
1687	18¢ Declaration of Independence,						
	by John Trumbull	6.00	—			7.50	1,983,000
	a. 18¢ John Adams, Roger Sherman,						
	Robert R. Livingston	.80	.55				1,983,000
	b. 18¢ Thomas Jefferson, Benjamin						
	Franklin	.80	.55				1,983,000
	c. 18¢ Thomas Nelson, Jr., Francis						
	Lewis, John Witherspoon,						
	Samuel Huntington	.80	.55				1,983,000
	d. 18¢ John Hancock,						
	Charles Thomson	.80	.55				1,983,000
	e. 18¢ George Read, John						
	Dickinson, Edward Rutledge	.80	.55				1,983,000
1688	24¢ Washington Crossing the						
	Delaware, by Emanuel Leutze/						
	Eastman Johnson	7.50	—			8.50	1,953,000
	a. 24¢ Boatsman	1.00	.75				1,953,000
	b. 24¢ George Washington	1.00	.75				1,953,000
	c. 24¢ Flagbearer	1.00	.75				1,953,000
	d. 24¢ Men in Boat	1.00	.75				1,953,000
	e. 24¢ Men on Shore	1.00	.75				1,953,000
1689	31¢ Washington Reviewing Army						
	at Valley Forge, by William T. Trego	9.00	—			9.50	1,903,000
	a. 31¢ Two Officers	1.25	.90				1,903,000
	b. 31¢ George Washington	1.25	.90				1,903,000
	c. 31¢ Officer and Black Horse	1.25	.90				1,903,000
	d. 31¢ Officer and White Horse	1.25	.90				1,903,000
	e. 31¢ Three Soldiers	1.25	.90				1,903,000

The Declaration of Independence, 4 July 1776 at Philadelphia
From a Painting by John Trumbull

1687

Washington Crossing the Delaware
From a Painting by Emanuel Leutze / Eastman Johnson

1688

Washington Reviewing His Ragged Army at Valley Forge
From a Painting by William T. Trego

1689

191

1976-1977

1690

1691   1692   1693   1694

1699

1700

1695   1696
1697   1698

1701

1702

1703

1704

1705

	1976 continued	Un	U	PB/LP #	FDC	Q
1690	13¢ Franklin and Map					
	of North America, 1776, June 1	.26	.05	1.30 (4)	.65	164,890,000
	American Bicentennial Issue, Declaration of Independence, by Trumbull, July 4					
1691	13¢	.26	.08	5.50 (20)	.65	51,008,750
1692	13¢	.26	.08		.65	51,008,750
1693	13¢	.26	.08		.65	51,008,750
1694	13¢	.26	.08	5.50 (20)	.65	51,008,750
	Strip of 4, #1691-1694	1.10	.75		2.00	
	Olympic Games Issue, July 16					
1695	13¢ Diving	.26	.08	3.40 (12)	.70	46,428,750
1696	13¢ Skiing	.26	.08		.70	46,428,750
1697	13¢ Running	.26	.08	3.40 (12)	.70	46,428,750
1698	13¢ Skating	.26	.08		.70	46,428,750
	Block of 4, #1695-1698	1.10	1.00		2.00	
1699	13¢ Clara Maass, Aug. 18	.26	.06	3.40 (12)	.65	130,592,000
1700	13¢ Adolph S. Ochs, Sept. 18	.26	.05	1.30 (4)	.65	158,332,800
	Christmas Issue, Oct. 27					
1701	13¢ Nativity,					
	by John Singleton Copley	.26	.05	3.40 (12)	.65	809,955,000
	Christmas Issue, Oct. 27, 1976 continued					
1702	13¢ "Winter Pastime",					
	by Nathaniel Currier	.26	.05	3.00 (10)	.65	481,685,000
1703	13¢ as 1702	.26	.05	5.70 (20)	.65	481,685,000

No. 1702 has overall tagging. Lettering at base is black and usually ½mm. below design. As a rule, no "snowflaking" in sky or pond. Pane of 50 has margins on 4 sides with slogans. No. 1703 has block tagging the size of the printed area. Lettering at base is gray black and usually ¾mm. below design. "Snowflaking" generally in sky and pond. Pane of 50 has margin only at right or left, and no slogans.

	Issues of 1977 American Bicentennial, Perf. 11					
1704	13¢ Washington,					
	by Charles Wilson Peale, Jan. 3	.26	.05	2.90 (10)	.65	150,328,000
1705	13¢ Tin Foil Phonograph, Mar. 23	.26	.05	1.30 (4)	.65	176,830,000

Ski Mail

One of the stamps issued for the 1976 Winter Olympic Games (#1696) honored skiing as a sport. John Thompson used his skis for transportation. Starting in 1858, he carried the mail between Placerville and Carson City, Nevada, traveling by skis.

For 20 winters, the Norseman skier was the only link from Carson City to California and the rest of the United States. He ran no set trail and used rocks, trees and peaks as his landmarks. Thompson slept on the snow at night with spruce boughs as his bed and the mailbag as his pillow. When Congress failed to appropriate money for his services for more than two years, the people on both sides of the mountain chipped in so that they could continue to receive mail.

Thompson's tombstone at Genoa, Colorado, reads, "Snowshoe Thompson" and has a pair of skis carved into the background. This hardy skier led the way for the pack trains, pony express and stagecoach.

	1977 continued	Un	U	PB/LP #	FDC	Q
	Pueblo Indian Art Issue, Apr. 13, Perf. 11					
1706	13¢ Zia Pot	.26	.08	3.00 (10)	.65	48,994,000
1707	13¢ San Ildefonso Pot	.26	.08		.65	48,994,000
1708	13¢ Hopi Pot	.26	.08	5.00 (16)	.65	48,994,000
1709	13¢ Acoma Pot	.26	.08		.65	48,994,000
	Block or strip of 4, #1706-1709	1.05	1.00		1.75	
1710	13¢ Spirit of St. Louis, May 20	.26	.05	3.65 (12)	.75	208,820,000
1711	13¢ Columbine and Rocky					
	Mountains, May 21	.26	.05	3.65 (12)	.65	192,250,000
	Butterfly Issue, June 6					
1712	13¢ Swallowtail	.26	.08	3.65 (12)	.65	54,957,500
1713	13¢ Checkerspot	.26	.08	3.65 (12)	.65	54,957,500
1714	13¢ Dogface	.26	.08		.65	54,957,500
1715	13¢ Orange Tip	.26	.08		.65	54,957,500
	Block of 4, #1712-1715	1.05	.90		1.75	
	American Bicentennial Issues					
1716	13¢ Marquis de Lafayette, June 13	.26	.05	1.30 (4)	.65	159,852,000
	Skilled Hands for Independence, July 4					
1717	13¢ Seamstress	.26	.08	3.65 (12)	.65	47,077,500
1718	13¢ Blacksmith	.26	.08	3.65 (12)	.65	47,077,500
1719	13¢ Wheelwright	.26	.08		.65	47,077,500
1720	13¢ Leatherworker	.26	.08		.65	47,077,500
	Block of 4, #1717-1720	1.05	.90		1.75	
	Perf. 11x10½					
1721	13¢ Peace Bridge and Dove,					
	Aug. 4	.26	.05	1.30 (4)	.65	163,625,000

Grenville Clark
(Great Americans Series)

Though he lived through two world wars, serving in one, Grenville Clark spent most of his life seeking peaceful alternatives on an international level. A lawyer with degrees from Harvard University, Clark served as a major and later lieutenant colonel in the Adjutant General's Department of the U.S. Army during World War I, helped found the Plattsburg Plan to establish the Military Training Camps Association and was one of the drafters of the Selective Service Act of 1940.

But the advocacy of peace and civil liberties through world federalism became Clark's life commitment. He held high offices in the United World Federalists, wrote numerous articles on both civil and world government, and, in 1958, published World Peace Through World Law. *His ideals continue today to guide the selection of grants and awards to world peace advocates through the Grenville Clark Fund at Dartmouth College.*

Zia Museum of New Mexico **Pueblo Art** USA 13c San Ildefonso Denver Art Museum **Pueblo Art** USA 13c

Hopi Heard Museum Phoenix **Pueblo Art** USA 13c Acoma School of American Research **Pueblo Art** USA 13c

1706 1707
1708 1709

1710

1711

Swallowtail USA 13C *Papilio oregonius* Checkerspot USA 13C *Euphydryas phaeton*

Dogface USA 13C *Colias eurydice* Orange-Tip USA 13C *Anthocaris midea*

1712 1713
1714 1715

Lafayette

US Bicentennial 13c

1716

the SEAMSTRESS for INDEPENDENCE USA 13c the BLACKSMITH for INDEPENDENCE USA 13c

the WHEELWRIGHT for INDEPENDENCE USA 13c the LEATHERWORKER for INDEPENDENCE USA 13c

1717 1718
1719 1720

United States & Canada Peace Bridge 1927-77 USA 13c

1721

Herkimer at Oriskany 1777 by Yohn
US Bicentennial 13 cents

722

ENERGY CONSERVATION USA 13c

ENERGY DEVELOPMENT USA 13c

1723
1724

First Civil Settlement·Alta California·1777

1725

Drafting the Articles of Confederation
York Town, Pennsylvania 1777 13c

726

13 USA
ANNIVERSARY YEAR

1727

Surrender at Saratoga 1777 by Trumbull
US Bicentennial 13 cents

1728

Christmas 13c USA

730

Carl Sandburg
USA 13c

1731

Alaska 1778
Capt. JAMES COOK
13c USA

Capt. JAMES COOK 13c USA
Hawaii 1778

1732
1733

USA 13c

1734

17

15c
USA

737

USA 15c USA 15c USA 15c USA 15c USA 15c
Virginia 1720 Rhode Island 1790 Massachusetts 1793 Illinois 1860 Texas 1890

USA 15c USA 15c USA 15c USA 15c USA 15c
Virginia 1720 Rhode Island 1790 Massachusetts 1793 Illinois 1860 Texas 1890

1977-1980

	1977 continued	Un	U	PB/LP	#	FDC	Q
	American Bicentennial Issue, Perf. 11						
1722	13¢ Herkimer at Oriskany,						
	by Frederick Yohn, Aug. 6	.26	.05	3.10	(10)	.65	156,296,000
	Energy Issue, Oct. 20						
1723	13¢ Energy Conservation	.26	.08	3.65	(12)	.65	79,338,000
1724	13¢ Energy Development	.26	.08			.65	79,338,000
	Pair, #1723-1724	.52	.35			1.00	
	American Bicentennial Issues						
1725	13¢ Farm House, Sept. 9	.26	.05	1.30	(4)	.65	154,495,000
	First civil settlement in Alta, California, 200th anniversary.						
1726	13¢ Articles of Confederation,						
	Sept. 30	.26	.05	1.30	(4)	.65	168,050,000
	200th anniversary of the Drafting of the Articles of Confederation, York Town, Pa.						
1727	13¢ Movie Projector and						
	Phonograph, Oct. 6	.26	.05	1.30	(4)	.75	156,810,000
	American Bicentennial Issue						
1728	13¢ Surrender of Saratoga,						
	by John Trumbull, Oct. 7	.26	.05	3.10	(10)	.65	153,736,000
	Christmas Issue, Oct. 21						
1729	13¢ Washington at Valley Forge	.26	.05	5.70	(20)	.65	882,260,000
1730	13¢ Rural Mailbox	.26	.05	3.10	(10)	.65	921,530,000
	Issues of 1978, Perf. 11						
1731	13¢ Carl Sandburg, Jan. 6	.26	.05	1.30	(4)	.65	156,580,000
	Capt. Cook Issue, Jan. 20						
1732	13¢ Capt. Cook	.26	.08	1.30	(4)	.75	101,095,000
1733	13¢ "Resolution" and "Discovery"	.26	.08	1.30	(4)	.75	101,095,000
	Pair, #1732-1733	.55	.30			1.50	
1734	13¢ Indian Head Penny, 1877,						
	Jan. 11	.26	.10	3.25	(4)	1.00	
1735	(15¢) Eagle (A), May 22	.30	.05	1.50	(4)	.65	
	Perf. 11x10½						
1736	(15¢) orange Eagle (1735), May 22	.30	.05			.65	
1736a	Booklet pane of 8	2.40	.60				
	Perf. 10						
1737	15¢ Roses, July 11	.30	.06			.65	
1737a	Booklet pane of 8	2.40	.60				
	Nos. 1736 and 1737 issued only in booklets.						
	1980 Windmills, Feb. 7, Perf. 11						
1738	15¢ Virginia, 1720	.30	.05			.65	
1739	15¢ Rhode Island, 1790	.30	.05			.65	
1740	15¢ Massachusetts, 1793	.30	.05			.65	
1741	15¢ Illinois, 1860	.30	.05			.65	
1742	15¢ Texas, 1890	.30	.05			.65	
	Booklet pane of 10	3.50	.60				

1978 continued	Un	U	PB/LP	#	FDC	Q
Coil Stamp, Perf. 10 Vertically						
1743 (15¢) orange Eagle (1735), May 22	.30	.05	1.00		.65	
Perf. 11						
1744 13¢ Harriet Tubman, Feb. 1	.26	.05	3.65	(12)	1.00	156,555,000
American Folk Art Issue, American Quilts, Mar. 8, 1978						
1745 13¢ Basket design, red & orange	.26	.08	3.65	(12)	.65	41,295,600
1746 13¢ Basket design, red	.26	.08	3.65	(12)	.65	41,295,600
1747 13¢ Basket design, orange	.26	.08			.65	41,295,600
1748 13¢ Basket design, black	.26	.08			.65	41,295,600
Block of 4, #1745-1748	1.05	.75			2.00	
American Dance Issue, Apr. 26						
1749 13¢ Ballet	.26	.08	3.65	(12)	.65	39,399,600
1750 13¢ Theater	.26	.08	3.65	(12)	.65	39,399,600
1751 13¢ Folk Dance	.26	.08			.65	39,399,600
1752 13¢ Modern Dance	.26	.08			.65	39,399,600
Block of 4, #1749-1752	1.05	.75			1.75	
1753 13¢ French Alliance, May 4	.26	.05	1.30	(4)	.65	102,920,000
Perf. 10½x11						
1754 13¢ Dr. Papanicolaou with						
Microscope, May 18	.26	.05	1.30	(4)	.65	152,355,000
Performing Arts Issue, Perf. 11						
1755 13¢ Jimmie Rodgers, May 24	.26	.05	3.65	(12)	.65	94,625,000
1756 15¢ George M. Cohan, July 3	.30	.05	4.20	(12)	.65	151,570,000

College Postage

College stamps actually attended college, but not as students. During the late 1800s, many business schools used simulated postage and revenue stamps as part of class procedure.

These labels were used to teach the students the correct handling of postage stamps, including their application on letters and packages, and the financial accounting procedures of expenses. In many cases, the labels were designed and printed by the students, but as the practice became generally accepted in business schools, commercial school supply houses listed them as part of their supplies.

As the labels became known to collectors, many bogus varieties appeared to satisfy the demand.

1744

1745   1746
1747   1748

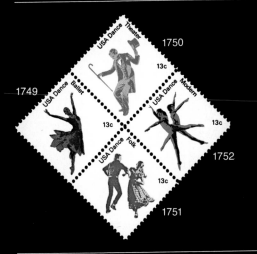

1749

1750

1752

1751

1753

1754

1755

1756

1757a,b,c,d

1757e,f,g,h

1757

1758

Viking missions to Mars

1759

1760   1761
1762   1763

1768

1769

1764   1765
1766   1767

200

1978

	1978 continued	Un	U	PB/LP	#	FDC	Q
1757	13¢ Souvenir sheet of 8, June 10	2.10	2.50	2.75	(8)	3.50	15,170,400
1757a	13¢ Cardinal	.26	.10				
1757b	13¢ Mallard	.26	.10				
1757c	13¢ Canada Goose	.26	.10				
1757d	13¢ Blue Jay	.26	.10				
1757e	13¢ Moose	.26	.10				
1757f	13¢ Chipmunk	.26	.10				
1757g	13¢ Red Fox	.26	.10				
1757h	13¢ Raccoon	.26	.10				
1758	15¢ Photographic Equipment, June 26	.30	.05	4.20	(12)	.65	163,200,000
1759	15¢ Viking I Landing on Mars, July 20	.30	.05	1.50	(4)	1.00	158,880,000
	American Owls, Aug. 26						
1760	15¢ Great Gray Owl	.30	.08	1.50	(4)	.65	46,637,500
1761	15¢ Saw-whet Owl	.30	.08	1.50	(4)	.65	46,637,500
1762	15¢ Barred Owl	.30	.08	1.50	(4)	.65	46,637,500
1763	15¢ Great Horned Owl	.30	.08	1.50	(4)	.65	46,637,500
	Block of 4, #1760-1763	1.25	.85			2.00	
	American Trees, Oct. 9						
1764	15¢ Giant Sequoia	.30	.08	4.20	(12)	.65	42,034,000
1765	15¢ White Pine	.30	.08	4.20	(12)	.65	42,034,000
1766	15¢ White Oak	.30	.08			.65	42,034,000
1767	15¢ Gray Birch	.30	.08			.65	42,034,000
	Block of 4, #1764-1767	1.25	.85			2.00	
	Christmas Issue, Oct. 18						
1768	15¢ Madonna and Child	.30	.05	4.20	(12)	.65	963,370,000
1769	15¢ Hobby Horse	.30	.05	4.20	(12)	.65	916,800,000

1979

	Issues of 1979, Perf. 11	Un	U	PB/LP	#	FDC	Q
1770	15¢ Robert F. Kennedy, Jan. 12	.30	.05	1.50	(4)	.65	159,297,600
1771	15¢ Martin Luther King, Jr., Jan. 13	.30	.05	4.20	(12)	.65	166,435,000
1772	15¢ Internt'l Year of the Child,						
	Feb. 15	.30	.05	1.50	(4)	.65	162,535,000
	Perf. 10½x11						
1773	15¢ John Steinbeck, Feb. 27	.30	.05	1.50	(4)	.65	155,000,000
1774	15¢ Albert Einstein, Mar. 4	.30	.05	1.50	(4)	.65	157,310,000
	American Folk Art Issue, Apr. 19, Pennsylvania Toleware, Perf. 11						
1775	15¢ Coffeepot	.30	.08	3.50	(10)	.65	43,524,000
1776	15¢ Tea Caddy	.30	.08			.65	43,524,000
1777	15¢ Sugar Bowl	.30	.08	5.40	(16)	.65	43,524,000
1778	15¢ Coffeepot	.30	.08			.65	43,524,000
	Block or strip of 4, #1775-1778	1.20	.85			2.00	174,096,000
	American Architecture Issue, June 4						
1779	15¢ Virginia Rotunda	.30	.08	1.50	(4)	.65	41,198,400
1780	15¢ Baltimore Cathedral	.30	.08	1.50	(4)	.65	41,198,400
1781	15¢ Boston State House	.30	.08	1.50	(4)	.65	41,198,400
1782	15¢ Philadelphia Exchange	.30	.08	1.50	(4)	.65	41,198,400
	Block of 4, #1779-1782	1.20	.85			2.00	164,793,600
	Endangered Flora Issue, June 7						
1783	15¢ Persistent Trillium	.30	.06	4.20	(12)	.65	40,763,750
1784	15¢ Hawaiian Wild Broadbean	.30	.08			.65	40,763,750
1785	15¢ Contra Costa Wallflower	.30	.08	4.20	(12)	.65	40,763,750
1786	15¢ Antioch Evening Primrose	.30	.08			.65	40,763,750
	Block of 4, #1783-1786	1.25	.85			2.00	163,055,000
1787	15¢ Seeing Eye Dogs, June 15	.30	.05	6.50	(20)	.65	161,860,000

Robert F. Kennedy
USA 15c

1770

Martin Luther King Jr.

Black Heritage USA 15c

1771

USA 15c

International Year of the Child

1772

John Steinbeck

USA 15c

1773

Einstein
USA 15c

1774

Pennsylvania Toleware
Folk Art USA 15c

Pennsylvania Toleware
Folk Art USA 15c

Pennsylvania Toleware
Folk Art USA 15c

Pennsylvania Toleware
Folk Art USA 15c

1775   1776
1777   1778

Jefferson 1743-1826 Virginia Rotunda
Architecture USA 15c

Latrobe 1764-1820 Baltimore Cathedral
Architecture USA 15c

Bulfinch 1763-1844 Boston State House
Architecture USA 15c

Strickland 1788-1854 Philadelphia Exchange
Architecture USA 15c

1779   1780
1781   1782

Endangered Flora

PERSISTENT TRILLIUM
15c USA

Endangered Flora

HAWAIIAN WILD BROADBEAN
15c USA

Endangered Flora

CONTRA COSTA WALLFLOWER
15c USA

Endangered Flora

ANTIOCH DUNES EVENING PRIMROSE
15c USA

USA 15c

Seeing For Me

1787

1788

1789

1790

1791
1793

1792
1794

1799

1800

1795
1797

1796
1798

1801

1802

1803

1804

1979-1980

		Un	U	PB/LP	#	FDC	Q
	1979 continued						
1788	15¢ Special Olympics, Aug. 9	.30	.05	3.50	(10)	.65	165,775,000
	Perf. 11x12						
1789	15¢ John Paul Jones,						
	by Charles Wilson Peale, Sept. 23	.30	.05	3.50	(10)	.65	160,000,000
	Olympic Games Issue, Perf. 11						
1790	10¢ Javelin, Sept. 5	.25	.22	3.75	(12)	1.00	67,195,000
1791	15¢ Running, Sept. 28	.35	.08	4.75	(12)	.75	46,726,250
1792	15¢ Swimming, Sept. 28	.35	.08	4.75	(12)	.75	46,726,250
1793	15¢ Canoeing, Sept. 28	.35	.08			.75	46,726,250
1794	15¢ Equestrian, Sept. 28	.35	.08			.75	46,726,250
	Block of 4, #1791-1794	1.50	.85			2.50	187,650,000
	Issues of 1980						
	Winter Olympic Games Issue, Feb. 1, Perf. 11x10½						
1795	15¢ Speed Skating	.45	.08	6.50	(12)	.75	
1796	15¢ Downhill Skiing	.45	.08	6.50	(12)	.75	
1797	15¢ Ski Jump	.45	.08			.75	
1798	15¢ Hockey Goaltender	.45	.08			.75	
	Block of 4, #1795-1798	1.90	.85			2.50	208,295,000
	Christmas Issue, Oct. 18, 1979, Perf. 11						
1799	15¢ Virgin and Child,						
	by Gerard David	.30	.05	4.25	(12)	.65	873,710,000
1800	15¢ Santa Claus	.30	.05	4.25	(12)	.65	931,880,000
1801	15¢ Will Rogers, Nov. 4	.30	.05	4.25	(12)	.65	161,290,000
1802	15¢ Vietnam Veterans, Nov. 11	.30	.05	3.50	(10)	1.25	172,740,000
	Perf. 11½x11½						
1803	15¢ W.C. Fields, Jan. 29	.30	.05	4.25	(12)	.65	168,995,000
	Perf. 11						
1804	15¢ Benjamin Banneker, Feb. 15	.30	.05	4.25	(12)	.65	160,000,000

	1980 continued	Un	U	PB/LP	#	FDC	Q
	Letter Writing Issue, Feb. 25						
1805	15¢ Letter Preserve Memories	.30	.08	11.00	(36)	.65	
1806	15¢ P.S. Write Soon	.30	.08			.65	
1807	15¢ Letters Lift Spirits	.30	.08			.65	
1808	15¢ P.S. Write Soon	.30	.08			.65	
1809	15¢ Letters Shape Opinions	.30	.08			.65	
1810	15¢ P.S. Write Soon	.30	.08	11.00	(36)	.65	
	Vertical Strip of 6, #1805-1810	1.80	1.25			3.00	233,598,000
	Perf. 10, Vertical Coil						
1811	1¢ Americana Type Coil, March 6	.05	.05	.15		.40	
1813	3.5¢ Coil, June 23	.08	.05	.30		.50	
1816	12¢ Freedom of Conscience,						
	Apr. 8	.24	.05	.75		.60	
	Perf. 11x10½						
1818	(18¢) "B" Mar. 15	.36	.05	1.80	(4)	.75	
	Perf. 10						
1819	(18¢) "B" Booklet, Mar. 15	.36	.05			.75	
	Perf. 10 Vert.						
1820	(18¢) "B" Coil, Mar. 15	.36	.05	1.00		.75	
	Perf. 10½x11						
1821	15¢ Frances Perkins, April 10	.30	.05	1.50	(4)	.65	163,510,000
	Perf. 11						
1822	15¢ Dolley Madison, May 20	.30	.05	1.50	(4)	.65	256,620,000
1823	15¢ Emily Bissell, May 31	.30	.05	1.50	(4)	.65	95,695,000
1824	15¢ Helen Keller/Anne Sullivan,						
	June 27	.30	.05	1.50	(4)	.80	153,975,000
1825	15¢ Veterans Administration,						
	July 21	.30	.05	1.50	(4)	.65	160,000,000
1826	15¢ General Bernardo de Galvez,						
	July 23	.30	.05	1.50	(4)	.65	103,855,000
	Coral Reefs Issue, Aug. 26						
1827	15¢ Brain Coral	.30	.08	4.50	(12)	.85	
1828	15¢ Elkhorn Coral	.30	.08			.85	
1829	15¢ Chalice Coral	.30	.08	4.50	(12)	.85	
1830	15¢ Finger Coral	.30	.08			.85	
	Block of 4, #1827-1830	1.20	.85			2.00	205,165,000

1811   1813

1805
1806

1807
1808

1809
1810

1822

1816   1818

Frances Perkins
USA 15c

Emily Bissell
Crusader Against Tuberculosis
USA 15c

1821   1823

1824   1825   1826

1827   1828
1829   1830

Organized Labor
Proud and Free
USA 15c

1831

Edith Wharton
USA 15c

1832

Glow by Josef Albers USA 15c
Learning
never ends

1833

Heiltsuk, Bella Bella
Indian Art USA 15c

Chilkat Tlingit
Indian Art USA 15c

Tlingit
Indian Art USA 15c

Bella Coola
Indian Art USA 15c

1834   1835
1836   1837

Renwick 1818-1895 Smithsonian Washington
Architecture USA 15c

Richardson 1838-1886 Trinity Church Boston
Architecture USA 15c

Furness 1839-1912 Penn Academy Philadelphia
Architecture USA 15c

AJ Davis 1803-1892 Lyndhurst Tarrytown NY
Architecture USA 15c

1838   1839
1840   1841

Christmas USA 15c

1842

USA 15c
Season's Greetings

1843

	1980 continued	Un	U	PB/LP #	FDC	Q
1831	15¢ Organized Labor, Sept. 1	.30	.05	4.50 (12)	.65	166,590,000
	Perf. 10½x11					
1832	15¢ Edith Wharton, Sept. 5	.30	.05	1.50 (4)	.65	163,275,000
	Perf. 11					
1833	15¢ American Education, Sept. 12	.30	.05	2.25 (6)	.65	160,000,000
	Indian Art—Masks Issue, Sept. 25					
1834	15¢ Bella Bella	.30	.08		.75	
1835	15¢ Chilkat	.30	.08		.75	
1836	15¢ Tlingit	.30	.08		.75	
1837	15¢ Bella Coola	.30	.08		.75	
	Block of 4, #1834-1837	1.20	.85	3.50 (10)	2.00	152,404,000
	American Architecture Issue, Oct. 9					
1838	15¢ Smithsonian	.30	.08		.75	
1839	15¢ Trinity Church	.30	.08		.75	
1840	15¢ Pennsylvania Academy of Fine Arts	.30	.08		.75	
1841	15¢ Lyndhurst	.30	.08		.75	
	Block of 4, #1838-1841	1.20	.85	1.50 (4)	2.00	155,024,000
1842	15¢ Christmas Stained Glass Windows, Oct. 31	.30	.05	4.25 (12)	.65	693,250,000
1843	15¢ Christmas Antique Toys, Oct. 31	.30	.05	6.50 (20)	.65	718,715,000

Walter Lippmann
(Great Americans Series)

Like many writers, editors and political philosophers, Walter Lippmann was always keenly aware of day-to-day occurrences. But it was his viewing of them as if they already were part of history that distinguished him from most American journalists. Called the "great elucidator" and "the man with the searching mind," Lippmann enjoyed credibility with a large audience throughout his career, despite a political about-face that took him from a staunch liberal persuasion in his early years to a recognized oracle of the conservative intellectuals in his later life.

After helping found the progressive New Republic *magazine in 1914, and serving on the staff of the* New York World *from 1921 to 1931, Lippmann began writing his Pulitzer Prize-winning syndicated column, "Today and Tomorrow"—first for the* New York Herald-Tribune *(1931-62) and later for the* Washington Post *(1962-67). His fascination with philosophy was evident in his column and numerous books on political theory, and his opinions were courted by political leaders throughout the world. Though the Lippmann writing style often was copied, few journalists ever mastered his ability to express complex theory in such readily understandable language.*

Great Americans Issue, 1980-1984

	Perf. 11	Un	U	PB/LP	#	FDC	Q
1844	1¢ Dorothea Dix, Sept. 23, 1983	.05	.05	1.00	(20)	.60	
	Perf. 10½x11						
1845	2¢ Igor Stravinsky, Nov. 18, 1982	.05	.05	.20	(4)	.60	
1846	3¢ Henry Clay, July 13, 1983	.06	.05	.30	(4)	.60	
1847	4¢ Carl Schurz, June 3, 1983	.08	.05	.40	(4)	.60	
1848	5¢ Pearl Buck, June 25, 1983	.10	.05	.50	(4)	.60	
	Perf. 11						
1853	10¢ Richard Russell, May 31, 1984	.20	.05	4.50	(20)	.65	
	Perf. 10½x11						
1855	13¢ Crazy Horse, Jan. 15, 1982	.26	.05	1.30	(4)	.65	
1857	17¢ Rachel Carson, May 28, 1981	.34	.05	1.75	(4)	.75	
1858	18¢ George Mason, May 7, 1981	.36	.05	1.75	(4)	.75	
1859	19¢ Sequoyah, Dec. 27, 1980	.38	.07	2.00	(4)	.80	
1860	20¢ Ralph Bunche, Jan. 12, 1982	.40	.05	2.00	(4)	.75	
1861	20¢ Thomas H. Gallaudet, June 10, 1983	.40	.05	2.00	(4)	.75	
	Perf. 11						
1862	20¢ Harry S. Truman, Jan. 26, 1984	.40	.05	8.50	(20)	.75	
1864	30¢ Frank C. Laubach, Sept. 2, 1984	.60	.08	12.50	(20)	.85	
1865	35¢ Dr. Charles Drew, June 3, 1981	.70	.08	3.50	(4)	1.00	
	Perf. 10½x11						
1866	37¢ Robert Millikan, Jan. 26, 1982	.75	.06	3.75	(4)	1.00	
	Perf. 11						
1868	40¢ Lillian M. Gilbreth, Feb. 24, 1984	.80	.08	17.50	(20)	1.00	

1844   1845   1846   1847   1848

1853   1855   1857   1858   1859

1860   1861   1862   1864   1865

1866   1868

USA 15c
Everett Dirksen

874

WhitneyMooreYoung

Black Heritage USA 15c

1875

Rose USA 18c

Camellia USA 18c

Dahlia USA 18c

Lily USA 18c

1876
1878

1877
1879

USA 18c USA 18c

USA 18c USA 18c

USA 18c USA 18c

USA 18c USA 18c

USA 18c USA 18c

1889a

USA 18c

...for amber waves of grain

1890

USA 18c

...from sea to shining sea

1891

6c 6c
USA USA

USA 18c ...for purple mountain majesties USA 18c ...for purple mountain majesties

USA 18c ...for purple mountain majesties USA 18c ...for purple mountain majesties

USA 18c ...for purple mountain majesties USA 18c ...for purple mountain majesties

1981

	Issues of 1981, Perf. 11	Un	U	PB/LP	#	FDC	Q
1874	15¢ Everett Dirksen, Jan. 4	.30	.05	1.50	(4)	.65	160,155,000
1875	15¢ Whitney Moore Young, Jr.,						
	Jan. 30	.30	.05	1.50	(4)	.65	159,505,000
	Flower Issue, April 23						
1876	18¢ Rose	.36	.08			.75	52,658,250
1877	18¢ Camellia	.36	.08			.75	52,658,250
1878	18¢ Dahlia	.36	.08			.75	52,658,250
1879	18¢ Lily	.36	.08			.75	52,658,250
	Block of 4, #1876-1879	1.50	.85	1.75	(4)	2.50	
	Wildlife Issue, May 14						
1880	18¢ Bighorned Sheep	.36	.05			.75	
1881	18¢ Puma	.36	.05			.75	
1882	18¢ Harbor Seal	.36	.05			.75	
1883	18¢ Bison	.36	.05			.75	
1884	18¢ Brown Bear	.36	.05			.75	
1885	18¢ Polar Bear	.36	.05			.75	
1886	18¢ Elk (wapiti)	.36	.05			.75	
1887	18¢ Moose	.36	.05			.75	
1888	18¢ White Tailed Deer	.36	.05			.75	
1889	18¢ Prong Horned Antelope	.36	.05			.75	
	Booklet Pane of 10, #1880-1889	3.60					
	Flag Issue, April 24						
1890	18¢ Flag and Anthem, for amber						
	waves of grain	.36	.05	7.50 (20)		.75	
	Perf. 10 Vert.						
1891	18¢ Flag and Anthem, from sea, coil	.36	.05			.75	
	Perf. 11						
1892	6¢ USA Circle of Stars, booklet	.12	.10			.75	
1893	18¢ Flag and Anthem, for purple						
	mountains majesties, booklet	.36	.05			.75	
1893a	Booklet Pane of 8,						
	2 #1892, 6 #1893	2.40	—				
1894	20¢ Flag over Supreme Court,						
	Dec. 17	.40	.05	8.50 (20)		.75	
	Perf. 10 Vert. Coil						
1895	20¢ Flag over Supreme Court,						
	Dec. 17	.40	.05	—		.75	
	Perf. 11 x 10½						
1896	20¢ Flag over Supreme Court	.40	.05	—		.75	
1896a	Booklet Pane of 6, Dec. 17	2.50					

1982-1984

	Transportation Issues, 1982-1984 Perf. 10 Vert.					
		Un	U	PB/LP #	FDC	Q
1897	1¢ Omnibus, Aug. 19, 1983	.05	.05	.15	.60	
1897A	2¢ Locomotive 1870's,					
	May 20, 1982	.05	.05	.15	.60	
1898	3¢ Railroad Handcar,					
	Mar. 25, 1983	.06	.05	.18	.60	
1898A	4¢ Stagecoach 1890's,					
	Aug. 19, 1982	.08	.05	.35	.60	
1899	5¢ Motorcycle, Oct. 10, 1983	.10	.05	.30	.60	
1900	5.2¢ Antique Sleigh,					
	Mar. 21, 1983	.12	.05	.36	.60	
1901	5.9¢ Bicycle 1870's, Feb. 17, 1982	.12	.05	.50	.60	
1902	7.4¢ Baby Buggy 1880s,					
	April 7, 1984	.15	.08		.65	
1903	9.3¢ Mail Wagon, Dec. 15, 1982	.20	.08	.60	.65	
1904	10.9¢ Hansom Cab 1890's,					
	Mar. 26, 1982	.22	.05	.70	.65	
1905	11¢ Railroad Caboose, Feb. 3, 1984	.22	.08			
1906	17¢ Electric Auto, June 25, 1982	.34	.05	1.00	.75	
1907	18¢ Surrey, May 15, 1982	.36	.05	1.00	.75	
1908	20¢ Fire Pumper, Dec. 10, 1982	.40	.05	1.20	.65	

Omnibus 1880s
USA 1c

1897

Locomotive 1870s
USA 2c

1897A

Handcar 1880s
USA 3c

1898

Stagecoach 1890s
USA 4c

1898A

Motorcycle
1913
USA 5c

1899

Sleigh 1880s
USA 5.2c Nonprofit
Org

1900

Bicycle 1870s
USA 5.9c

1901

Baby Buggy 1880s
USA 7.4c

1902

Mail Wagon 1880s
USA 9.3c

1903

Hansom Cab 1890s
USA 10.9c

1904

RR Caboose 1890s
USA 11c
Bulk Rate

1905

Electric Auto 1917
USA 17c

1906

Surrey 1890s
USA 18c

1907

Fire Pumper
1860s
USA 20c

1908

1909

1910

1911

1912   1913   1914   1915

1981-1983

		Un	U	PB/LP	#	FDC	Q
1909	$9.35 Express Mail, Aug. 12, 1983	19.00	5.00	—		25.00	
	Booklet Pane of 3	60.00	—				
	Perf. 11x10½						
1910	18¢ American Red Cross, May 1	.36	.05	1.75	(4)	.75	165,175,000
	Perf. 11						
1911	18¢ Savings and Loan, May 8	.36	.05	1.75	(4)	.75	107,240,000
	Space Achievement Issue, May 21						
1912	18¢ Exploring the Moon	.36	.10			.75	42,227,375
1913	18¢ Benefitting Mankind	.36	.10			.75	42,227,375
1914	18¢ Benefitting Mankind	.36	.10			.75	42,227,375
1915	18¢ Understanding the Sun	.36	.10			.75	42,227,375
1916	18¢ Probing the Planets	.36	.10			.75	42,227,375
1917	18¢ Benefitting Mankind	.36	.10			.75	42,227,375
1918	18¢ Benefitting Mankind	.36	.10			.75	42,227,375
1919	18¢ Comprehending the						
	Universe	.36	.10			.75	42,227,375
	Block of 8, #1912-1919	3.00	2.25	3.00	(8)	5.00	

The Unknown

For many years, the proposed voyage of Christopher Columbus was turned down by Spain and Portugal for the following reasons:
1. *A voyage to Asia would require three years;*
2. *The Western Ocean was infinite;*
3. *Of the five climatic zones, only three were habitable;*
4. *If he did reach the other side, he could not get back;*
5. *So many years after the creation, it was doubtful that anyone could find unknown lands of any value.*

Fortunately, Columbus found a friend in the Court who helped overturn the decision. The explorer was on his history-making trip the following year. And the tradition of exploration is still being carried on by the men and women who venture into space.

In the relatively short span of time from Columbus to the shuttle, minutes in terms of the history of mankind, the ability of man to live and work in space has proved sound. The Space Transportation System has been able to take astronauts to areas of space in order to drop off satellites, perform scientific and biological experiments and pick up and repair space vehicles.

In addition to the eight Space Shuttle stamps (#1912-19), there are many other stamps related to space exploration. These range from the Communications for Peace (#1173) and other scientific space issues to the series of manned space achievements starting with Project Mercury (#1193).

Future postage stamps are certain to include illustrations of space stations and probes of the planets. Indeed, exploration of the world has been enlarged to exploration of the universe.

	1981 continued	Un	U	PB/LP	#	FDC	Q
1920	18¢ Professional Management,						
	June 18	.36	.05	1.75	(4)	.75	99,420,000
	Wildlife Habitat Issue, June 26						
1921	18¢ Wetland Habitats	.36	.08			.75	46,732,500
1922	18¢ Grassland Habitats	.36	.08			.75	46,732,500
1923	18¢ Mountain Habitats	.36	.08			.75	46,732,500
1924	18¢ Woodland Habitats	.36	.08			.75	46,732,500
	Block of 4, #1921-1924	1.50	.85	1.75	(4)	2.50	
1925	18¢ International Year of the						
	Disabled, June 29	.36	.05	1.75	(4)	.75	100,265,000
1926	18¢ Edna St. Vincent Millay,						
	July 10	.36	.05	1.75	(4)	.75	99,615,000
1927	18¢ Alcoholism, Aug. 19	.36	.05	8.00	(20)	.75	97,535,000

Non-denominated Stamps

*The practice of issuing stamps without denominations was begun in the
1850s when several British colonies used identical designs but changed the
color to indicate different values. The countries did this to save money since
only one die or plate was needed. Inflation was so severe in Hungary in 1946
that stamps and postal stationery were sold at the going rate on that
particular day. The gold yuan currency of China in the spring of 1949
kept increasing every day, making stamps worthless even before they
came off the printing press. Between May and July 1949, a set of four
non-denominated stamps was released with a design symbolizing the
designated service. These included ordinary mail, airmail, express and
registered letters.*

*The first stamps issued without value by the United States were two
Christmas stamps (#1579-80) released on October 14, 1975, when an
increase from 10 cents to 13 cents was expected. The rate hike was delayed
and the stamps remained at 10 cents. The situation repeated itself in 1981 for
the Christmas pair (#1939-40) and these stamps have a value of 20 cents.*

*Continued uncertainty over the possibility of increased rates led the Postal
Service to issue "letter stamps" to cover the domestic rate. The orange "A"
stamp (#1735) has a value of 15 cents and was issued May 22, 1978. The
violet "B" stamp (#1818) came out on March 15, 1980, and has a face value of
18 cents. The brown "C" stamp (#1946), distributed on October 11, 1981, has
a value of 20 cents. The newest addition to the series is the green "D" stamp,
issued February 1, 1985, with a face value of 22 cents. All of the U.S. stamps
are still valid for postage and can be used in combination with other stamps
to make the current domestic rate.*

*Universal Postal Union regulations state that all stamps used for
international mail must have the value printed on the face of the stamp.
Therefore, the United States non-denominated stamps are valid only for
domestic use.*

1920

1921   1922
1923   1924

1925

1926

1927

1932

1933

1928
1930

1929
1931

1934

1935

1936

1937

1938

1939

1940

1941

	1981 continued	Un	U	PB/LP	#	FDC	Q
	American Architecture Issue, Aug. 28						
1928	18¢ NYU Library	.36	.08			.75	41,827,000
1929	18¢ Biltmore House	.36	.08			.75	41,827,000
1930	18¢ Palace of the Arts	.36	.08			.75	41,827,000
1931	18¢ National Farmer's Bank	.36	.08			.75	41,827,000
	Block of 4, #1928-1931	1.50	.85	1.75	(4)	2.50	
	Perf. 10½x11						
1932	18¢ Babe Zaharias, Sept. 22	.36	.05	1.75	(4)	.75	101,625,000
1933	18¢ Bobby Jones, Sept. 22	.36	.05	1.75	(4)	.75	99,170,000
	Perf. 11						
1934	18¢ Remington Sculpture, Oct. 9	.36	.05	1.75	(4)	.75	101,155,000
1935	18¢ James Hoban, Oct. 13	.60	.35	3.00	(4)	.75	101,200,000
1936	20¢ James Hoban, Oct. 13	.40	.05	2.00	(4)	.75	167,360,000
1937	18¢ Yorktown 1781, Oct. 16	.36	.06			.75	81,210,000
1938	18¢ Virginia Capes 1781, Oct. 16	.36	.06			.75	81,210,000
	Pair, #1937-1938	.72	.15	1.75	(4)	1.00	
1939	(20¢) Christmas Madonna,						
	Oct. 28	.40	.05	2.00	(4)	.75	597,720,000
1940	(20¢) Christmas Child Art, Oct. 28	.40	.05	2.00	(4)	.75	792,600,000
1941	20¢ John Hanson, Nov. 5	.40	.05	2.00	(4)	.75	167,130,000

Chester W. Nimitz
(Great Americans Series)

About a month after his appointment to the Naval Academy at the tender age of 15, Chester Nimitz got so seasick during a Sunday afternoon sailing excursion that he nearly lost the seagoing aspirations that later fueled his stunning military career. The sea was nevertheless to be Nimitz' second home, and the "calm, frosty-faced, steel-blue-eyed Texan" became one of the Navy's best strategists and administrators, a man whose tactics and leadership were instrumental in key Naval victories during World War II.

Four years out of Annapolis, Ensign Nimitz asked for battleship duty and was given a submarine assignment. At the time, undersea craft were regarded as a "cross between a Jules Verne fantasy and a whale," but the young sailor perservered, eventually commanding a flotilla comprising all the submarines in the Atlantic.

In 1941, the Admiral was given command of the Pacific Fleet. As master strategist behind the heroic Battle of Midway, his astute positioning of carriers enabled U.S. bombers to sink four Japanese carriers, allowing the Allies to shift to the offensive. Nimitz' forces went on to aid in the capture of Iwo Jima and Okinawa, hastening the end of the war in the Pacific. He was awarded the Distinguished Service Medal for his role, and after the war served as Chief of Naval Operations and U.N. Commissioner to India and Pakistan.

1981-1982	Un	U	PB/LP	#	FDC	Q
U.S. Desert Plants Issue, December 11						
1942	20¢ Barrel Cactus	.40	.06			.75	47,890,000
1943	20¢ Agave	.40	.06			.75	47,890,000
1944	20¢ Beavertail Cactus	.40	.06			.75	47,890,000
1945	20¢ Saguaro	.40	.06			.75	47,890,000
	Block of 4, #1942-1945	1.60	.85	2.00	(4)	2.50	
Perf. 11x10½						
1946	(20¢) "C" Eagle, Oct. 11	.40	.05	2.00	(4)	.75	
Perf. 10 Vert.						
1947	(20¢) "C" Eagle, coil, Oct. 11	.40	.05	1.00		.75	
1948	(20¢) "C" Eagle, booklet, Oct. 11	.40	.05			.75	
Perf. 11x10½						
1948a	Booklet Pane of 10	4.25	—				
Issues of 1982, Perf. 11						
1949	20¢ Bighorn, booklet, Jan. 8	.40	.05			.75	
1949a	Booklet Pane of 10	4.00	—			8.00	
1950	20¢ Franklin D. Roosevelt, Jan. 3	.40	.05	2.00	(4)	.75	163,939,200
1951	20¢ Love, Feb. 1	.40	.05	2.00	(4)	.75	
1952	20¢ George Washington, Feb. 22	.40	.05	2.00	(4)	.75	180,700,000

Sinclair Lewis
(Great Americans Series)

The eyes and ears with which Sinclair "Red" Lewis saw small-town, Midwestern America in the 1920s were harsh and unforgiving, but his literary assaults on what he viewed as the contradictions and banalities of middle-class lifestyles by 1930 earned him the first Nobel Prize for literature which was awarded to an American.

Using his hometown of Sauk Centre, Minnesota, as a model, Lewis published Main Street, *in 1920, which thrust his extraordinary talent for capturing detail, mimicking American speech and molding Dickens-like caricatures into the public spotlight. He continued his satire of the narrow, restricted life of the small town by describing a shallow American businessman in* Babbit *(1922); he attacked commercialism in the medical profession in* Arrowsmith *(1925), and hypocrisy in evangelical religion in* Elmer Gantry *(1927). His efforts, though worthy of the Nobel Prize, won him perhaps as many detractors as friends.*

In the end, though, his reputation was solid—one of the great depictors of the 1920s, a brilliant satirist, creator of the social history of an era—and most critics acknowledge the tremendous impact Lewis had on American literature. Although he earned his reputation as a novelist, Lewis was also a prolific writer of short stories for magazines that included Redbook, Cosmopolitan *and* Saturday Evening Post, *and as book editor for* Newsweek.

1946

1942   1943   1945

1944

1950

1949

1951

1952

Alabama USA 20c	**Alaska** USA 20c	**Arizona** USA 20c	**Arkansas** USA 20c	**California** USA 20c
Yellowhammer & Camellia	*Willow Ptarmigan & Forget-Me-Not*	*Cactus Wren & Saguaro Cactus Blossom*	*Mockingbird & Apple Blossom*	*California Quail & California Poppy*
1953	1954	1955	1956	1957
Colorado USA 20c	**Connecticut** USA 20c	**Delaware** USA 20c	**Florida** USA 20c	**Georgia** USA 20c
Lark Bunting & Rocky Mountain Columbine	*Robin & Mountain Laurel*	*Blue Hen Chicken & Peach Blossom*	*Mockingbird & Orange Blossom*	*Brown Thrasher & Cherokee Rose*
1958	1959	1960	1961	1962
Hawaii USA 20c	**Idaho** USA 20c	**Illinois** USA 20c	**Indiana** USA 20c	**Iowa** USA 20c
Hawaiian Goose & Hibiscus	*Mountain Bluebird & Syringa*	*Cardinal & Violet*	*Cardinal & Peony*	*Eastern Goldfinch & Wild Rose*
1963	1964	1965	1966	1967
Kansas USA 20c	**Kentucky** USA 20c	**Louisiana** USA 20c	**Maine** USA 20c	**Maryland** USA 20c
Western Meadowlark & Sunflower	*Cardinal & Goldenrod*	*Brown Pelican & Magnolia*	*Chickadee & White Pine Cone and Tassel*	*Baltimore Oriole & Black-Eyed Susan*
1968	1969	1970	1971	1972

	1982 continued	Un	U	PB/LP	#	FDC	Q
	State Birds & Flowers Issue, Apr. 14, Perf. 10½x11						
1953	20¢ Alabama	.40	.25			.75	13,339,900
1954	20¢ Alaska	.40	.25			.75	13,339,900
1955	20¢ Arizona	.40	.25			.75	13,339,900
1956	20¢ Arkansas	.40	.25			.75	13,339,900
1957	20¢ California	.40	.25			.75	13,339,900
1958	20¢ Colorado	.40	.25			.75	13,339,900
1959	20¢ Connecticut	.40	.25			.75	13,339,900
1960	20¢ Delaware	.40	.25			.75	13,339,900
1961	20¢ Florida	.40	.25			.75	13,339,900
1962	20¢ Georgia	.40	.25			.75	13,339,900
1963	20¢ Hawaii	.40	.25			.75	13,339,900
1964	20¢ Idaho	.40	.25			.75	13,339,900
1965	20¢ Illinois	.40	.25			.75	13,339,900
1966	20¢ Indiana	.40	.25			.75	13,339,900
1967	20¢ Iowa	.40	.25			.75	13,339,900
1968	20¢ Kansas	.40	.25			.75	13,339,900
1969	20¢ Kentucky	.40	.25			.75	13,339,900
1970	20¢ Louisiana	.40	.25			.75	13,339,900
1971	20¢ Maine	.40	.25			.75	13,339,900
1972	20¢ Maryland	.40	.25			.75	13,339,900

Mr. ZIP

The postal zoning system in the United States began in 1943 with the introduction of the one or two digit zone number. These numbers identified a delivery station of a metropolitan post office. On July 1, 1963, Mr. ZIP introduced the Zone Improvement Plan. This was a five-digit national coding system used to identify each postal delivery section. The first digit identifies one of ten geographical areas, with the second digit denoting a state, part of a heavily populated state, or two or three less populated states. The third digit designates a major metropolitan postal facility or sectional center, with the fourth and fifth digits picking up the original zone number.

The Federal German Post Office became the first to use the current postal code system to speed delivery. The function of a code system is to help in address scanning and the automated processing of mail, and to speed up mail sorting. Approximately 97 percent of all mail delivered in the United States uses the Zip Code. In 1974, the USPS issued a postage stamp (#1511) to publicize the numerical system.

The new improved version, ZIP + 4—a nine-digit code—will narrow the sorting down to individual streets, office buildings, and large users. Many collectors save the single stamps or block of four stamps with Mr. ZIP printed on the margins.

	1982 continued	Un	U	PB/LP	#	FDC	Q
1973	20¢ Massachusetts	.40	.25			.75	13,339,900
1974	20¢ Michigan	.40	.25			.75	13,339,900
1975	20¢ Minnesota	.40	.25			.75	13,339,900
1976	20¢ Mississippi	.40	.25			.75	13,339,900
1977	20¢ Missouri	.40	.25			.75	13,339,900
1978	20¢ Montana	.40	.25			.75	13,339,900
1979	20¢ Nebraska	.40	.25			.75	13,339,900
1980	20¢ Nevada	.40	.25			.75	13,339,900
1981	20¢ New Hampshire	.40	.25			.75	13,339,900
1982	20¢ New Jersey	.40	.25			.75	13,339,900
1983	20¢ New Mexico	.40	.25			.75	13,339,900
1984	20¢ New York	.40	.25			.75	13,339,900
1985	20¢ North Carolina	.40	.25			.75	13,339,900
1986	20¢ North Dakota	.40	.25			.75	13,339,900
1987	20¢ Ohio	.40	.25			.75	13,339,900
1988	20¢ Oklahoma	.40	.25			.75	13,339,900
1989	20¢ Oregon	.40	.25			.75	13,339,900
1990	20¢ Pennsylvania	.40	.25			.75	13,339,900
1991	20¢ Rhode Island	.40	.25			.75	13,339,900
1992	20¢ South Carolina	.40	.25			.75	13,339,900

Post or Postal Cards?

Deltiology is the collecting and study of postcards. The word comes from delti (little picture) and logy (the theory or study of).

A postcard is a privately-printed mailing card used for sending a message. It can be sent through the mail without an envelope at the First-Class card rate. A postal card is sold by the U.S. Postal Service with postage already printed on the card.

The first U.S. postal card was issued May 1, 1873, with a one-cent stamp printed in the upper righthand corner. It featured a profile of the Goddess of Liberty with the words, "U.S. Postage" and "One Cent." The first known cancellation was applied 12 days later. Airmail postal cards were issued on January 10, 1949, with a four-cent rate and depicted an eagle in flight.

Picture postcards made their first appearance in the U.S. in 1893 and were issued to commemorate the Columbian Exposition held in Chicago. The manufacturer printed scenes of the exposition on government postal cards. Austria issued the world's first postal card in 1869, but cards with advertising messages on them existed for many years prior to that date. The firms that used these early private advertising cards had to pay letter rates.

Massachusetts USA 20c	Michigan USA 20c	Minnesota USA 20c	Mississippi USA 20c	Missouri USA 20c
Black-Capped Chickadee & Mayflower	Robin & Apple Blossom	Common Loon & Showy Lady Slipper	Mockingbird & Magnolia	Eastern Bluebird & Red Hawthorn
1973	1974	1975	1976	1977

Montana USA 20c	Nebraska USA 20c	Nevada USA 20c	New Hampshire USA 20c	New Jersey USA 20c
Western Meadowlark & Bitterroot	Western Meadowlark & Goldenrod	Mountain Bluebird & Sagebrush	Purple Finch & Lilac	American Goldfinch & Violet
1978	1979	1980	1981	1982

New Mexico USA 20c	New York USA 20c	North Carolina USA 20c	North Dakota USA 20c	Ohio USA 20c
Roadrunner & Yucca Flower	Eastern Bluebird & Rose	Cardinal & Flowering Dogwood	Western Meadowlark & Wild Prairie Rose	Cardinal & Red Carnation
1983	1984	1985	1986	1987

Oklahoma USA 20c	Oregon USA 20c	Pennsylvania USA 20c	Rhode Island USA 20c	South Carolina USA 20c
Scissor-tailed Flycatcher & Mistletoe	Western Meadowlark & Oregon Grape	Ruffed Grouse & Mountain Laurel	Rhode Island Red & Violet	Carolina Wren & Carolina Jessamine
1988	1989	1990	1991	1992

South Dakota
USA 20c

Ring-Necked Pheasant & *Pasqueflower*

1993

Tennessee
USA 20c

Mockingbird & *Iris*

1994

Texas
USA 20c

Mockingbird & *Bluebonnet*

1995

Utah
USA 20c

California Gull & *Sego Lily*

1996

Vermont
USA 20c

Hermit Thrush & *Red Clover*

1997

Virginia
USA 20c

Cardinal & *Flowering Dogwood*

1998

Washington
USA 20c

American Goldfinch & *Rhododendron*

1999

West Virginia
USA 20c

Cardinal & *Rhododendron Maximum*

2000

Wisconsin
USA 20c

Robin & *Wood Violet*

2001

Wyoming
USA 20c

Western Meadowlark & *Indian Paintbrush*

2002

20c
USA
1982 USA THE NETHERLANDS

2003

Library of Congress
USA 20c

2004

Wise shoppers
stretch dollars

Consumer
Education

USA 20c

2005

USA 20c
Breeder reactor Knoxville World's Fair

USA 20c
Fossil fuels Knoxville World's Fair

USA 20c
Solar energy Knoxville World's Fair

USA 20c
Synthetic fuels Knoxville World's Fair

2006
2008

2007
2009

Horatio Alger

USA 20c

2010

THE BARRYMORES

Performing Arts USA 20c

2012

Aging
together

USA
20c

2011

	1982 continued	Un	U	PB/LP	#	FDC	Q
1993	20¢ South Dakota	.40	.25			.75	13,339,900
1994	20¢ Tennessee	.40	.25			.75	13,339,900
1995	20¢ Texas	.40	.25			.75	13,339,900
1996	20¢ Utah	.40	.25			.75	13,339,900
1997	20¢ Vermont	.40	.25			.75	13,339,900
1998	20¢ Virginia	.40	.25			.75	13,339,900
1999	20¢ Washington	.40	.25			.75	13,339,900
2000	20¢ West Virginia	.40	.25			.75	13,339,900
2001	20¢ Wisconsin	.40	.25			.75	13,339,900
2002	20¢ Wyoming	.40	.25			.75	13,339,900
	Sheet of 50			22.00			
	Perf. 11						
2003	20¢ USA/Netherlands, Apr. 20	.40	.05	8.50 (20)		.75	109,245,000
2004	20¢ Library of Congress, Apr. 21	.40	.05	2.00		.75	112,535,000
	Perf. 10 Vert.						
2005	20¢ Consumer Education, Apr. 27	.40	.05	1.10		.75	
	World's Fair Issue, Apr. 29, Perf. 11						
2006	20¢ Solar Energy	.40	.08			.75	31,160,000
2007	20¢ Synthetic Fuels	.40	.08			.75	31,160,000
2008	20¢ Breeder Reactor	.40	.08			.75	31,160,000
2009	20¢ Fossil Fuels	.40	.08			.75	31,160,000
	Plate Block of 4, (#2006-2009)			2.00			
2010	20¢ Horatio Alger, Apr. 30	.40	.05	2.00		.75	107,605,000
2011	20¢ Aging Together, May 21	.40	.05	2.00		.75	173,160,000
2012	20¢ The Barrymores, June 8	.40	.05	2.00		.75	107,285,000

Stamps Used As Currency

There was a period in the history of the United States when you could go to the local store and pay for your purchase with postage stamps. Due to the shortage of coins during the Civil War, Congress passed an act on July 17, 1862, authorizing the Treasury Department to issue "postage currency." Francis Skinner, the Treasurer of the United States, attached a postage stamp to imprinted Treasury paper to be used as small denomination currency.

A Boston sewing machine salesman, John Gault, invented and patented a method of encasing postage stamps in metal framed discs with a transparent mica front and advertisements embossed on the back. He used the stamps of the 1861 definitive series with values ranging from one to ninety cents. Both stamp and coin collectors seek these encased stamps, and the retail value is generally based on the scarcity of the ad on the reverse side.

1982

	1982 continued	Un	U	PB/LP	#	FDC	Q
2013	20¢ Dr. Mary Walker, June 10	.40	.05	2.00	(4)	.75	109,040,000
2014	20¢ International Peace Garden,						
	June 30	.40	.05	2.00	(4)	.75	183,270,000
2015	20¢ America's Libraries, July 13	.40	.05	2.00	(4)	.75	169,495,000
	Black Heritage Series, Aug. 2, Perf. 11x10½						
2016	20¢ Jackie Robinson	.40	.05	2.00	(4)	.75	164,235,000
	Perf. 11						
2017	20¢ Touro Synagogue, Aug. 22	.40	.05	8.50 (20)		.75	110,130,000
2018	20¢ Wolf Trap Farm Park, Sept. 1	.40	.05	2.00	(4)	.75	110,995,000
	American Architecture Issue, September 30						
2019	20¢ Fallingwater	.40	.08			.75	41,335,000
2020	20¢ Illinois Institute of Technology	.40	.08			.75	41,335,000
2021	20¢ Gropius House	.40	.08			.75	41,335,000
2022	20¢ Dulles Airport	.40	.08			.75	41,335,000
	Block of 4, (#2019-2022)	1.60	.85	2.00	(4)	2.50	
2023	20¢ Francis of Assisi, Oct. 7	.40	.05	2.00	(4)	.75	174,180,000
2024	20¢ Ponce de Leon, Oct. 2	.40	.05	8.50 (20)		.75	110,261,000
2025	13¢ Puppy and Kitten, Nov. 3	.26	.05	1.30	(4)	.75	
2026	20¢ Christmas, Madonna						
	and Child—Tiepolo, Oct. 28	.40	.05	8.50 (20)		.75	703,295,000
	Seasons Greetings Issue, Oct. 28						
2027	20¢ Sledding	.40	.05			.75	197,220,000
2028	20¢ Snowman	.40	.05			.75	197,220,000
2029	20¢ Skating	.40	.05			.75	197,220,000
2030	20¢ Tree	.40	.05			.75	197,220,000
	Block of 4, #2027-2030	1.60	.85	2.00	(4)	2.50	

2013

2014

2015

2016

2017

2019
2021

2020
2022

2018

2023

2024

2025

2026

2027
2029

2028
2030

2031

2032

2033
2034

2035

2036

2037

2038

2039

2040

2041

2042

2043

Issues of 1983, Perf. 11	Un	U	PB/LP	#	FDC	Q
2031 20¢ Science & Industry, Jan. 19	.40	.05	2.00	(4)	.75	118,555,000
Balloon Issue, March 31						
2032 20¢ Intrepid	.40	.08			.75	
2033 20¢ Hot Air Balloons	.40	.08			.75	
2034 20¢ Hot Air Balloons	.40	.08			.75	
2035 20¢ Explorer	.40	.08			.75	
Block of 4, #2032-2035	1.60	.85	2.00	(4)	2.50	226,128,000
2036 20¢ Swedish-American Treaty,						
March 24	.40	.05	2.00	(4)	.75	118,225,000
2037 20¢ Civilian Conservation Corps,						
March 24	.40	.05	2.00	(4)	.75	114,290,000
2038 20¢ Joseph Priestley, April 13	.40	.05	2.00	(4)	.75	165,000,000
2039 20¢ Voluntarism, April 5	.40	.05	8.50	(20)	.75	120,430,000
2040 20¢ U.S./Germany Concord,						
April 29	.40	.05	2.00	(4)	.75	117,025,000
2041 20¢ Brooklyn Bridge, May 5	.40	.05	2.00	(4)	.75	181,700,000
2042 20¢ TVA, May 18	.40	.05	8.50	(20)	.75	114,250,000
2043 20¢ Physical Fitness, May 14	.40	.05	8.50	(20)	.75	111,775,000

Railway Post Office

Various stamps in the Transportation Series (#1897-1907) recall the days when mail trains were the fastest means of moving letters from city to city. At one point, after World War II, more than 30,000 mail clerks worked on the trains as they criss-crossed the United States.

At first, the trains were used strictly to carry the mail. Then it was suggested that mail could be sorted en route, saving a great deal of time. The first traveling Railway Post Office began operating between Liverpool and Birmingham, England, in 1837. Mail was sorted on a train in motion for the first time in the United States in July 1862.

The mail clerk had a difficult job as the train sped through the towns. He had to snare the mail pouch as it hung from a crane with a steel "catcher" arm, and at the same time throw out a mail pouch for the residents of the town. The clerks worked in wooden cars with potbellied stoves, and fires were a common hazard. Of course, bandits who robbed the mail cars were legendary, and many stories have been written about trains being stopped and the railway clerks being forced to give up their precious cargo.

The last run of a mail train was on June 30, 1977, but a new Fast Mail service was established between Washington and Boston on October 28, 1984.

	1983 continued	Un	U	PB/LP	#	FDC	Q
	Black Heritage Issues, June 9						
2044	20¢ Scott Joplin	.40	.05	2.00	(4)	.75	115,200,000
2045	20¢ Medal of Honor, June 7	.40	.05	2.00	(4)	.75	108,820,000
	American Sports Series, July 6, Perf. 10½x11						
2046	20¢ George Herman "Babe" Ruth	.40	.05	2.00	(4)	.75	184,950,000
	Literary Arts Series, July 8, Perf. 11						
2047	20¢ Nathaniel Hawthorne	.40	.05	2.00	(4)	.75	110,925,000
	Summer Olympic Games, July 28						
2048	13¢ Discus	.26	.05			.75	
2049	13¢ High Jump	.26	.05			.75	
2050	13¢ Archery	.26	.05			.75	
2051	13¢ Boxing	.26	.05			.75	
	Block of 4, #2048-2051	1.05	.65	1.30	(4)	2.50	
2052	20¢ Treaty of Paris, Sept. 2	.40	.05	2.00	(4)	.75	104,340,000
2053	20¢ Civil Service, Sept. 9	.40	.05	8.50	(20)	.75	114,725,000
2054	20¢ Metropolitan Opera, Sept. 14	.40	.05	2.00	(4)	.75	112,525,000
	American Inventors Issue, Sept. 14						
2055	20¢ Charles Steinmetz	.40	.05			.75	
2056	20¢ Edwin Armstrong	.40	.05			.75	
2057	20¢ Nikola Tesla	.40	.05			.75	
2058	20¢ Philo T. Farnsworth	.40	.05			.75	
	Block of 4, #2055-2058	1.60	.85	2.00	(4)	2.50	193,055,000

Baseball

Not only has baseball been adopted as this nation's favorite pastime, but it has also been the subject of stamps (#855 and 1381). A formal commission which, from 1905-1908, investigated the origin of baseball credited General Abner Doubleday with the game's invention at Cooperstown, New York.

The Doubleday claim has been criticized by many who cite several instances of baseball being played as a children's game long before Doubleday's era. The first example is a children's book of alphabets, A Little Pretty Book, published in London in 1744 that uses " 'B' is for Baseball. A batter heads the field and runs from base to base." The book was later published in New York in 1762 and may have been the reason for the legend that baseball originated in the United States.

Further research revealed that an unknown writer in 1857 traced baseball to the 11th century, where the game was known as "bace" and later as "prisoner's base." As additional evidence, Abner Doubleday was in West Point as a cadet when he was supposed to have been in Cooperstown. Doubleday graduated from the Point in 1842 and went on to become a Union general in the Civil War.

1983

2044

2045

2046

2047

2052

2048
2050

2049
2051

2053

2054

2055
2057

2056
2058

2063

2059
2061

2060
2062

2064

2065

2066

2071

2072

2067
2069

2068
2070

	1983 continued	Un	U	PB/LP	#	FDC	Q
	Streetcars Issue, Oct. 8						
2059	20¢ First American Streetcar	.40	.05			.75	
2060	20¢ Early Electric Streetcar	.40	.05			.75	
2061	20¢ "Bobtail" Horsecar	.40	.05			.75	
2062	20¢ St. Charles Streetcar	.40	.05			.75	
	Block of 4, #2059-2062	1.60	.85	2.00	(4)	2.50	207,725,000
2063	20¢ Christmas Raphael, Oct. 28	.40	.05	2.00	(4)	.75	
2064	20¢ Christmas Santa Claus, Oct. 28	.40	.05	8.50	(20)	.75	
2065	20¢ Martin Luther, Nov. 11	.40	.05	2.00	(4)	.75	
	Issues of 1984, Perf. 11						
2066	20¢ Alaska Statehood, Jan. 3	.40	.05	2.00	(4)	.75	
	Winter Olympics Issue, Jan. 6, Perf. 10½x11						
2067	20¢ Ice Dancing	.40	.05			.75	
2068	20¢ Alpine Skiing	.40	.05			.75	
2069	20¢ Nordic Skiing	.40	.05			.75	
2070	20¢ Hockey	.40	.05			.75	
	Block of 4, #2067-2070	1.60	.85	2.00	(4)	2.50	
	Perf. 11						
2071	20¢ Federal Deposit Insurance Corp.,						
	Jan. 12	.40	.05	2.00	(4)	.75	
2072	20¢ Love, Jan. 31	.40	.05	8.50	(20)	.75	

First Days

First day cover collecting is a popular part of the stamp collecting hobby. The earliest known U.S. first day covers feature the Franklin/Washington stamps (#7 and #10) issued July 1, 1851. On July 12, 1922, the Post Office Department announced a specific first day city for the 10-cent Special Delivery (#E 12) stamp. This started the policy of helping the collector by announcing the first day cities and dates.

The reason that the Rutherford B. Hayes (#563) first day cover is so expensive is that only four sheets of 100 stamps each were available on the first day and approximately 100 covers exist. The rest of the stamps were collected in unused condition and either placed in albums or used later for postage. The first stamps officially issued outside of the Continental United States were the Hawaii overprint issue (#647-8) issued at Honolulu, Hawaii, on August 13, 1928. The "First Day of Issue" slogan cancel was used first in the machine cancel on the Northwest Ordinance stamp (#795). The same slogan cancel was used first in a hand cancel for the Washington Irving stamp (#859) on January 29, 1940.

The first commercially made cachet for a first day cover was prepared by George Linn for the Harding Memorial stamp (#610). Since cachets were unknown in the early days of stamp collecting, the only method of determining a first day cover was to check the date in the postmark to see if it matched the date of issue of the stamp. When looking through a collection of older covers, it is important to know the first day of issue of the stamps and covers.

	1984 continued	Un	U	PB/LP	#	FDC	Q
	Black Heritage Issues, Feb. 1, Perf. 11						
2073	20¢ Carter G. Woodson	.40	.05	2.00	(4)	.75	
2074	20¢ Soil and Water Conservation,						
	Feb. 6	.40	.05	2.00	(4)	.75	
2075	20¢ Credit Union, Feb. 10	.40	.05	2.00	(4)	.75	
	Orchids Issue, Mar. 5						
2076	20¢ Wild pink	.40	.05			.75	
2077	20¢ Yellow Lady's-slipper	.40	.05			.75	
2078	20¢ Spreading Pogonia	.40	.05			.75	
2079	20¢ Pacific Calypso	.40	.05			.75	
	Block of 4, #2076-2079	1.60	.85	2.00	(4)	2.50	
2080	20¢ Hawaii Statehood, Mar. 12	.40	.05	2.00	(4)	.75	
2081	20¢ National Archives, Apr. 16	.40	.05	2.00	(4)	.75	
	Summer Olympics, May 4						
2082	20¢ Diving	.40	.05			.75	
2083	20¢ Long Jump	.40	.05			.75	
2084	20¢ Wrestling	.40	.05			.75	
2085	20¢ Kayak	.40	.05			.75	
	Block of 4, #2082-2085	1.60	.85	2.00	(4)	2.50	
2086	20¢ Louisiana World Exposition,						
	May 11	.40	.05	2.00	(4)	.75	
2087	20¢ Health Research, May 17	.40	.05	2.00	(4)	.75	

Painters and Paintings

People are the primary subjects of stamps. In general, they are good people who have done good works deserving recognition. Objects, however, are also popular inspirations for stamps; paintings fall under this second category.

Of the 36 painters honored by stamps, less than half had stamps especially issued to honor them—the other artists had their works reproduced on stamps with only their names included in the designs. These painting stamps were used to commemorate other persons or events, not the painters themselves.

American painters are represented by 22 of these stamps; the others depict European artists or their works including six Italians, five Dutchmen, one Englishman, one Spaniard and one Swiss. Nine other artists or their works also appear on stamps: a cartoonist, four graphic artists, four sculptors and a silversmith.

If they were still alive today, these creative geniuses would probably have no misgivings about their works gaining fame instead of themselves. Their works, after all, were the proud product of their imaginations, and the men will live on forever through their work—on canvas or stamp.

1984

2073

2074

2075

2080

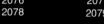

2076
2078

2077
2079

2081

2082
2084

2083
2085

2086

2087

DOUGLAS FAIRBANKS

Performing Arts USA 20c

2088

Jim Thorpe

USA 20c

2089

JOHN McCORMACK

Performing Arts USA 20c

2090

USA 20c 1959-1984 Saint Lawrence Seaway

2091

Preserving Wetlands 1934 1984

USA 20c

2092

Roanoke Voyages North Carolina 1584

USA 20c

2093

Herman Melville

USA 20c

2094

Horace Moses Founder, Junior Achievement USA 20c

2095

SMOKEY

USA 20c

2096

Roberto Clemente

USA 20c

2097

USA 20c

USA 20c

Beagle, Boston Terrier

Chesapeake Bay Retriever, Cocker Spaniel

USA 20c

USA 20c

Alaskan Malamute, Collie

Black and Tan Coonhound, American Foxhound

2098   2099
2100   2101

	1984 continued	Un	U	PB/LP	#	FDC	Q
	Performing Arts Series, May 23, Perf. 11						
2088	20¢ Douglas Fairbanks	.40	.05	8.50	(20)	.75	
2089	20¢ Jim Thorpe, May 24	.40	.05	2.00	(4)	.75	
	Performing Arts Series, June 6						
2090	20¢ John McCormack	.40	.05	2.00	(4)	.75	
2091	20¢ St. Lawrence Seaway,						
	June 26	.40	.05	2.00	(4)	.75	
2092	20¢ Preserving Wetlands, July 2	.40	.05	2.00	(4)	.75	
2093	20¢ Roanoke Voyages, July 13	.40	.05	2.00	(4)	.75	
	Literary Arts Series, Aug. 1						
2094	20¢ Herman Melville	.40	.05	2.00	(4)	.75	
2095	20¢ Horace Moses, Aug. 6	.40	.05	8.50	(20)	.75	
2096	20¢ Smokey the Bear, Aug. 13	.40	.05	2.00	(4)	.75	
2097	20¢ Roberto Clemente, Aug. 17	.40	.05	2.00	(4)	.75	
	Dogs, Sept. 7						
2098	20¢ Beagle and Boston Terrier	.40	.08			.75	
2099	20¢ Chesapeake Bay Retriever						
	and Cocker Spaniel	.40	.08			.75	
2100	20¢ Alaskan Malamute and Collie	.40	.08			.75	
2101	20¢ Black and Tan Coonhound						
	and American Foxhound	.40	.08			.75	
	Block of 4, #2098-2101	1.60	.85	2.00	(4)	2.50	

Collecting Made Easy

Six days a week, your letter carrier brings mail to your home or office. Each day's delivery may contain letters, postcards or packages that can open an exciting world of stamp collecting. Here are some of the items that can make for an interesting collection:

First of all, look at the stamps used on the mail. Put aside one of each of all United States stamps that are on the letters. Look for shade and color varieties among the duplicates.

After looking at a stamp, examine the postmark. Many people collect cancellations from every city or town in their state, or if that job sounds too big, try collecting them from every city in your county. Arrange them alphabetically and leave room for variations. Many cities use different cancels and the variety might amaze you.

Another popular part of the hobby is meter collecting. Cut around the meter cancel, making sure not to cut into the imprint. There are a number of meter manufacturers, each using a different symbol in the meter. Many meters also have slogans advertising the company's products. You can specialize in meters featuring tires, sewing machines or whatever you feel is interesting.

The Postal Service routinely prints slogan cancels on mail to promote various projects or events. A collection of one specific slogan cancel from different cities, for example, can be fascinating.

	1984 continued	Un	U	PB/LP	#	FDC	Q
2102	20¢ Crime Prevention, Sept. 26	.40	.05	2.00	(4)	.75	
2103	20¢ Hispanic Americans Oct. 31	.40	.05				
2104	20¢ Family Unity, Oct. 1	.40	.05	8.50	(20)	.75	
2105	20¢ Eleanor Roosevelt, Oct. 11	.40	.05	2.00	(4)	.75	
2106	20¢ A Nation of Readers, Oct. 16	.40	.05	2.00	(4)	.75	
2107	20¢ Christmas Lippi, Oct. 30	.40	.05			.75	
2108	20¢ Christmas Santa Claus,						
	Oct. 30	.40	.05			.75	
	Perf. 10½						
2109	20¢ Vietnam Veterans' Memorial,						
	Nov. 10	.40	.05			.75	

Postage Free

There is an institution in Stateville, Illinois, where the 2,251 inhabitants are permitted to mail up to three one-ounce letters every week with the administration paying the postage. The local post office has nine employees who work from 9 a.m. to 5 p.m. five days per week. None of the residents pay any local, state or federal taxes.

This "Utopia" is the Stateville Correctional Center located on the outskirts of Joliet, Illinois. The maximum security facility has 2,200 acres, 14 of which are surrounded by a 33-foot high wall. Stateville is the largest penal institution in the United States. It has 1,000 employees—500 are guards and the balance handle administrative functions.

The average incoming daily mail is 3,000 letters and 100 packages. The nine postal employees open every letter and parcel, with certain exceptions, and examine each for contraband. Typical contraband consists of drugs, currency and unused postage stamps. Mint, unused stamps are considered currency and have been used to barter for illegal items from other prisoners or guards. The letters themselves are not read, only the contents examined. Letters that are not opened are from appointed officials, attorneys, courts and the news media.

Ninety per cent of the incoming packages contain magazines or books. The mail clerks examine each page to see that they are not glued together with contraband between the leaves. An X-ray machine is on the post office premises so that other items may be checked. Outgoing letters are not opened, censored or marked in any manner. A postage meter cancellation is applied with Joliet, Illinois, as the point of mailing.

A prisoner recently sued the warden of the institution claiming that his civil rights were being violated since his mail was being opened without his permission. The Court ruled that since his mail was not read, and only the contents examined for illegal material, the facility had the legal right to continue to open prisoners' mail.

2102

2103

2104

2105

2106

2107

2108

2109

Jerome Kern (22¢, #2110)

Type: Commemorative
Date of Issue: January 23, 1985
Place of Issue: New York, New York
Designer: Jim Sharpe
Printing: Gravure
Colors: Yellow, Red, Blue, Black, Line Red (Burgundy)

Jerome Kern composed more than 1,000 songs and 108 theatrical scores, earning two Academy Awards for his music. This "King of the American Musical Stage" served as an inspiration for other musical giants, such as Richard Rodgers and George Gershwin.

Mary McLeod Bethune (22¢, #2137)

Type: Commemorative (Black Heritage USA Series)
Date of Issue: March 5, 1985
Place of Issue: Washington, D.C.
Designer: Jerry Pinkney
Printing: Gravure
Colors: Yellow, Red, Blue, Black, Purple, Green

Issued in conjunction with the 50th anniversary of the National Council of Negro Women, this stamp depicts the organization's founder, Mary McLeod Bethune.

Duck Decoys (22¢, (4) #2138-2141)

Type: Commemorative (Folk Art Series)
Date of Issue: March 22, 1985
Place of Issue: Shelburne, Vermont
Designer: Stevan Dohanos
Printing: Gravure
Colors: Black Line, Yellow, Magenta, Cyan, Black Tone

The duck decoys depicted on these stamps are based on actual decoys carved by artisans of the late 19th and early 20th centuries. Two of the decoys are displayed in the Shelburne Museum in Shelburne, Vermont.

Winter Special Olympics (22¢, #2142)

Winter Special Olympics

Type: Commemorative
Date of Issue: March 25, 1985
Place of Issue: Park City, Utah
Designer: Jeff Cornell
Printing: Gravure
Colors: Yellow, Magenta, Cyan, Black, Special Yellow, Special Blue

The International Special Olympic Games were founded in Chicago in 1968.

Seashells (22¢, #2117-2121, single stamps; #2121a,
            booklet pane of 10)

Type: Definitive
Date of Issue: April 4, 1985
Place of Issue: Boston, Massachusetts
Designer: Peter Cocci
Printing: Intaglio
Colors: #2117 and #2119: Black, Brown
        #2118 and #2121: Black, Brown, Purple
        #2120: Black, Purple

Issued in conjunction with the 75th anniversary of the
Boston Malacological Club, these stamps depict typical
seashells found on coastlines that ring the U.S.: Alaska
to California; Texas to Brazil; Canada to Massachusetts;
and the Carolinas to Texas.

Love (22¢, #2143)

Type: Special
Date of Issue: April 17, 1985
Place of Issue: Hollywood, California
Designer: Corita Kent
Printing: Gravure
Colors: Yellow, Orange, Red, Green, Blue, Purple

1985 ISSUES

Abraham Baldwin (7¢, #1846)

Type: Definitive (Great Americans Series)
Date of Issue: January 25, 1985
Place of Issue: Athens, Georgia
Designer: Richard Sparks
Printing: Intaglio
Color: Red

One of the signers of the U.S. Constitution, Abraham Baldwin believed that a popular government could succeed only if its citizens were educated. In 1785 he wrote the charter for Franklin College, the oldest college at the University of Georgia, which established the first state university in the United States.

Alden Partridge (11¢, #1846F)

Type: Definitive (Great Americans Series)
Date of Issue: February 12, 1985
Place of Issue: Northfield, Vermont
Designer: Robert Anderson
Printing: Intaglio
Color: Blue

West Point graduate Alden Partridge is widely considered the "spiritual father" of the Reserve Officer Training Corps (ROTC). In 1819, Partridge founded the American Literary, Scientific and Military Academy (later Norwich University) and implemented a curriculum designed to produce what he called "citizen soldiers."

Chester W. Nimitz (50¢, #1869)

Type: Definitive (Great Americans Series)
Date of Issue: February 22, 1985
Place of Issue: Fredericksburg, Texas
Designer: Christopher Calle
Printing: Intaglio
Color: Brown

The tactics and leadership of Admiral Chester W. Nimitz were instrumental in key Naval victories in the Pacific during World War II.

Grenville Clark (39¢, #1867)

Type: Definitive (Great Americans Series)
Date of Issue: March 20, 1985
Place of Issue: Hanover, New Hampshire
Designer: Roy Andersen
Printing: Intaglio
Color: Purple

Military expert Grenville Clark was key to U.S. preparedness through both world wars. Also a lawyer, he was at the same time recognized as a leading advocate of peace, and helped draft the landmark Selective Service Act of 1940. Clark published a respected book, *World Peace Through World Law,* as well as many articles on both civil and world government.

Sinclair Lewis (14¢, #1856)

Type: Definitive (Great Americans Series)
Date of Issue: March 21, 1985
Place of Issue: Sauk Centre, Minnesota
Designer: Bradbury Thompson
Printing: Intaglio
Color: Gray

This stamp honors novelist Sinclair Lewis, and was issued on his 100th birthday. In 1930, Lewis became the first American to be awarded a Nobel Prize for Literature. The native Minnesotan wrote about Middle America and cast a critical eye on 1920s middle class lifestyles.

John James Audubon (22¢, #1863)

Type: Definitive (Great Americans Series)
Date of Issue: April 23, 1985
Place of Issue: New York, New York
Designer: Christopher Calle
Printing: Intaglio
Color: Blue

John James Audubon devoted his life to the study and accurate rendering of birds. His monumental work, *The Birds of America,* was a huge endeavor containing highly precise, minutely detailed and scaled drawings of hundreds of species of American birds.

Sylvanus Thayer (9¢, #1846E)

Type: Definitive (Great Americans Series)
Date of Issue: June 7, 1985
Place of Issue: Braintree, Massachusetts
Designer: Robert Alexander Anderson
Printing: Intaglio
Color: Green

Sylvanus Thayer is considered the father of technical education. As superintendent of the U.S. Military Academy beginning in 1817, Thayer instituted reforms which made the Academy the first purely technological school in America.

General Henry Knox (8¢, #1851)

Type: Definitive (Great Americans Series)
Date of Issue: July 25, 1985
Place of Issue: Thomaston, Maine
Designer: Arthur Lidov
Printing: Intaglio
Color: Olive

General Henry Knox, a trusted adviser and close friend of George Washington, joined the Continental Army in 1775. Through his strategic activity during the Revolutionary War, Knox helped establish such military traditions as the U.S. Army Artillery and the U.S. Military Academy at West Point. At the end of the war, he succeeded Washington as General-in-Chief of the Army. In 1785, Knox was appointed Secretary of War under the Articles of Confederation and was retained in this position as a member of President Washington's cabinet, formed in 1789.

Walter Lippmann (6¢, #1849)

Type: Definitive (Great Americans Series)
Date of Issue: September 19, 1985
Place of Issue: Minneapolis, Minnesota
Designer: Dennis Lyall
Printing: Intaglio
Color: Orange

Walter Lippmann—writer, editor, political philosopher—was the object of millions of newspaper readers' wrath or praise. His syndicated column, "Today and Tomorrow," ran in the New York *Herald-Tribune* from 1931 to 1962 and in the Washington Post from 1962 until Lippmann's retirement in 1967.

Iceboat (14¢, #2134)

Type: Definitive (Transportation Series)
Date of Issue: March 23, 1985
Place of Issue: Rochester, New York
Designer: William H. Bond
Printing: Intaglio
Color: Blue

During winters in the late 1800s, our American ancestors in the Great Lakes and Northeast regions adopted a method of transportation long used on frozen canals in the Netherlands: the iceboat. Today, iceboats are vehicles for sport; racing iceboats can reach speeds that exceed 100 miles per hour.

Stanley Steamer (12¢, #2131)

Type: Definitive (Transportation Series)
Date of Issue: April 2, 1985
Place of Issue: Kingfield, Maine
Designer: Ken Dallison
Printing: Intaglio
Color: Blue

Francis and Freelan Stanley produced the first Stanley Steamer in 1897; by 1902 they had organized the Stanley Motor Carriage Company to manufacture their steampowered automobiles. A Stanley racer set the 1906 world speed record of more than two miles per minute.

Oil Wagon (10.1¢, #2129)

Type: Definitive (Transportation Series)
Date of Issue: April 18, 1985
Place of Issue: Oil Center, New Mexico
Designer: James Schleyer
Printing: Intaglio
Color: Blue

The pen and ink rendering of an oil wagon evokes a feeling of the late 19th century, when they were fixtures of everday life. The wagons delivered oil for home heating and stove and lantern fuel.

Pushcart (12.5¢, #2132)

Type: Definitive (Transportation Series)
Date of Issue: April 18, 1985
Place of Issue: Oil Center, New Mexico
Designer: James Schleyer
Printing: Intaglio
Color: Olive

In the 19th century, pushcarts were used by merchants as movable shops. The two-wheeled variety pictured here is filled with produce and equipped with the tools of the trade: a hanging scale, placards and an umbrella to protect the grocer's wares.

Tricycle (6¢, #2127)

Type: Definitive (Transportation Series)
Date of Issue: May 6, 1985
Place of Issue: Childs, Maryland
Designer: James Schleyer
Printing: Intaglio
Color: Brown

The tricycle was at one time considered *adult* transportation. Still used by grown-ups in Great Britain, the three-wheeled vehicles were developed when two-wheelers began to sport front wheels of some 52 inches in diameter. These huge wheels made seats dangerously high for the average adult.

School Bus (3.4¢, #2123)

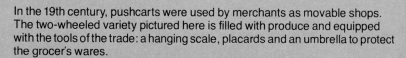

Type: Definitive (Transportation Series)
Date of Issue: June 8, 1985
Place of Issue: Arlington, Virginia
Designer: Lou Nolan
Printing: Intaglio
Color: Green

This Transportation Series stamp pictures a Model T school bus typical of those seen across the nation in the 1920s. The first "school bus" was actually a farmer's wagon hired by a school district in 1859. This idea has grown today to include thousands of local, suburban and intercity school transit vehicles.

Stutz Bearcat (11¢, #2130)

Type: Definitive (Transportation Series)
Date of Issue: June 11, 1985
Place of Issue: Baton Rouge, Louisiana
Designer: Ken Dallison
Printing: Intaglio
Color: Green

Harry C. Stutz was one of the great American automobile pioneers. His Stutz Motorcar Company manufactured the first Bearcat in 1914. The car became a symbol of the Roaring Twenties era, then ceased production in 1935 as a result of the Great Depression.

Ambulance (8.3¢, #2128)

Type: Definitive (Transportation Series)
Date of Issue: June 21, 1985
Place of Issue: Reno, Nevada
Designer: James Schleyer
Printing: Intaglio
Color: Green

The Civil War-era ambulance pictured in this stamp's pen-and-ink rendering was a light, horse-drawn wagon stocked with medical supplies.

Buckboard (4.9¢, #2125)

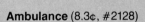

Type: Definitive (Transportation Series)
Date of Issue: June 21, 1985
Place of Issue: Reno, Nevada
Designer: William H. Bond
Printing: Intaglio
Color: Brown

Buckboards were a basic form of American transportation in the late 1800s. The "buckboard" was a flexible plank set between the front and rear axles of a horse-drawn vehicle. The passenger portion of the wagon was then built upon the board.

1985 ISSUES

Lawrence and Elmer Sperry (39¢, #C114)

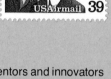

Type: International Airmail
Date of Issue: February 13, 1985
Place of Issue: Garden City, New York
Designer: Howard Koslow
Printing: Gravure
Colors: Yellow, Magenta, Cyan, Black, Blue

Elmer Sperry and his son, Lawrence, were aviation inventors and innovators who revolutionized flying. Elmer was awarded more than 400 patents on aviation-related devices. Lawrence helped develop and test the automatic pilot, retractable landing gear and the first guided missile. The stamp pictures the first amphibious flying boat, built by Lawrence using many of Elmer's inventions.

Alfred Verville (33¢, #C113)

Type: International Airmail
Date of Issue: February 13, 1985
Place of Issue: Garden City, New York
Designer: Ken Dallison
Printing: Gravure
Colors: Yellow, Magenta, Cyan, Black, Blue

Aviation pioneer Alfred Verville worked with Lawrence Sperry (see #C114) to design and produce the Verville-Sperry R-3 Army Racer. Featured in the stamp's design, the plane set a 216-m.p.h. speed record in 1924 and, nearly 50 years later, was recognized as one of the 12 most significant aircraft of all time. Verville also worked with aviation designer Glenn Curtiss.

Transpacific Airmail (44¢, #C115)

Type: International Airmail
Date of Issue: February 15, 1985
Place of Issue: San Francisco, California
Designer: Chuck Hodgson
Printing: Gravure
Colors: Yellow, Magenta, Cyan, Black

The China Clipper began the first transpacific mail flight 100 years after the first clipper ship sailed into San Francisco harbor. The historic flight from San Francisco to Manila, in The Philippines, took over 59 hours. The Clipper was designed to carry passengers as well as mail, and played an essential part in the war effort when it was loaned to the U.S. Navy in 1942.

Rural Electrification Administration (22¢, #2144)

Type: Commemorative
Date of Issue: May 11, 1985
Place of Issue: Madison, South Dakota
Designer: Howard Koslow
Printing: Gravure/Intaglio
Colors: Black, Cyan, Magenta, Yellow

President Franklin D. Roosevelt created the Rural Electrification Administration in 1935. At that time, just one in ten farms had electricity; since then, the REA has approved almost $60 billion in loans to assist millions of electricity consumers and telephone service subscribers.

AMERIPEX '86 (22¢, #2145)

Type: Commemorative
Date of Issue: May 25, 1985
Place of Issue: Rosemont, Illinois
Designer: Richard D. Sheaff
Printing: Offset/Intaglio
Colors: Blue, Red, Black (Intaglio), Tan, Gray (Offset)

A Chicago suburb, Rosemont, will host AMERIPEX '86, May 22-June 1. More than 100,000 people are expected to attend, and over 50 countries will exhibit at the largest philatelic exhibition ever to be held in North America.

Abigail Adams (22¢, #2146)

Type: Commemorative
Date of Issue: June 14, 1985
Place of Issue: Quincy, Massachusetts
Designer: Bart Forbes
Printing: Gravure
Colors: Yellow, Magenta, Cyan, Black

Abigail Adams is often referred to as America's first fully emancipated woman. Her marriage to statesman John Adams, who became President of the U.S., thrust her into the highest circles of political life. The First Lady was an established writer as well as her husband's trusted advisor, and she became the nation's "First Mother" when her son took over at the White House.

1985 ISSUES

Frederic Auguste Bartholdi (22¢, #2147)

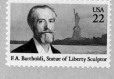

Type: Commemorative
Date of Issue: July 18, 1985
Place of Issue: New York, New York
Designer: Howard Paine
Printing: Offset/Intaglio
Colors: Yellow, Magenta, Cyan and Black (Offset); Black (Intaglio)

The issuance of this stamp presages the centennial of The Statue of Liberty's dedication in 1986, and commemorates its French sculptor Frederic Auguste Bartholdi's 150th birthday.

Social Security Act (22¢, #2153)

Type: Commemorative
Date of Issue: August 14, 1985
Place of Issue: Baltimore, Maryland
Designer: Robert Brangwyne
Printing: Gravure
Colors: Light Blue, Dark Blue

Social insurance came to the United States in 1908, with a law providing workers' compensation for some federal employees. Several states passed workers' compensation laws in 1911; however, due to the economy's long-retained agricultural character, no significant, comprehensive social security laws were passed until the Social Security Act of 1935. Today, approximately 37 million people receive benefits totaling more than $15 billion a month.

Junipero Serra (44¢)

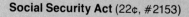

Type: Commemorative
Date of Issue: August 22, 1985
Place of Issue: San Diego, California
Designer: Richard Schlecht
Printing: Gravure
Colors: Yellow, Magenta, Cyan, Black

Father Junipero Serra was among the Spanish explorers who first claimed the land that today is California. Father Serra established nine missions that eventually grew to include 21 settlements from San Diego to San Francisco.

World War I Veterans (22¢)

Type: Commemorative
Date of Issue: August 26, 1985
Place of Issue: Milwaukee, Wisconsin
Designer: Richard Sheaff
Printing: Intaglio
Colors: Green, Red

World War I introduced technologies of modern warfare on the battlefields of Europe; as a result, its casualties far exceeded those of any previous war. More than eight million soldiers and 13 million civilians died during four years of fighting—some 350,000 were American "doughboys." Many of the Americans died not of wounds, but of the disease that raged among the unsanitary trenches characteristic of the Great War.

Korean War Veterans (22¢, #2152)

Type: Commemorative
Date of Issue: July 26, 1985
Place of Issue: Washington, D.C.
Designer: Richard Sheaff
Printing: Intaglio
Colors: Green, Red

The Korean War was the first conflict in which U.S. troops fought under the flag of the United Nations. The stamp's design was based on a photograph that showed weary troops trudging through a mountain pass on the march seaward after the intervention by Chinese Communist forces. More than 50,000 Americans died before a truce ended the three-year trauma.

Help End Hunger (22¢)

Type: Commemorative
Date of Issue: October 15, 1985
Place of Issue: Washington, D.C.
Designer: Jerry Pinkney
Printing: Gravure
Colors: Yellow, Magenta, Cyan, Line Black, Tone Black

1985 ISSUES

Public Education in America (22¢)

Type: Commemorative
Date of Issue: October 1, 1985
Place of Issue: Boston, Massachusetts
Designer: Uldis Purins
Printing: Gravure
Colors: Yellow, Magenta, Cyan, Line Black, Tone Black

This stamp marks the 350th anniversary of the Boston Latin School and features objects associated with a teacher's desk in the early years of public education in the U.S.

Horses (22¢)

Type: Commemorative
  (Block of four)
Date of Issue: September
  25, 1985
Place of Issue: Lexington,
  Kentucky
Designer: Roy Andersen
Printing: Gravure
Colors: Yellow, Magenta,
  Cyan, Line Black, Tone
  Black

Spanish conquistador Hernando Cortez introduced horses to North America in 1519, when he landed in Mexico with 17 of them.

International Youth Year (22¢)

Type: Commemorative
  (Block of four)
Date of Issue: October 7, 1985
Place of Issue: Chicago, Illinois
Designer: Dennis Luzak
Printing: Gravure
Colors: Yellow, Magenta, Cyan,
  Line Black, Tone Black

The United Nations General Assembly proclaimed 1985 as "International Youth Year."

Envelopes Stamp (17.5¢ & 21.1¢)

Design not available at press time.

Type: Regular (Zip +4 rate)
Date of Issue: October 22, 1985 (21.1¢) Date undetermined (17.5¢)
Place of Issue: Washington, D.C.
Printing: Gravure

Poinsettia (22¢)

Type: Christmas (Contemporary)
Date of Issue: October 30, 1985
Place of Issue: Nazareth, Michigan
Designer: James Dean
Printing: Gravure
Colors: Yellow, Magenta, Cyan, Black

Madonna and Child (22¢)

Type: Christmas (Traditional)
Date of Issue: October 30, 1985
Place of Issue: Detroit, Michigan
Designer: Bradbury Thompson
Printing: Gravure
Colors: Yellow, Magenta, Cyan, Black

George Washington/Washington Monument
(18¢, #2149)

Type: Regular
Date of Issue: November 6, 1985
Place of Issue: Washington, D.C.
Designer: Thomas Szumowski
Printing: Gravure
Colors: Yellow, Magenta, Cyan, Black

Commemorating the centennial of the dedication of the Washington
Monument, the U.S. Postal Service issued this stamp featuring the monument
along with its inspiration, George Washington. This rendering of the first
President was based upon a famous portrait by Gilbert Stuart.

1985 ISSUES

First Class D Stamp (nondenominated, #2111, sheet;
               #2112, coil; #2113, booklet;
               #2113a, pane of 10)

Type: Special
Date of Issue: February 1, 1985
Place of Issue: Los Angeles, California
Designer: Bradbury Thompson
Printing: Stamps and Coils , Gravure; Booklet , Intaglio
Color: Green

The nondenominated D stamp was issued to accommodate the First-Class letter rate increase from 20¢ to 22¢.

Flag Over Capitol (22¢, #2114, sheet: #2115, coil;
               #2116, booklet;
               #2116a, booklet pane of 5)

2114

Type: Special
Date of Issue: March 29, 1985
Place of Issue: Waubeka, Wisconsin, booklet
Washington, D.C, sheet and coil
Designer: Frank Waslick
Printing: Intaglio
Colors: Red, Blue, Black

2116a

The booklet version of this stamp was issued
in Waubeka, Wisconsin, where the first observance of Flag Day is believed to have taken place in 1885. The horizontally-oriented stamp is a new size, twice the width of an ordinary booklet stamp; the booklet pane is the first issued in the U.S. to offer a single row of five stamps.

Express Mail ($10.75, #2122, single stamp;
#2122a, booklet pane of 3)

Type: Definitive (Booklet Pane of 3)
Date of Issue: April 29, 1985
Place of Issue: San Francisco, California
Designer: Young & Rubicam
Printing: Gravure
Colors: Yellow, Magenta, Cyan, Red, Black

The use of Express Mail Next Day Service has increased steadily since its introduction; the availability of this stamp offers a convenient way to pay postage, especially for customers using collection boxes.

Penalty Mail (22¢, #0136, coil; 14¢, #0129A,
sheet; nondenominated, #0138,
postcard-rate sheet; #0139,
D-rate coil)

0138

Type: Definitive
Date of Issue: May 15, 1985
Place of Issue: Washington, D.C.
Designer: Bradbury Thompson
Printing: Intaglio
Colors: Black, Red, Blue

Previously called "Official Mail" stamps, the designation "Penalty Mail" refers to the legend which appears on these stamps: "Penalty for private use $300."

Postage Due (17¢, #J104)

*Design not available
at press time.*

Type: Definitive
Date of Issue: June 10, 1985
Place of Issue: Washington, D.C.
Printing: Intaglio
Colors: Red, Black

Since many post offices now use meter or handstamped markings instead of postage due stamps, the new 17-cent issue is available by mail order only. Because they are not valid for prepayment of postage, the stamps by themselves are not eligible to receive cancellation; if, however, postage due stamps are positioned adjacent to regular prepayment stamps, they will be cancelled.

1918-1935

C1

C2

C3

C3a

C4

C5

C6

C7

C10

C11

C12

C13

C14

C15

C18

C20

	Air Post Stamps	Un	U	PB/LP	#	FDC	Q
	For prepayment of postage on all mailable matter sent by airmail. All unwatermarked.						
	Issue of 1918, Perf. 11						
C1	6¢ Curtiss Jenny	120.00	45.00	1,500.00	(6)	*16,000.00*	3,395,854
C2	16¢ Curtiss Jenny	160.00	52.50	3,000.00	(6)	*16,000.00*	3,793,887
C3	24¢ Curtiss Jenny	160.00	65.00	850.00	(4)	*19,000.00*	2,134,888
C3a	Center Inverted	*110,000.00*					
	Issue of 1923						
C4	8¢ Wooden Propeller and						
	Engine Nose	45.00	20.00	750.00	(6)	500.00	6,414,576
C5	16¢ Air Service Emblem	160.00	50.00	4,500.00	(6)	850.00	5,309,275
C6	24¢ De Havilland Biplane	200.00	40.00	5,250.00	(6)	1,000.00	5,285,775
	Issue of 1926-27						
C7	10¢ Map of U.S.						
	and Two Mail Planes	5.00	.50	75.00	(6)	65.00	42,092,800
C8	15¢ olive brown (C7)	6.00	2.75	90.00	(6)	75.00	15,597,307
C9	20¢ yellow green (C7)	17.50	2.25	225.00	(6)	115.00	17,616,350
	Issue of 1927						
C10	10¢ Lindbergh's "Spirit of						
	St. Louis", June 18	13.00	3.00	250.00	(6)	25.00	20,379,179
C10a	Booklet pane of 3	140.00	*60.00*				
	Nos. C1-C10 inclusive were also available for ordinary postage.						
	Issue of 1928						
C11	5¢ Beacon on Rocky Mountains,						
	July 25	6.00	.65	80.00	(6)	50.00	106,887,675
C12	5¢ Winged Globe, Feb. 10	17.50	.45	300.00	(6)	20.00	97,641,200
	Graf Zeppelin Issue, Apr. 19						
C13	65¢ Zeppelin over Atlantic Ocean	350.00	275.00	4,500.00	(6)	2,250.00	93,536
C14	$1.30 Zeppelin between						
	Continents	800.00	550.00	11,000.00	(6)	1,600.00	72,428
C15	$2.60 Zeppelin Passing Globe	1,350.00	850.00	17,000.00	(6)	2,500.00	61,296
	Issued for use on mail carried on the first Europe-Pan-American round-trip flight of Graf Zeppelin, May 1930.						
	Issues of 1931-32, Perf. 10½x11						
C16	5¢ violet (C12)	10.00	.50	175.00	(4)	250.00	57,340,050
C17	8¢ olive bistre (C12)	4.00	.30	65.00	(4)	20.00	76,648,803
	Issue of 1933, Perf. 11						
C18	50¢ Century of Progress, Oct. 2	130.00	110.00	1,500.00	(6)	275.00	324,070
	Issue of 1934, Perf. 10½ x 11						
C19	6¢ dull orange (C12), July 1	4.25	.12	35.00	(4)	*200.00*	302,205,100
	Issue of 1935, Perf. 11						
C20	25¢ Transpacific, Nov. 22	2.00	1.25	35.00	(6)	40.00	10,205,400

	Issue of 1937	Un	U	PB/LP	#	FDC	Q
C21	20¢ The "China Clipper," over the						
	Pacific, Feb. 15	17.50	2.25	200.00	(6)	40.00	12,794,600
C22	50¢ carmine (C21)	16.00	6.50	190.00	(6)	40.00	9,285,300
	Issue of 1938						
C23	6¢ Eagle Holding Shield,						
	Olive Branch, and Arrows, May 14	.50	.06	11.00	(4)	20.00	349,946,500
	Issue of 1939						
C24	30¢ Transatlantic, May 16	17.50	1.50	285.00	(6)	45.00	19,768,150
	Issues of 1941-44, Perf. 11x10½						
C25	6¢ Twin-motor Transport Plane,						
	1941	.18	.05	1.00	(4)	2.25	4,476,527,700
C25a	Booklet pane of 3	6.50	1.00				
	Singles No. C25a are imperf. at sides or imperf. at sides and bottom.						
C26	8¢ olive green (C25), 1944	.25	.05	1.50	(4)	3.75	1,744,876,650
C27	10¢ violet (C25), 1941	2.00	.20	16.00	(4)	7.00	67,117,400
C28	15¢ brown carmine (C25), 1941	4.50	.35	22.00	(4)	10.00	78,434,800
C29	20¢ bright green (C25), 1941	3.25	.30	19.00	(4)	10.00	42,359,850
C30	30¢ blue (C25), 1941	4.00	.30	21.00	(4)	16.00	59,880,850
C31	50¢ orange (C25), 1941	22.50	4.00	135.00	(4)	40.00	11,160,600
	Issue of 1946						
C32	5¢ DC-4 Skymaster, Sept. 25	.15	.05	.75	(4)	2.00	864,753,100
	Issues of 1947, Perf. 10½x11						
C33	5¢ DC-4 Skymaster, Mar. 26	.12	.05	.75	(4)	2.00	971,903,700
	Perf. 11x10½						
C34	10¢ Pan American Union Building,						
	Washington, D.C., Aug. 30	.30	.06	2.25	(4)	2.00	207,976,550
C35	15¢ Statue of Liberty/						
	N.Y. Skyline, Aug. 20	.35	.05	2.50	(4)	2.75	756,186,350
C36	25¢ Plane over San Francisco-						
	Oakland Bay Bridge, July 30	1.60	.12	7.50	(4)	3.50	132,956,100
	Issues of 1948						
	Coil Stamp, Perf. 10 Horizontally						
C37	5¢ carmine (C33), Jan. 15	2.00	1.10	13.50		2.00	Unlimited
	Perf. 11x10½						
C38	5¢ New York City, July 31	.18	.18	20.00	(4)	1.75	38,449,100
	Issues of 1949						
	Perf. 10½x11						
C39	6¢ carmine (C33), Jan. 18	.18	.05	.85	(4)	1.50	5,070,095,200
C39a	Booklet pane of 6	13.50	5.00				
	Perf. 11x10½						
C40	6¢ Alexandria 200th Anniv., May 11	.18	.10	.95	(4)	1.25	75,085,000
	Coil Stamp, Perf. 10 Horizontally						
C41	6¢ carmine (C33), Aug. 25	4.50	.05	20.00		1.25	Unlimited
	Universal Postal Union Issue, Perf. 11x10½						
C42	10¢ Post Office Dept. Bldg., Nov. 18	.35	.35	3.25	(4)	1.75	21,061,300

1937-1949

C21

C23

C24

C25

C32

C33

C34

C35

C36

C38

C40

C42

1948-1966

C43

C44

C45

C46

C47

C48

C49

C51

C53

C54

C55

C56

C57

C58

C59

C60

	1949 continued	Un	U	PB/LP	#	FDC	Q
C43	15¢ Globe and Doves Carrying						
	Messages, Oct. 7	.50	.50	2.75	(4)	2.25	36,613,100
C44	25¢ Boeing Stratocruiser						
	and Globe, Nov. 30	.85	.85	11.00	(4)	2.75	16,217,100
C45	6¢ Wright Brothers, Dec. 17	.20	.10	1.00	(4)	3.75	80,405,000
	Issue of 1952						
C46	80¢ Diamond Head, Honolulu,						
	Hawaii, Mar. 26	12.50	1.50	80.00	(4)	17.50	18,876,800
	Issue of 1953						
C47	6¢ Powered Flight, May 29	.16	.10	.85	(4)	1.50	78,415,000
	Issue of 1954						
C48	4¢ Eagle in Flight, Sept. 3	.12	.08	5.00	(4)	.75	50,483,600
	Issue of 1957						
C49	6¢ Air Force, Aug. 1	.20	.10	1.50	(4)	1.75	63,185,000
	Issues of 1958						
C50	5¢ rose red (C48), July 31	.22	.15	5.00	(4)	.80	72,480,000
	Perf. 10½x11						
C51	7¢ Silhouette of Jet Liner, July 31	.22	.05	1.30	(4)	.75	532,410,300
C51a	Booklet pane of 6	16.50	6.50				1,326,960,000
	Coil Stamp, Perf. 10 Horizontally						
C52	7¢ blue (C51)	4.50	.20	22.50		.90	157,035,000
	Issues of 1959, Perf. 11x10½						
C53	7¢ Alaska Statehood, Jan. 3	.25	.12	1.50	(4)	.65	90,055,200
	Perf. 11						
C54	7¢ Balloon Jupiter, Aug. 17	.25	.12	1.50	(4)	1.10	79,290,000
	Issued for the 100th anniversary of the carrying of mail by the balloon Jupiter from Lafayette to Crawfordsville, Indiana.						
	Perf. 11x10½						
C55	7¢ Hawaii Statehood, Aug. 21	.25	.12	1.50	(4)	1.00	84,815,000
	Perf. 11						
C56	10¢ Pan-American Games, Aug. 27	.40	.40	5.00	(4)	.90	38,770,000
	Issue of 1959-66						
C57	10¢ Liberty Bell, June 10, 1960	3.00	1.00	15.00	(4)	1.50	39,960,000
C58	15¢ Statue of Liberty, Jan. 13, 1961	.75	.06	4.00	(4)	1.10	Unlimited
C59	25¢ Abraham Lincoln, Apr. 22, 1960	.75	.06	4.00	(4)	1.50	Unlimited
	Issue of 1960, Perf. 10½x11						
C60	7¢ Jet Airliner (C51), Aug. 12	.30	.05	1.50	(4)	.70	289,460,000
C60a	Booklet pane of 6	22.50	7.00				
	Coil Stamp, Perf. 10 Horizontally						
C61	7¢ carmine (C60), Oct. 22	8.00	.25	50.00		1.00	87,140,000

	Issue of 1961, Perf. 11	Un	U	PB/LP	#	FDC	Q
C62	13¢ Liberty Bell, June 28, 1961	.65	.10	7.00	(4)	.80	Unlimited
C63	15¢ Statue of Liberty, Jan. 13, 1961	.40	.08	2.25	(4)	1.00	Unlimited
	No. C63 has a gutter between the two parts of the design; No. C58 does not.						
	Issue of 1962, Perf. 10½x11						
C64	8¢ Jetliner over Capitol, Dec. 5	.22	.05	1.10	(4)	.60	Unlimited
	Booklet pane of 5 + label	7.50	1.25				
	Coil Stamp, Perf. 10 Horizontally						
C65	8¢ carmine (C64), Dec. 5	.50	.08	4.00		.80	Unlimited
	Issue of 1963, Perf. 11						
C66	15¢ Montgomery Blair, May 3	1.30	.75	7.00	(4)	1.35	42,245,000
	Issues of 1963-64, Perf. 11x10½						
C67	6¢ Bald Eagle, July 12, 1963	.20	.15	3.50	(4)	.50	Unlimited
	Perf. 11						
C68	8¢ Amelia Earhart, July 24, 1963	.30	.15	3.00	(4)	2.50	63,890,000
C69	8¢ Robert H. Goddad, Oct. 5, 1964	.90	.15	5.00	(4)	2.75	65,170,000
	Issues of 1967						
C70	8¢ Alaska Purchase, Mar. 30	.45	.20	4.00	(4)	.70	64,710,000
C71	20¢ "Columbia Jays" by Audubon,						
	Apr. 26	1.50	.15	8.50	(4)	2.00	165,430,000
	Issues of 1968, Perf. 11x10½						
C72	10¢ 50-Star Runway, Jan. 5	.30	.05	2.25	(4)	.60	Unlimited
C72b	Booklet pane of 8	4.00	.75				
C72c	Booklet pane of 5 + label	2.50	.75				
C73	10¢ carmine (C72), Coil, Perf. 10	.65	.05			.60	Unlimited
	Air Mail Service Issue, Perf. 11						
C74	10¢ Curtiss Jenny, May 15	.60	.15	5.00	(4)	1.50	74,180,000
C75	20¢ U.S.A. and Jet, Nov. 22	.85	.06	5.00	(4)	1.10	Unlimited
	Issue of 1969						
C76	10¢ Moon Landing, Sept. 9	.30	.15	2.50	(4)	3.50	152,364,800
	Issues of 1971-73, Perf. 10½x11, 11x10½						
C77	9¢ Plane, May 15, 1971	.22	.15	2.00	(4)	.50	Unlimited
C78	11¢ Silhouette of Jet, May 7, 1971	.30	.05	1.75	(4)	.50	Unlimited
C78a	Booklet pane of 4 + 2 labels	1.50	.40				
C79	13¢ Winged Airmail Envelope,						
	Nov. 16, 1973	.32	.10	1.65	(4)	.55	Unlimited
C79a	Booklet pane of 5 + label,						
	Dec. 27, 1973	1.35	.70				
	Perf. 11						
C80	17¢ Statue of Liberty, July 13, 1971	.55	.15	2.75	(4)	.60	Unlimited
	Perf. 11x10½						
C81	21¢ red, blue and black (C75)						
	May 21, 1971	.55	.10	2.75	(4)	.75	Unlimited

C62

C63

C64

C66

C67

C68

C69

C70

C71

C72

C74

C75

C76

C77

C78

C79

C80

C81

1972-1980

C84

C85

C86

C87

C88

C89

C90

C97

C91
C92

C93
C94

C95
C96

C98

C99

C100

	1971-1973 continued	Un	U	PB/LP	#	FDC	Q
	Coil Stamps, Perf. 10 Vertically						
C82	11¢ Silhouette of Jet (C78),						
	May 7, 1971	.40	.06	2.25		.50	Unlimited
C83	13¢ red (C79), Dec. 27, 1973	.40	.10	2.10		.50	
	Issues of 1972, Perf. 11						
C84	11¢ City of Refuge, May 3	.30	.15	2.00	(4)	.65	78,210,000
	Perf. 11x10½						
C85	11¢ Skiing and Olympic Rings,						
	Aug. 17	.30	.15	3.50	(10)	.50	96,240,000
	Issue of 1973						
C86	11¢ De Forest Audions, July 10	.30	.15	1.75	(4)	.50	58,705,000
	Issues of 1974, Perf. 11						
C87	18¢ Statue of Liberty, Jan. 11	.45	.45	2.50	(4)	.65	Unlimited
C88	26¢ Mt. Rushmore National						
	Memorial, Jan. 2	.60	.15	2.85	(4)	.85	Unlimited
	Issue of 1976						
C89	25¢ Plane & Globes, Jan. 2	.60	.18	3.25	(4)	.85	
C90	31¢ Plane, Globes & Flag, Jan. 2	.62	.10	3.25	(4)	.85	
	Issues of 1978, Wright Brothers Issue, Sept. 23						
C91	31¢ Orville & Wilbur Wright	.90	.15	5.00	(4)	1.15	
C92	31¢ Orville & Wilbur Wright	.90	.15	5.00	(4)	1.15	
	Pair, #C91-C92	1.85	.65			2.30	
	Issues of 1979, Octave Chanute Issue, March 29						
C93	21¢ Octave Chanute	.90	.32			1.00	
C94	21¢ Octave Chanute	.90	.32	5.00	(4)	1.00	
	Pair, #C93-C94	1.85	.75			2.00	
	Wiley Post Issue, Nov. 20						
C95	25¢ Wiley Post	.90	.35			1.00	
C96	25¢ Wiley Post	.90	.35	5.00	(4)	1.00	
	Pair, #C95-C96	1.85	.85	1.85		2.00	
	Olympic Games Issue						
C97	31¢ High Jump	.90	.30	12.00	(12)	1.15	47,200,000
	Issues of 1980						
C98	40¢ Philip Mazzei, Oct. 13	.90	.30	12.00	(12)	1.35	80,935,000
C99	28¢ Blanche Stuart Scott, Dec. 30	.70	.15	9.00	(12)	1.10	20,190,000
C100	35¢ Glenn Curtiss, Dec. 30	.70	.15	10.00	(12)	1.25	22,945,000

		Un	U	PB/LP	#	FDC		Q
	Issues of 1983, Olympics Issues, Perf. 11, June 17							
C101	28¢ Gymnastics	.56	.28			1.10		
C102	28¢ High Jump	.56	.28			1.10		
C103	28¢ Basketball	.56	.28			1.10		
C104	28¢ Soccer	.56	.28			1.10		
	Block of 4, #C101-C104	2.25	1.75	2.75	(4)	3.75		Unlimited
	Olympics Issues Perf. 11, April 8							
C105	40¢ Shotput	.80	.40			1.35		
C106	40¢ Gymnastics	.80	.40			1.35		
C107	40¢ Swimming	.80	.40			1.35		
C108	40¢ Weightlifting	.80	.40			1.35		
	Block of 4, #C105-C108	3.50	2.00	4.00	(4)	5.00		Unlimited
	Olympics Issues, Perf. 11, Nov. 4							
C109	35¢ Fencing	.70	.35			1.25		
C110	35¢ Bicycling	.70	.35			1.25		
C111	35¢ Volleyball	.70	.35			1.25		
C112	35¢ Pole Vault	.70	.35			1.25		
	Block of 4, #C109-C112	3.00	1.85	3.50	(4)	4.50		
	Air Post Special Delivery Stamps							
	Issue of 1934, Perf. 11							
CE1	16¢ dark blue (CE2)	.85	.85	27.50	(6)	25.00		
	For imperforate variety see No. 771.							
	Issue of 1936							
CE2	16¢ Great Seal of United States	.40	.25	12.00	(4)	17.50		

Universal Postal Union

In the 19th century, figuring the cost of a letter mailed from the United States to another country was complicated. The rate depended on the U.S. domestic rate, sea postage, the rate of the receiving country, and the transit rate assessed by each country through which the letter traveled. The recipient of the letter usually paid all these fees. The receiving post office had to compute the postage due, then change this figure into gold centimes, a universal money exchange. This money had to be returned to the country where the letter originated. This led to postal agreements between individual countries, and sometimes sections of countries.

The basis of the Universal Postal Union (#1530-37) was that a letter written to another country usually prompts a letter in response.

This situation existed for almost 100 years, until Colombia complained at the 1969 UPU Congress that they received much more mail than they sent. They also stated that it cost them more money to deliver a letter in their country than it cost in an industrialized nation. A letter delivered to a remote area frequently was carried by train, bus, horse and boat before it reached its destination. In 1971, a system of balancing payments went into effect whereby "sender" countries pay other nations who receive more mail than they send to the "senders".

C105   C106
C107   C108

C101   C102
C103   C104

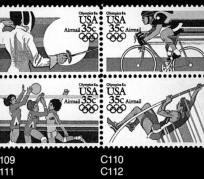

C109   C110
C111   C112

CE1   CE2

		Un	U	PB/LP	#	FDC	Q
	Special Delivery Stamps.						
	Unwmkd., Issue of 1885, Perf. 12						
E1	10¢ Messenger Running	250.00	30.00	*13,500.00*	(8)	*8,000.00*	
	Issue of 1888						
E2	10¢ blue (E3)	250.00	7.50	*13,500.00*	(8)		
	Issue of 1893						
E3	10¢ Messenger Running	165.00	14.00	*8,500.00*	(8)		
	Issue of 1894, Line under "Ten Cents"						
E4	10¢ Messenger Running	725.00	17.50	*16,500.00*	(6)		
	Issue of 1895, Wmkd. (191)						
E5	10¢ blue (E4)	135.00	2.50	*5,500.00*	(6)		
	Issue of 1902						
E6	10¢ Messenger on Bicycle	90.00	2.50	*3,500.00*	(6)		
	Issue of 1908						
E7	10¢ Mercury Helmet and						
	Olive Branch	60.00	27.50	1,100.00	(6)		
	Issue of 1911, Wmdk. (190)						
E8	10¢ ultramarine (E6)	90.00	4.00	*3,000.00*	(6)		
	Issue of 1914, Perf. 10						
E9	10¢ ultramarine (E6)	185.00	5.25	*5,250.00*	(6)		
	Unwmkd., Issue of 1916						
E10	10¢ ultramarine (E6)	325.00	21.00	*7,000.00*	(6)		
	Issue of 1917, Perf. 11						
E11	10¢ ultramarine (E6)	15.00	.30	250.00	(6)		
	Issue of 1922						
E12	10¢ Postman and Motorcycle	22.50	.15	450.00	(6)	550.00	
	Issue of 1925						
E13	15¢ Postman and Motorcycle	22.50	.65	250.00	(6)	275.00	
E14	20¢ Post Office Truck	3.00	1.75	45.00	(6)	150.00	
	Issue of 1927, Perf. 11x10½						
E15	10¢ Postman and Motorcycle	.70	.05	6.00	(4)	100.00	
	Issue of 1931						
E16	15¢ orange (E12)	.80	.08	6.50	(4)	135.00	
	Issue of 1944						
E17	13¢ Postman and Motorcycle	.65	.06	4.00	(4)	12.00	
E18	17¢ Postman and Motorcycle	5.00	2.25	28.50	(4)	12.00	
	Issue of 1951						
E19	20¢ black (E14)	2.00	.12	12.00	(4)	5.00	
	Issue of 1954-57						
E20	20¢ Delivery of Letter	.60	.08	4.00	(4)	3.00	
E21	30¢ Delivery of Letter	.90	.05	5.00	(4)	2.25	
	Issue of 1969-71, Perf. 11						
E22	45¢ Arrows	2.25	.20	11.00	(4)	3.50	
E23	60¢ Arrows	1.20	.12	5.50	(4)	3.50	

1885-1971

E1

E3

E4

E6

E7

E12

E13

E14

E15

E17

E18

E20

E21

E22

E23

1879-1959

F1

FA1

JQ1

JQ2

J2

J19

J25

J33

J69

J78

J88

J98

J101

	Un	U	PB/LP	#	FDC	Q

Registration Stamp

Issued for the prepayment of registry; not usable for postage. Sale discontinued May 28, 1913.

Issue of 1911, Perf. 12, Wmkd. USPS (190)

		Un	U	PB/LP	#	FDC	Q
F1	10¢ Bald Eagle	75.00	4.50	*2,100.00*	(6)	*9,000.00*	

Certified Mail Stamp

For use on first-class mail for which no indemnity value is claimed, but for which proof of mailing and proof of delivery are available at less cost than registered mail.

Issue of 1955, Perf. 10½x11

		Un	U	PB/LP	#	FDC	Q
FA1	15¢ Letter Carrier	.50	.30	6.25	(4)	3.25	54,460,300

		Un	U

Postage Due Stamps

For affixing by a postal clerk to any mail to denote amount to be collected from addressee because of insufficient prepayment of postage.

Printed by American Bank Note Company Issue of 1879, Design of J2, Perf. 12, Unwmd.

		Un	U
J1	1¢ brown	22.50	5.00
J2	2¢ Figure of Value	150.00	4.00
J3	3¢ brown	17.50	2.50
J4	5¢ brown	225.00	20.00
J5	10¢ brown	300.00	10.00
J6	30¢ brown	125.00	20.00
J7	50¢ brown	200.00	30.00

Special Printing

		Un	U
J8	1¢ deep brown	*5,000.00*	—
J9	2¢ deep brown	*3,250.00*	—
J10	3¢ deep brown	*3,000.00*	—
J11	5¢ deep brown	*2,500.00*	—
J12	10¢ deep brown	*1,450.00*	—
J13	30¢ deep brown	*1,450.00*	—
J14	50¢ deep brown	*1,450.00*	

Regular Issue of 1884-89, Design of J19

		Un	U
J15	1¢ red brown	25.00	2.50
J16	2¢ red brown	32.50	2.50
J17	3¢ red brown	425.00	90.00
J18	5¢ red brown	200.00	10.00
J19	10¢ Figure of Value	165.00	5.00
J20	30¢ red brown	90.00	22.50
J21	50¢ red brown	900.00	125.00

Issue of 1891-93, Design of J25

		Un	U
J22	1¢ bright claret	8.50	.50
J23	2¢ bright claret	11.50	.45
J24	3¢ bright claret	22.50	2.75
J25	5¢ Figure of Value	25.00	2.75
J26	10¢ bright claret	50.00	7.50
J27	30¢ bright claret	200.00	75.00
J28	50¢ bright claret	225.00	85.00

Printed by the Bureau of Engraving and Printing, Issue of 1894, Design of J33, Perf. 12

		Un	U
J29	1¢ vermillion	450.00	75.00
J30	2¢ vermillion	190.00	32.50

Parcel Post Postage Due Stamps

For affixing by a postal clerk to any parcel post package to denote the amount to be collected from the addressee because of insufficient prepayment of postage.

Beginning July 1, 1913, these stamps were valid for use as regular postage due stamps.

Issue of 1912, Design of JQ1 and JQ5, Perf. 12

		Un	U
JQ1	1¢ Figure of Value	9.00	3.00
JQ2	2¢ dark green	80.00	15.00
JQ3	5¢ dark green	11.50	3.50
JQ4	10¢ dark green	150.00	35.00
JQ5	25¢ Figure of Value	75.00	3.50

		Un	U	PB/LP	#	FDC	Q
J31	1¢ deep claret	15.00	3.00	375.00	(6)		
J32	2¢ deep claret	12.50	1.75	325.00	(6)		
J33	3¢ Figure of Value	60.00	17.50	850.00	(6)		
J34	5¢ deep claret	65.00	22.50	950.00	(6)		
J35	10¢ deep rose	60.00	12.50	850.00	(6)		
J36	30¢ deep claret	175.00	45.00				
J37	50¢	400.00	90.00				
	Issue of 1895, Design of J33, Wmkd. (191)						
J38	1¢ deep claret	4.00	.30	190.00	(6)		
J39	2¢ deep claret	4.00	.20	190.00	(6)		
J40	3¢ deep claret	25.00	1.00	425.00	(6)		
J41	5¢ deep claret	25.00	1.00	450.00	(6)		
J42	10¢ deep claret	27.50	2.00	550.00	(6)		
J43	30¢ deep claret	225.00	17.50	3,750.00	(6)		
J44	50¢ deep claret	150.00	18.00	2,250.00	(6)		
	Issue of 1910-12, Design of J33, Wmkd. (190)						
J45	1¢ deep claret	17.50	2.00	400.00	(6)		
J46	2¢ deep claret	17.50	.15	350.00	(6)		
J47	3¢ deep claret	325.00	15.00	3,850.00	(6)		
J48	5¢ deep claret	45.00	2.50	600.00	(6)		
J49	10¢ deep claret	50.00	6.00	1,150.00	(6)		
J50	50¢ deep claret	550.00	65.00	6,500.00	(6)		
	Issue of 1914-15, Design of J33, Perf. 10						
J52	1¢ carmine lake	35.00	6.00	550.00	(6)		
J53	2¢ carmine lake	22.50	.20	350.00	(6)		
J54	3¢ carmine lake	350.00	12.50	4,500.00	(6)		
J55	5¢ carmine lake	17.50	1.50	285.00	(6)		
J56	10¢ carmine lake	30.00	.85	675.00	(6)		
J57	30¢ carmine lake	125.00	12.00	2,350.00	(6)		
J58	50¢ carmine lake	*4,500.00*	300.00	*33,500.00*	(6)		
	Issue of 1916, Design of J33, Unwmkd.						
J59	1¢ rose	800.00	135.00	7,250.00	(6)		
J60	2¢ rose	67.50	5.00	800.00	(6)		
	Issue of 1917, Design of J33, Perf. 11						
J61	1¢ carmine rose	1.50	.08	40.00	(6)		
J62	2¢ carmine rose	1.25	.05	35.00	(6)		
J63	3¢ carmine rose	6.50	.08	100.00	(6)		
J64	5¢ carmine	6.50	.08	95.00	(6)		
J65	10¢ carmine rose	9.00	.20	125.00	(6)		
J66	30¢ carmine rose	50.00	.40	575.00	(6)		
J67	50¢ carmine rose	65.00	.12	750.00	(6)		

		Un	U	PB/LP	#	FDC	Q
	Issue of 1925, Design of J33						
J68	½¢ dull red	.50	.06	11.00	(6)		
	Issue of 1930-31, Design of J69						
J69	½¢ Figure of Value	3.50	.70	35.00	(6)		
J70	1¢ carmine	2.50	.15	27.50	(6)		
J71	2¢ carmine	3.50	.15	40.00	(6)		
J72	3¢ carmine	22.50	1.00	240.00	(6)		
J73	5¢ carmine	20.00	1.50	225.00	(6)		
J74	10¢ carmine	42.50	.50	400.00	(6)		
J75	30¢ carmine	120.00	1.00	1,000.00	(6)		
J76	50¢ carmine	135.00	.30	1,150.00	(6)		
	Design of J78						
J77	$1 carmine	30.00	.06	275.00	(6)		
J78	$5 "FIVE" on $	40.00	.12	375.00	(6)		
	Issue of 1931-56, Design of J69, Perf 11x10½						
J79	½¢ dull carmine	1.25	.08	22.50	(4)		
J80	1¢ dull carmine	.15	.05	2.00	(4)		
J81	2¢ dull carmine	.15	.05	2.00	(4)		
J82	3¢ dull carmine	.25	.05	3.00	(4)		
J83	5¢ dull carmine	.35	.05	4.00	(4)		
J84	10¢ dull carmine	1.10	.05	8.50	(4)		
J85	30¢ dull carmine	8.50	.08	45.00	(4)		
J86	50¢ dull carmine	9.50	.06	57.50	(4)		
	Perf. 10½x11						
J87	$1 scarlet, same design as J78	45.00	.20	325.00	(4)		
	Issue of 1959, Perf. 11x10½, Design of J88 and J98						
J88	½¢ Figure of Value	1.25	.85	125.00	(4)		
J89	1¢ carmine rose	.05	.05	.50	(4)		
J90	2¢ carmine rose	.06	.05	.60	(4)		
J91	3¢ carmine rose	.07	.05	.70	(4)		
J92	4¢ carmine rose	.08	.05	1.25	(4)		
J93	5¢ carmine rose	.10	.05	.75	(4)		
J94	6¢ carmine rose	.12	.05	1.40	(4)		
J95	7¢ carmine rose	.14	.06	1.60	(4)		
J96	8¢ carmine rose	.16	.05	1.75	(4)		
J97	10¢ carmine rose	.20	.05	1.25	(4)		
J98	30¢ Figure of Value	.70	.05	5.50	(4)		
J99	50¢ carmine rose	1.10	.05	6.50	(4)		
	Design of J101						
J100	$1 carmine rose	2.00	.05	10.00	(4)		
J101	$5 Outline Figure of Value	8.00	.15	40.00	(4)		
	Design of J88						
J102	11¢ carmine rose	.22	.05	1.10	(4)		
J103	13¢ carmine rose	.26	.05	1.30	(4)		

1873-1911

O7

O14

O18

O34

O44

O52

O57

O71

O76

O91

O93

O95

O101

O114

O121

0127

0128

0129

0130

0132

0133

0135

278

Official Stamps

The franking privilege having been abolished as of July 1, 1873, these stamps were provided for each of the departments of Government for the prepayment of official matter.

These stamps were supplanted on May 1, 1879 by penalty envelopes and on July 5, 1884 were declared obsolete.

Designs are as follows: Post Office officials, figures of value and department name; all other departments, various portraits and department names.

Issues of 1873
Printed by the Continental Bank Note Co. Thin Hard Paper
Department of Agriculture: Yellow

		Un	U
O1	1¢ Franklin	55.00	30.00
O2	2¢ Jackson	37.50	13.50
O3	3¢ Washington	30.00	3.50
O4	6¢ Lincoln	40.00	12.50
O5	10¢ Jefferson	95.00	47.50
O6	12¢ Clay	130.00	70.00
O7	15¢ Webster	90.00	47.50
O8	24¢ Winfield Scott	110.00	55.00
O9	30¢ Hamilton	150.00	85.00

Executive Dept.

		Un	U
O10	1¢ carmine, Franklin	225.00	85.00
O11	2¢ Jackson	150.00	70.00
O12	3¢ carmine,		
	Washington	175.00	65.00
O13	6¢ carmine, Lincoln	275.00	140.00
O14	10¢ Jefferson	250.00	140.00

Dept. of the Interior: Vermilion

		Un	U
O15	1¢ Franklin	15.00	2.25
O16	2¢ Jackson	12.00	1.50
O17	3¢ Washington	20.00	1.50
O18	6¢ Lincoln	15.00	1.50
O19	10¢ Jefferson	12.50	3.50
O20	12¢ Clay	20.00	2.50
O21	15¢ Webster	37.50	7.25
O22	24¢ W. Scott	27.50	5.50
O23	30¢ Hamilton	37.50	5.75
O24	90¢ Perry	85.00	12.50

Dept. of Justice: Purple

		Un	U
O25	1¢ Franklin	35.00	17.50
O26	2¢ Jackson	57.50	20.00
O27	3¢ Washington	60.00	7.00
O28	6¢ Lincoln	52.50	10.00
O29	10¢ Jefferson	60.00	25.00

		Un	U
O30	12¢ Clay	37.50	12.00
O31	15¢ Webster	95.00	47.50
O32	24¢ W. Scott	275.00	120.00
O33	30¢ Hamilton	250.00	85.00
O34	90¢ Perry	375.00	175.00

Navy Dept: Ultramarine

		Un	U
O35	1¢ Franklin	30.00	10.00
O36	2¢ Jackson	20.00	8.00
O37	3¢ Washington	24.00	3.00
O38	6¢ Lincoln	20.00	4.50
O39	7¢ Stanton	150.00	60.00
O40	10¢ Jefferson	26.00	10.00
O41	12¢ Clay	37.50	8.25
O42	15¢ Webster	65.00	22.50
O43	24¢ W. Scott	65.00	30.00
O44	30¢ Hamilton	55.00	12.50
O45	90¢ Perry	275.00	80.00

Post Office Dept: Black

		Un	U
O47	1¢ Figure of Value	7.25	3.00
O48	2¢ Figure of Value	7.00	2.50
O49	3¢ Figure of Value	2.50	.75
O50	6¢ Figure of Value	7.00	1.65
O51	10¢ Figure of Value	32.50	16.50
O52	12¢ Figure of Value	17.50	3.75
O53	15¢ Figure of Value	20.00	6.50
O54	24¢ Figure of Value	25.00	8.25
O55	30¢ Figure of Value	25.00	7.00
O56	90¢ Figure of Value	40.00	11.00

Dept. of State

		Un	U
O57	1¢ dark green Franklin	35.00	10.00
O58	2¢ dark green Jackson	80.00	25.00
O59	3¢ bright green		
	Washington	30.00	7.50
O60	6¢ bright green Lincoln	27.50	7.50
O61	7¢ dark green Stanton	55.00	15.00
O62	10¢ dark green		
	Jefferson	35.00	12.50
O63	12¢ dark green Clay	70.00	27.50
O64	15¢ dark green		
	Webster	55.00	15.00
O65	24¢ dark green		
	W. Scott	150.00	75.00
O66	30¢ Hamilton	135.00	60.00

1873-1983

1873 continued

		Un	U
O67	90¢ dark green Perry	300.00	120.00
O68	$2 green and black		
	Seward	500.00	225.00
O69	$5 green and black		
	Seward	4,000.00	2,000.00
O70	$10 green and black		
	Seward	2,500.00	1,300.00
O71	$20 Seward	2,150.00	1,100.00

Treasury Dept.: Brown

		Un	U
O72	1¢ Franklin	12.00	1.75
O73	2¢ Jackson	18.00	1.75
O74	3¢ Washington	10.00	1.00
O75	6¢ Lincoln	17.50	1.00
O76	7¢ Stanton	35.00	11.00
O77	10¢ Jefferson	35.00	3.50
O78	12¢ Clay	35.00	1.50
O79	15¢ Webster	35.00	3.25
O80	24¢ W. Scott	165.00	55.00
O81	30¢ Hamilton	50.00	3.25
O82	90¢ Perry	55.00	3.00

War Dept.: Rose

		Un	U
O83	1¢ Franklin	50.00	3.25
O84	2¢ Jackson	45.00	5.00
O85	3¢ Washington	42.50	1.00
O86	6¢ Lincoln	200.00	4.00
O87	7¢ Stanton	45.00	25.00
O88	10¢ Jefferson	15.00	3.00
O89	12¢ Clay	45.00	2.00
O90	15¢ Webster	12.00	1.20
O91	24¢ W. Scott	12.50	1.75
O92	30¢ Hamilton	14.00	1.50
O93	90¢ Perry	35.00	10.00

Issues of 1879
Printed by the American Bank Note Co. Soft, Porous Paper, Dept. of Agriculture: Yellow

O94	1¢ Franklin, issued		
	without gum	*1,350.00*	—
O95	3¢ Washington	160.00	25.00

Dept. of the Interior: Vermilion

O96	1¢ Franklin	110.00	60.00
O97	2¢ Jackson	2.50	.75
O98	3¢ Washington	2.00	.60

		Un	U
O99	6¢ Lincoln	3.00	1.00
O100	10¢ Jefferson	27.50	17.50
O101	12¢ Clay	50.00	30.00
O102	15¢ Webster	125.00	60.00
O103	24¢ W. Scott	1,000.00	—

Dept. of Justice: Bluish Purple

O106	3¢ Washington	40.00	17.50
O107	6¢ Lincoln	100.00	60.00

Post Office Dept.: Black

O108	3¢ Figure of Value	6.50	1.40

Treasury Dept.: Brown

O109	3¢ Washington	21.00	2.50
O110	6¢ Lincoln	42.50	17.50
O111	10¢ Jefferson	60.00	15.00
O112	30¢ Hamilton	675.00	135.00
O113	90¢ Perry	700.00	135.00

War Dept.: Rose Red

O114	1¢ Franklin	1.75	.75
O115	2¢ Jackson	2.75	1.00
O116	3¢ Washington	2.75	.65
O117	6¢ Lincoln	2.50	.70
O118	10¢ Jefferson	15.00	6.00
O119	12¢ Clay	12.00	1.75
O120	30¢ Hamilton	37.50	25.00

Official Postal Savings Mail, Perf. 12
These stamps were used to prepay postage on official correspondence of the Postal Savings Division of the Post Office Department. Discontinued Sept. 23, 1914

Issues of 1911, Wmkd. (191)

O121	2¢ Official Postal Savings	9.00	1.10
O122	50¢ Official Postal Savings	100.00	32.50
O123	$1 Official Postal Savings	95.00	9.50

Wmkd. (190)

O124	1¢ Official Postal Savings	4.00	1.00
O125	2¢ Official Postal Savings	30.00	3.50
O126	10¢ Official Postal Savings	8.50	1.00

Issues of 1983

O127	1¢ Official Mail U.S.A.	.05	—
O128	4¢ Official Mail U.S.A.	.08	—
O129	13¢ Official Mail U.S.A.	.26	—
O130	17¢ Official Mail U.S.A.	.34	—
O132	1.00 Official Mail U.S.A.	2.00	—
O133	5.00 Official Mail U.S.A.	10.00	—
O135	20¢ Official Mail U.S.A.	.40	.40

1861-1863

1 2 3 6

5

8 9 13 14

11

		Un	U
	General Issues, All Imperf.		
	Issue of 1861: Lithographed, Unwatermarked		
1	5¢ Jefferson Davis	195.00	110.00
2	10¢ Thomas Jefferson	250.00	200.00
	Issue of 1862		
3	2¢ Andrew Jackson	600.00	725.00
4	5¢ blue J. Davis (6)	125.00	105.00
5	10¢ Thomas Jefferson	900.00	625.00
	Typographed		
6	5¢ J. Davis		
	(London print)	12.00	20.00
7	5¢ blue (6) (local print)	16.00	17.00
	Issues of 1863, Engraved		
8	2¢ Andrew Jackson	67.50	285.00

	Thick or Thin Paper		
9	10¢ Jefferson Davis	800.00	650.00
10	10¢ blue (9), (with		
	rectangular frame)	3,500.00	1,750.00
	Prices of No. 10 are for copies showing parts of lines on at least two sides of frame.		
11	10¢ Jefferson Davis,		
	die Ia	13.00	15.00
12	10¢ blue J. Davis,		
	die B (11)	14.00	16.00
	Dies A and B differ in that B has an extra line outside its corner ornaments.		
13	20¢ George Washington	47.50	275.00
	Issue of 1862, Typographed		
14	1¢ John C. Calhoun		
	(This stamp was never		
	put in use.)	135.00	—

865-1880

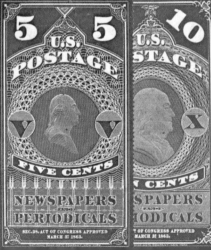

		Un	U
	Newspaper Stamps **Perf. 12, Issues of 1865** **Printed by the National Bank Note Co.,** **Thin, Hard Paper, No Gum, Unwmkd.,** **Colored Borders**		
PR1	5¢ Washington	150.00	—
PR2	10¢ Franklin	75.00	—
PR3	25¢ Lincoln	75.00	—
	White Border, Yellowish Paper		
PR4	5¢ light blue (PR1)	30.00	25.00
	Reprints of 1875 **Printed by the Continental Bank Note Co.,** **Hard, White Paper, No Gum**		
PR5	5¢ dull blue (PR1),		
	white border	55.00	—
PR6	10¢ dark bluish green,		
	(PR2), colored border	32.50	—
PR7	25¢ dark carmine		
	(PR3), colored border	65.00	—
	Issue of 1880 **Printed by the American Bank Note Co.,** **Soft, Porous Paper, White Border**		
PR8	5¢ dark blue (PR1)	110.00	—
	Issue of 1875 **Printed by the Continental Bank Note Co.,** **Thin, Hard Paper**		
	PR9-PR15; "Statue of Freedom" (PR15)		
PR9	2¢ black	8.00	8.00
PR10	3¢ black	11.00	11.00
PR11	4¢ black	9.00	9.00
PR12	6¢ black	12.50	12.50
PR13	8¢ black	17.50	17.50
PR14	9¢ black	40.00	40.00
PR15	10¢ Statue of Freedom	17.50	15.00
	PR16-PR23: "Justice" (PR18)		
PR16	12¢ rose	40.00	30.00
PR17	24¢ rose	50.00	35.00
PR22	84¢ rose	175.00	100.00
PR23	96¢ rose	110.00	85.00
PR24	$1.92 Ceres	130.00	90.00
PR25	$3 "Victory"	175.00	110.00
PR26	$6 Clio	325.00	150.00
PR27	$9 Minerva	425.00	185.00
PR28	$12 Vesta	500.00	250.00
PR29	$24 "Peace"	500.00	275.00
PR30	$36 "Commerce"	550.00	325.00
PR31	$48 red brown Hebe		
	(PR78)	700.00	425.00
PR32	$60 violet Indian		
	Maiden (PR79)	700.00	375.00
	Special Printing, Hard, White Paper, **Without Gum**		
	PR33-PR39: Statue of Freedom (PR15)		
PR33	2¢ gray black	60.00	—
PR34	3¢ gray black	65.00	—
PR35	4¢ gray black	80.00	—
PR36	6¢ gray black	110.00	—
PR37	8¢ gray black	130.00	—
PR38	9¢ gray black	150.00	—
PR39	10¢ gray black	185.00	—
	PR40-PR47: "Justice" (PR18)		
PR40	12¢ pale rose	210.00	—
PR41	24¢ pale rose	275.00	—
PR42	36¢ pale rose	375.00	—
PR43	48¢ pale rose	425.00	—
PR44	60¢ pale rose	500.00	—
PR45	72¢ pale rose	650.00	—
PR46	84¢ pale rose	675.00	—
PR47	96¢ pale rose	800.00	—
PR48	$1.92 dark brown		
	Ceres (PR24)	*2,400.00*	—
PR49	$3 vermilion "Victory"		
	(PR25)	*5,000.00*	—
PR50	$6 ultra. Clio (PR26)	*6,000.00*	—
PR51	$9 yel. Minerva		
	(PR27)	*11,000.00*	—
PR52	$12 bl. grn. Vesta		
	(PR28)	*10,000.00*	—
PR53	$24 dark gray violet		
	"Peace" (PR29)	—	—
PR54	$36 brown rose		
	"Commerce" (PR30)	—	—
PR55	$48 red brown Hebe		
	(PR78)	—	—
PR56	$60 violet Indian		
	Maiden (PR79)	—	—

All values of this issue Nos. PR33 to PR56 exist imperforate but were not regularly issued.

1879-1895

Issue of 1879, Printed by the American Bank Note Co., Soft, Porous Paper

PR57-PR62: Statue of Freedom (PR15)

		Un	U
PR57	2¢ black	4.00	3.50
PR58	3¢ black	5.00	4.50
PR59	4¢ black	5.00	4.50
PR60	6¢ black	10.50	9.00
PR61	8¢ black	10.50	9.00
PR62	10¢ black	10.50	9.00

PR63-PR70: "Justice" (PR18)

PR63	12¢ red	30.00	20.00
PR64	24¢ red	30.00	18.50
PR65	36¢ red	110.00	85.00
PR66	48¢ red	80.00	50.00
PR67	60¢ red	60.00	50.00
PR68	72¢ red	145.00	90.00
PR69	84¢ red	110.00	75.00
PR70	96¢ red	80.00	55.00
PR71	$1.92 pale brown		
	Ceres (PR24)	65.00	50.00
PR72	$3 red vermilion		
	"Victory" (PR25)	65.00	50.00
PR73	$6 blue Clio (PR26)	110.00	75.00
PR74	$9 org. Minerva (PR27)	70.00	50.00
PR75	$12 yellow green		
	Vesta (PR28)	110.00	75.00
PR76	$24 dark violet		
	"Peace" (PR29)	145.00	100.00
PR77	$36 Indian red		
	"Commerce" (PR30)	185.00	120.00
PR78	$48 Hebe	250.00	150.00
PR79	$60 Indian Maiden	275.00	150.00

All values of the 1879 issue except Nos. PR63 to PR66 and PR68 to PR70 exist imperforate but were not regularly issued.

**Issue of 1883
Special Printing**

PR80	2¢ intense black Statue		
	of Freedom (PR15)	130.00	—

Regular Issue of 1885

PR81	1¢ black Statue of		
	Freedom (PR15)	5.50	3.50

PR82-PR89: "Justice" (PR18)

		Un	U
PR82	12¢ carmine	17.50	8.50
PR83	24¢ carmine	20.00	12.50
PR84	36¢ carmine	30.00	15.00
PR85	48¢ carmine	40.00	25.00
PR86	60¢ carmine	60.00	35.00
PR87	72¢ carmine	70.00	40.00
PR88	84¢ carmine	140.00	85.00
PR89	96¢ carmine	100.00	70.00

All values of the 1885 issue exist imperforate but were not regularly issued.

**Issue of 1894
Printed by the Bureau of Engraving and Printing, Soft Wove Paper**

PR90-PR94: Statue of Freedom (PR90)

PR90	1¢ Statue of Freedom	30.00	
PR91	2¢ intense black	30.00	—
PR92	4¢ intense black	40.00	—
PR93	6¢ intense black	750.00	—
PR94	10¢ intense black	75.00	—

PR95-PR99: "Justice" (PR18)

PR95	12¢ pink	350.00	—
PR96	24¢ pink	325.00	—
PR97	36¢ pink	*2,200.00*	—
PR98	60¢ pink	*2,200.00*	—
PR99	96¢ pink	*3,500.00*	—
PR100	$3 sclt. "Victory" (PR25)	*4,500.00*	—
PR101	$6 pl. blue Clio (PR26)	*5,250.00*	*3,000.00*

**Issue of 1895, Unwmkd.
PR102-PR105: Statue of Freedom (PR116)**

PR102	1¢ black	17.50	5.00
PR103	2¢ black	18.50	5.00
PR104	5¢ black	25.00	8.50
PR105	10¢ black	55.00	25.00
PR106	25¢ cme "Justice" (PR118)	75.00	25.00
PR107	50¢ cme. "Justice" (PR119)	175.00	75.00
PR108	$2 sclt. "Victory" (PR120)	200.00	45.00
PR109	$5 ultra Clio (PR121)	325.00	135.00

PR15

PR18

PR24

PR25

PR26

PR27

PR28

PR29

PR30

PR78

PR79

PR90

PR116

PR118

PR119

PR120

PR121

PR122

PR123

PR124

PR125

Q1   Q2   Q3

Q4   Q5   Q6

Q7   Q8   Q9

Q10   Q11   Q12

QE1   QE2   QE3

QE4

	Un	U
PR110	$10 green Vesta		
	(PR122)	300.00	150.00
PR111	$20 slate "Peace"		
	(PR123)	600.00	275.00
PR112	$50 dull rose		
	"Commerce" (PR124)	625.00	275.00
PR113	$100 purple Indian		
	Maiden (PR125)	700.00	325.00

Issue of 1895-97
Wmkd. (191), Yellowish Gum

PR114-PR117: Statue of Freedom (PR116)

		Un	U
PR114	1¢ black	2.50	2.00
PR115	2¢ black	2.50	1.50
PR116	5¢ black	4.00	3.00
PR117	10¢ black	2.50	2.00
PR118	25¢ "Justice"	4.00	3.75
PR119	50¢ "Justice"	5.00	3.50
PR120	$2 "Victory"	7.50	8.50
PR121	$5 Clio	17.50	20.00
PR122	$10 Vesta	15.00	25.00
PR123	$20 "Peace"	16.00	27.50
PR124	$50 "Commerce"	17.50	27.50
PR125	$100 Indian Maiden	20.00	35.00

In 1899, the Government sold 26,989 sets of these stamps, but, as the stock of the high values was not sufficient to make up the required number, the $5, $10, $20, $50 and $100 were reprinted. These are virtually indistinguishable from earlier printings.

Parcel Post Stamps

Issued for the prepayment of postage on parcel post packages only.

Beginning July 1, 1913, these stamps were valid for all postal purposes.

		Un	U
	Issue of 1912-13, Perf. 12		
Q1	1¢ Post Office Clerk	4.00	.90
Q2	2¢ City Carrier	4.50	.70
Q3	3¢ Railway Postal Clerk	10.00	5.00
Q4	4¢ Rural Carrier	27.50	2.00
Q5	5¢ Mail Train	27.50	1.25
Q6	10¢ Steamship and		
	Mail Tender	40.00	1.75
Q7	15¢ Automobile		
	Service	65.00	9.00
Q8	20¢ Airplane Carrying		
	Mail	140.00	17.50
Q9	25¢ Manufacturing	75.00	4.50
Q10	50¢ Dairying	225.00	35.00
Q11	75¢ Harvesting	75.00	25.00
Q12	$1 Fruit Growing	425.00	20.00

Special Handling Stamps

For use on parcel post packages to secure the same expeditious handling accorded to first class mail matter.

		Un	U
	Issue of 1925-29, Design of QE3, Perf. 11		
QE1	10¢ Special Handling	1.50	.90
QE2	15¢ Special Handling	1.65	.90
QE3	20¢ Special Handling	2.00	1.75
QE4	25¢ Special Handling	20.00	7.50

With First Day Cancellations

The Postal Service offers Souvenir Pages for new stamps. The series began with a page for the Yellowstone Park Centennial stamp issued March 1, 1972. The pages feature one or more stamps tied by the first day cancel, technical data and information on the subject of the issue. More than just collectors' items, Souvenir Pages make wonderful show and conversation pieces. Souvenir Pages are issued in limited editions.

1972

1	Yellowstone Park,	$150.00
1a	Same with Parsons Wmk.	$175.00
1A	Family Planning (sold only with FD cancellation by USPS at INTERPEX '72 show in NYC),	$500.00
2	Cape Hatteras,	$150.00
2a	Same with Parsons Wmk.	$175.00
3	Fiorello La Guardia,	$150.00
3a	Same with Parsons Wmk.	$200.00
4	City of Refuge,	$150.00
4a	Same with Parsons Wmk.	$175.00
5	Wolf Trap Farm,	$50.00
5a	Wolf Trap Farm with '72 Eagle Wmk.,	$50.00
5b	Wolf Trap Farm with Star and Parsons Wmk.	$60.00
6	Colonial Craftsman, (4),	$40.00
7	Mount McKinley,	$50.00
8	Olympic Games, (4),	$25.00
9	Parent Teachers Association,	$15.00
10	Wildlife Conservation, (4),	$15.00
11	Mail Order,	$15.00
12	Osteopathic Medicine,	$15.00
13	Tom Sawyer,	$15.00
14	Benjamin Franklin,	$15.00
15	Christmas, (2),	$20.00
16	Pharmacy,	$12.00
17	Stamp Collecting,	$12.00

1973

18	Eugene O'Neill Coil,	$25.00
18a	Eugene O'Neil Coil, Bottom line ends 1973 0-509-757 (Wmk. '73)	$500.00
19	Love,	$20.00
20	Pamphleteer,	$12.00
21	George Gershwin,	$12.00
22	Posting Broadside,	$10.00
23	Copernicus,	$10.00
24	Postal Service Employees, (10),	$12.00
25	Harry S. Truman,	$10.00

26	Postrider,	$10.00
27	Giannini,	$10.00
28	Boston Tea Party, (4),	$12.00
29	Progress in Electronics, (4),	$12.00
30	Robinson Jeffers,	$6.00
31	Lyndon B. Johnson,	$6.00
32	Henry O. Tanner,	$6.00
33	Willa Cather,	$6.00
34	Colonial Drummer,	$8.00
35	Angus Cattle,	$6.00
36	Christmas, (2),	$12.00
37	13¢ Airmail sheet stamp,	$5.00
38	10¢ Crossed Flags,	$5.00
39	Jefferson Memorial,	$5.00
40	13¢ Airmail Coil,	$5.00

1974

41	Mount Rushmore,	$5.00
41a	Mount Rushmore with Wmk.	$40.00
42	ZIP Code,	$5.00
42a	ZIP Code with error date,	$600.00
43	Statue of Liberty,	$5.00
43a	Statue of Liberty with Wmk.	$50.00
44	Elizabeth Blackwell,	$5.00
45	Veterans of Foreign Wars,	$5.00
46	Robert Frost,	$5.00
47	EXPO '74,	$5.00
48	Horse Racing,	$5.00
49	Skylab with Wmk.,	$8.00
49a	Skylab without Wmk.	$30.00
50	Universal Postal Union, (8),	$10.00
51	Mineral Heritage, (4),	$8.00
52	Fort Harrod,	$5.00
53	Continental Congress, (4),	$8.00
54	Chautauqua,	$5.00
55	Kansas Wheat,	$5.00
56	Energy Conservation,	$5.00
57	6.3¢ Bulk Rate, (2),	$5.00
58	Sleepy Hollow,	$5.00
59	Retarded Children,	$5.00
60	Christmas, (3),	$9.00

1975

61	Benjamin West,	$5.00
62	Pioneer,	$8.00
63	Collective Bargaining,	$5.00

64	Sybil Ludington,	$5.00
65	Salem Poor,	$5.00
66	Haym Salomon,	$5.00
67	Peter Francisco,	$5.00
68	Mariner,	$8.00
69	Lexington & Concord,	$5.00
70	Paul Laurence Dunbar,	$5.00
71	D.W. Griffith,	$5.00
72	Bunker Hill,	$5.00
73	Military Uniforms, (4),	$9.00
74	Apollo Soyuz, (2),	$9.00
75	International Women's Year,	$5.00
76	Postal Bicentennial, (4),	$8.00
77	World Peace Through Law,	$5.00
78	Banking & Commerce, (2),	$5.00
79	Christmas, (2),	$6.00
80	Francis Parkman,	$4.00
81	Freedom of the Press,	$4.00
82	Old North Church,	$4.00
83	Flag & Independence Hall,	$4.00
84	Freedom to Assemble,	$4.00
85	Liberty Bell Coil,	$4.00
86	American Eagle & Shield,	$4.00

1976

87	Spirit of '76, (3),	$7.00
87a	Spirit of '76 with error cancellation,	$600.00
88	25¢ & 31¢ Airmails, (2),	$5.00
89	Interphil,	$5.00
90	Fifty State Flag Series,	$60.00
91	Freedom to Assemble Coil,	$4.00
92	Telephone Centennial,	$4.00
93	Commercial Aviation,	$4.00
94	Chemistry,	$4.00
95	7.9¢ Bulk Rate,	$4.00
96	Benjamin Franklin,	$4.00
97	Bicentennial SS,	$60.00
98	Declaration of Independence, (4),	$8.00
99	Olympics, (4),	$9.00
100	Clara Maass,	$4.00
101	Adolph S. Ochs,	$4.00
102	Christmas, (3),	$6.00
103	7.7¢ Bulk Rate,	$4.00

1977

104 Washington at Princeton, $4.00
105 $1 Vending Machine Booklet Pane, perf. 10, $30.00
106 Sound Recording, $4.00
107 Pueblo Art, (4), $5.00
108 Lindbergh Flight, $5.00
109 Colorado Centennial, $5.00
110 Butterflies, (4), $5.00
111 Lafayette, $4.00
112 Skilled Hands, (4), $5.00
113 Peace Bridge, $4.00
114 Herkimer at Oriskany, $4.00
115 Alta, California, $4.00
116 Articles of Confederation, $4.00
117 Talking Pictures, $4.00
118 Surrender at Saratoga, $4.00
119 Energy, (2), $4.00
120 Christmas Mailbox, $4.00
121 Christmas, Valley Forge, $4.00
122 Petition for Redress Coil, (2), $4.00
123 Petition for Redress sheet stamp, $4.00
124 1¢, 2¢, 3¢, 4¢ Americana, $4.00

1978

125 Carl Sandburg, $4.00
126 Indian Head Penny, $4.00
127 Captain Cook, Anchorage, $5.00
128 Captain Cook, Honolulu, $5.00
129 Harriet Tubman, $4.00
130 American Quilts, (4), $5.00
131 16¢ Statue of Liberty, $4.00
132 Sandy Hook Lighthouse, $4.00
133 American Dance, (4), $5.00
134 French Alliance, $4.00

135 Dr. Papanicolaou, $4.00
136 "A" Stamp, (2), $4.00
137 Jimmie Rodgers, $4.00
138 CAPEX '78, (SS), $8.00
139 Oliver Wendell Holmes, $4.00
140 Photography, $4.00
141 Fort McHenry Flag, (2), $4.00
142 George M. Cohan, $4.00
143 Rose Booklet single, $4.00
144 8.4¢ Bulk Rate, $4.00
145 Viking Missions, $5.00
146 Remote Outpost, $4.00
147 American Owls, (4), $5.00
148 Wright Brothers, (2), $5.00
149 American Trees, $5.00
150 Hobby Horse, $4.00
151 Andrea della Robbia, $4.00
152 $2 Kerosene Lamp, $12.00

1979

153 Robert F. Kennedy, $4.00
154 Martin Luther King, Jr., $4.00
155 International Year of the Child, $4.00
156 John Steinbeck, $4.00
157 Albert Einstein, $4.00
158 Octave Chanute, (2), $5.00
159 Pennsylvania Toleware, (4), $5.00
160 American Architecture, (4), $5.00
161 Endangered Flora, (4), $5.00
162 Seeing Eye Dogs, $4.00
163 $1 Americana, $10.00
164 Special Olympics, $4.00
165 $5 Americana, $30.00
166 30¢ Americana, $6.00
167 Olympics, $5.00
168 50¢ Americana, $6.00
169 John Paul Jones, $4.00
170 15¢ Olympic, (4), $8.00
171 Gerard David Madonna, $4.00

172 Santa Claus, $4.00
173 3.1¢ Coil, $5.00
174 31¢ Olympic, $8.00
175 Will Rogers, $4.00
176 Vietnam Veterans, $4.00
177 Wiley Post, $5.00

1980

178 W. C. Fields, $4.00
179 Winter Olympics, (4), $8.00
180 Windmills Booklet, $8.00
181 Benjamin Banneker, $3.50
182 Letter Writing, (6), $5.00
183 1¢ Quill Pen Coil, $3.50
184 Frances Perkins, $3.50
185 Dolley Madison, $3.50
186 Emily Bissell, $3.50
187 3.5¢ Non-Profit Bulk Rate Coil, $5.00
188 Helen Keller/ Anne Sullivan, $3.50
189 Veterans Administration, $3.50
190 General Bernardo de Galvez, $3.50
191 Coral Reefs, (4), $4.50
192 Organized Labor, $3.50
193 Edith Wharton, $3.50
194 American Education, $3.50
195 Northwest Indian Masks, (4), $4.50
196 Architecture, (4), $4.50
197 Phillip Mazzei, $4.00
198 Stained Glass Window, $4.00
199 Antique Toys, $4.00
200 19¢ Sequoyah, $3.50
201 28¢ Scott A/M, $3.50
202 35¢ Curtiss A/M, $3.50

1981

203 Everett Dirksen, $3.50
204 Whitney M. Young, $3.50
205 "B" Sheet & Coil, $3.50
206 "B" Booklet Pane, $4.50
207 12¢ Americana S & C, $3.50
208 Flowers Block, {4), $3.50
209 18¢ Flag Sheet & Coil, $3.50
210 18¢ Flag Booklet Pane, $4.50
211 American Red Cross, $3.50
212 George Mason, $3.50
213 Savings & Loan, $3.50
214 Animals Booklet Pane, $6.00
215 18¢ Surrey Coil, $3.50
216 Space Achievement, (8), $10.00
217 17¢ Rachel Carson, $3.50
218 35¢ Dr. Charles Drew, $3.50
219 Professional Management, $3.50
220 17¢ Electric Car Coil, $3.50
221 Wildlife Habitat, (4), $4.00
222 International Year Disabled, $3.50
223 Edna St. Vincent Millay, $3.50
224 Alcoholism, $3.50
225 Architecture, (4), $4.00
226 Zaharis, $3.50
227 Bobby Jones, $3.50
228 Frederic Remington, $3.50
229 "C" Sheet/Coil, $3.50
230 "C" Booklet, $5.00

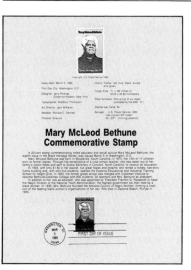

Mary McLeod Bethune Commemorative Stamp

A 22-cent stamp commemorating noted educator and social activist Mary McLeod Bethune, the eighth issue in the Black Heritage Series, was issued March 5 in Washington, D.C. Mary McLeod Bethune was born in Mayesville, South Carolina, in 1875, the 15th of 17 children born to former slaves. Through the beneficence of a rural school teacher, she was taken out of her cotton-picking environment and offered a chance to become educated in a missionary school. In 1904, with only $1.50 in her pocket, but great hopes and dreams, she rented a rickety, two-story frame building and, with only five students, opened the Daytona Educational and Industrial Training School for Negro Girls. In 1923, the former grade school was merged with Cookman Institute to become Bethune-Cookman College with 600 students, 32 teachers and Mrs. Bethune as president. In addition to her role as educator, she was appointed by President Franklin D. Roosevelt to head the Negro Division of the National Youth Administration, the highest government job then held by a black woman. In 1935, Mrs. Bethune founded the National Council of Negro Women, forming a coalition of the leading black women's organizations of her day. She died in Daytona Beach, Florida in 1955.

WASHINGTON D.C. MAR 5 1985 20004 FIRST DAY OF ISSUE

231	18¢/20¢ Hoban, (2),	$3.50
232	Yorktown, (2),	$3.50
233	Teddybear-Christmas,	$3.50
234	Art-Christmas '81,	$3.50
235	John Hanson,	$3.50
236	20¢ Pumper, Coil,	$4.00
237	Desert Plant, (4),	$4.00
238	9.3¢ Wagon, (3),	$3.50
239	20¢ Reg + Coil,	$3.50
240	20¢ Booklet,	$4.50

1982

241	Sheep Booklet,	$5.00
242	20¢ Ralph Bunche,	$3.00
243	13¢ Crazy Horse,	$3.00
244	37¢ Millikan,	$3.00
245	Roosevelt, FD.,	$3.00
246	20¢ LOVE,	$3.00
247	5.9¢ Bicycle, (4),	$3.00
248	20¢ Washington,	$3.00
249	10.9¢ Cab Coil,	$3.00
250	Birds & Flowers,	$40.00
250a	Birds & Flowers with all 10½ x 11 Perfs,	$70.00
250b	Birds & Flowers with all 11 x 11 Perfs,	$75.00
251	Netherlands,	$3.00
252	Library of Congress,	$3.00
253	20¢ Consumer Coil,	$3.00
254	World's Fair, (4),	$3.50
255	Horatio Alger,	$3.00
256	2¢ Locomotive Coil,	$3.00
257	20¢ Aging,	$3.00
258	20¢ Barrymores,	$3.00
259	Mary Walker,	$3.00
260	Peace Garden,	$3.00
261	America's Libraries,	$3.00
262	Jackie Robinson,	$4.00
263	Stagecoach,	$3.00
264	Touro Synagogue,	$3.00
265	Wolf Trap,	$3.00
266	Architecture, (4),	$3.50
267	Francis of Assisi,	$3.00
268	Ponce de Leon,	$3.00
269	Snow Scenes, (4),	$4.00
270	Art-Christmas,	$3.00
271	Kitten & Puppy,	$3.00
272	Igor Stravinsky,	$3.00

1983

273	Officials (7 stamps-3 pgs),	$30.00
274	Science,	$2.50
275	Sleigh Coil,	$2.50
276	Sweden,	$2.50
277	Handcar Coil,	$2.50
278	Ballooning, (4),	$4.00
279	Civilian Conservation Corps,	$2.50
280	40¢ Olympics, (4),	$5.00
281	Priestley,	$2.50
282	Voluntarism,	$2.50
283	German Immigrants,	$2.50
284	Physical Fitness,	$2.50
285	Brooklyn Bridge,	$2.50
286	Tennessee Valley Authority,	$2.50
287	Carl Schurz,	$2.50
288	Medal of Honor,	$2.50
289	Scott Joplin,	$2.50
290	Thomas H. Gallaudet,	$2.50
291	28¢ Olympics, (4),	$4.00
292	Pearl S. Buck,	$2.50
293	Babe Ruth,	$4.00

294	Nathaniel Hawthorne,	$2.50
295	Henry Clay,	$2.50
296	13¢ Olympics, (4),	$4.00
297	$9.35 Eagle,	$30.00
297A	$9.35 Eagle Booklet Pane of 3,	$80.00
298	Omnibus,	$2.50
299	Treaty of Paris,	$2.50
300	Civil Service,	$2.50
301	Metropolitan Opera,	$2.50
302	Inventors, (4),	$3.50
303	Dorothea Dix,	$2.50
304	Streetcars, (4),	$3.50
305	Motorcycle Coil,	$2.50
306	Contemporary Christmas,	$2.50
307	Art Masterpiece Christmas,	$2.50
308	35¢ Olympic, (4),	$4.50
309	Martin Luther,	$2.50
310	Flag Booklet Pane,	$5.00

1984

311	Alaska,	$2.50
312	Winter Olympics, (4),	$4.00
313	FDIC,	$2.50
314	Truman,	$2.50
315	LOVE,	$2.50
316	Carter G. Woodson,	$2.50
317	Railroad Caboose Coil,	$2.50
318	Soil & Water Conservation,	$2.50
319	Credit Union,	$2.50
320	Lillian Gilbreth,	$2.50
321	Orchids, (4),	$4.00
322	Hawaii,	$2.50
323	Baby Buggy Coil,	$2.50
324	National Archives,	$2.50
325	Summer Olympics, (4),	$4.00
326	New Orleans World's Fair,	$2.50
327	Health Research,	$2.50
328	Douglas Fairbanks,	$2.50
329	Jim Thorpe,	$3.50
330	Richard Russell,	$2.50
331	John McCormack,	$2.50
332	St. Lawrence Seaway,	$2.50
333	Duck Stamp 50th Anniversary,	$3.00
334	Roanoke Voyages,	$2.50
335	Herman Melville,	$2.50
336	Horace Moses,	$2.50
337	Smokey Bear,	$3.00
338	Roberto Clemente,	$3.50
339	Dr. Frank Laubach,	$2.50
340	Dogs, (4),	$3.50
341	Crime Prevention,	$2.50
342	Family Unity,	$2.50
343	Eleanor Roosevelt,	$2.50
344	Nation of Readers,	$2.50
345	Santa Claus,	$2.50
346	Madonna & Child,	$2.50
347	Hispanic Americans,	$2.50
348	Vietnam Veterans Memorial,	$2.50

1985*

349	Jerome Kern,	$2.50
350	Abraham Baldwin,	$2.50
351	D sheet & coil pair,	$2.50
352	D booklet pane, (10),	$5.00

353	Non. dem. Penalty Mail Sheet & coil pair,	$2.50
354	Alden Partridge,	$2.50
355	Alfred Verville airmail,	$2.50
356	Lawrence & Elmer Sperry,	$2.50
357	Transpacific airmail,	$2.50
358	Chester Nimitz,	$2.50
359	Mary McLeod Bethune,	$2.50
360	Grenville Clark,	$2.50
361	Sinclair Lewis,	$2.50
362	Duck Decoys, (4),	$3.00
363	Iceboat coil pair,	$2.50
364	Winter Special Olympics,	$2.50
365	Flag over Capital, Sheet & coil pair,	$2.50
366	Booklet pane, (5),	$3.00
367	Stanley Steamer coil pair,	$2.50
368	Seashells booklet pane, (10),	$5.00
369	Love,	$2.50
370	Oil Wagon coil strip,	$2.50
371	Pushcart coil pair,	$2.50
372	John J. Audubon,	$2.50
373	Express Mail,	$25.00
373A	Eagle Booklet pane,	$70.00
374	Tricycle coil strip,	$2.50
375	Rural Electrification Administration,	$2.50
376	14¢ and 22¢ Penalty Mail sheet and coil pair,	$2.50
377	Ameripex '86,	$2.50
378	Sylvanus Thayer,	$2.50
379	School bus coil strip,	$2.50
380	Stutz Bearcat coil pair,	$2.50
381	Abigail Adams,	$2.50
382	Ambulance coil strip,	$2.50
383	Buckboard coil strip,	$2.50
384	Henry Knox,	$2.50
385	Korean War Veterans,	$2.50
386	George Washington coil,	$2.50
387	Social Security Act,	$2.50
388	Father Junipero Serra airmail,	$2.50
389	World War I Veterans,	$2.50
390	Walter Lippmann,	$2.50
391	Horses, (4),	$3.00
392	International Youth Year, (4),	$3.00
393	Holiday Postcard,	$2.50
394	Christmas Contemporary,	$2.50
395	Madonna & Child,	$2.50
396	Presort Zip + 4,	$2.50
397	Frederic Auguste Bartholdi,	$2.50
398	Help End Hunger,	$2.50
399	Public Education,	$2.50

Prices are courtesy of Charles D. Simmons, a stamp dealer specializing in Souvenir Pages.

*Numbers and pricing for 1985 issues subject to change.

The Postal Service offers American Commemorative Panels for each new commemorative stamp and special Christmas stamp issued. The series first began September 20, 1972, with the issuance of the Wildlife Commemorative Panel and will total over 250 panels by the end of 1985. The panels feature stamps in mint condition complemented by reproductions of steel line engravings and stories behind the commemorated subject.

1972

1	Wildlife,	$17.50
2	Mail Order,	$17.50
3	Osteopathic Medicine,	$17.50
4	Tom Sawyer,	$17.50
5	Pharmacy,	$17.50
6	Christmas 1972,	$22.00
7	'Twas the Night Before Christmas,	$22.00
8	Stamp Collecting,	$17.50

1973

9	Love,	$17.50
10	Pamphleteers,	$22.00
11	George Gershwin,	$22.00
12	Posting Broadside,	$22.00
13	Copernicus,	$17.50
14	Postal People,	$22.00
15	Harry S. Truman,	$23.50
16	Post Rider,	$29.00
17	Boston Tea Party,	$57.50
18	Electronics,	$17.50
19	Robinson Jeffers,	$17.50
20	Lyndon B. Johnson,	$23.50
21	Henry O. Tanner,	$17.50
22	Willa Cather,	$17.50
23	Drummer,	$29.00
24	Angus Cattle,	$17.50
25	Christmas 1973,	$22.00
26	Christmas Needlepoint,	$22.00

1974

27	Veterans of Foreign Wars,	$17.50
28	Robert Frost,	$17.50
29	EXPO '74,	$22.00
30	Horse Racing,	$22.00
31	Skylab,	$22.00
32	Universal Postal Union,	$23.50
33	Mineral Heritage,	$17.50
34	Fort Harrod,	$17.50
35	Continental Congress,	$17.50
36	Chautauqua,	$17.50
37	Kansas Wheat,	$17.50
38	Energy Conservation,	$17.50
39	Sleepy Hollow,	$17.50
40	Retarded Children,	$17.50
41	Christmas "The Road-Winter",	$22.00
42	Christmas Angel Altarpiece,	$22.00

1975

43	Benjamin West,	$17.50
44	Pioneer,	$22.00
45	Collective Bargaining,	$17.50
46	Contributors to the Cause,	$22.00
47	Mariner,	$22.00
48	Lexington & Concord,	$22.00
49	Paul Laurence Dunbar,	$17.50
50	D. W. Griffith,	$17.50
51	Bunker Hill,	$22.00
52	Military Services,	$22.00
53	Apollo Soyuz,	$22.00

54	World Peace Through Law,	$17.50
55	International Women's Year,	$17.50
56	Postal Bicentennial,	$22.00
57	Banking and Commerce,	$17.50
58	Early Christmas Card,	$22.00
59	Christmas Madonna,	$22.00

1976

60	Spirit of '76,	$22.00
61	Interphil 76,	$22.00
62	State Flags,	$36.00
63	Telephone, Centennial,	$17.50
64	Commercial Aviation,	$17.50
65	Chemistry,	$17.50
66	Benjamin Franklin,	$22.00
67	Declaration of Independence,	$22.00
68	Olympics,	$22.00
69	Clara Maass,	$22.00
70	Adolph S. Ochs,	$17.50
71	Currier Winter Pastime,	$22.00
72	Copley Nativity,	$22.00

1977

73	Washington at Princeton,	$26.00
74	Sound Recording,	$32.50
75	Pueblo Art,	$150.00
76	Lindbergh Flight,	$150.00
77	Colorado Centennial,	$32.50
78	Butterflies,	$36.00
79	Lafayette,	$32.50
80	Skilled Hands,	$32.50
81	Peace Bridge,	$32.50
82	Herkimer at Oriskany,	$32.50

83	Alta, California,	$32.50
84	Articles of Confederation,	$32.50
85	Talking Pictures,	$32.50
86	Surrender at Saratoga,	$32.50
87	Energy Conservation & Development,	$32.50
88	Christmas, Washington at Valley Forge,	$36.00
89	Christmas, Rural Mailbox,	$36.00

1978

90	Carl Sandburg,	$22.00
91	Captain Cook,	$36.00
92	Harriet Tubman,	$22.00
93	American Quilts,	$32.50
94	American Dance,	$22.00
95	French Alliance,	$27.50
96	Dr. Papanicolaou,	$22.00
97	Jimmie Rodgers,	$22.00
98	Photography,	$22.00
99	George M. Cohan,	$22.00
100	Viking Missions,	$36.00
101	American Owls,	$32.50
102	American Trees,	$32.50
103	Madonna and Child,	$22.00
104	Christmas Hobby Horse,	$22.00

1979

105	Robert F. Kennedy,	$22.00
106	Martin Luther King, Jr.	$22.00
107	Year of the Child,	$22.00
108	John Steinbeck,	$22.00
109	Albert Einstein,	$29.00
110	Pennsylvania Toleware,	$22.00
111	American Architecture,	$22.00
112	Endangered Flora,	$22.00
113	Seeing Eye Dogs,	$22.00

114	Special Olympics,	$22.00
115	John Paul Jones,	$36.00
116	15 ¢ Olympic Games,	$29.00
117	Virgin and Child,	$22.00
118	Santa Claus,	$22.00
119	Will Rogers,	$22.00
120	Vietnam Veterans,	$36.00
121	10 ¢, 31 ¢ Olympic Games,	$29.00

1980

122	W.C. Fields,	$22.00
123	Winter Olympics,	$29.00
124	Benjamin Banneker,	$22.00
125	Frances Perkins,	$22.00
126	Emily Bissell,	$22.00
127	Helen Keller/ Anne Sullivan,	$22.00
128	Veterans Administration,	$22.00
129	General Bernardo de Galvez,	$22.00
130	Coral Reefs,	$22.00
131	Organized Labor,	$22.00
132	Edith Wharton,	$22.00
133	American Education,	$22.00
134	Northwest Indian Masks,	$27.50
135	American Architecture,	$22.00
136	Christmas Stained Glass Window,	$22.00
137	Christmas Antique Toys,	$22.00

1981

138	Everett Dirksen,	$17.50
139	Whitney Moore Young,	$17.50
140	American Flowers,	$22.00
141	American Red Cross,	$17.50
142	Savings & Loan,	$17.50
143	Space Achievement,	$22.00

* 1985 issues subject to change.

Prices are courtesy of Frank Riolo, a stamp dealer specializing in Commemorative Panels.

These cards were issued as souvenirs of the philatelic gatherings at which they were distributed by the United States Postal Service, its predecessor the United States Post Office Department, or the Bureau of Engraving and Printing. They were not valid for postage.

The forerunner of the souvenir cards is the 1938 Philatelic Truck souvenir sheet which the Post Office Department issued and distributed in various cities visited by the Philatelic Truck. It shows the White House, printed in blue on white paper. Issued with and without gum. Price with gum, $80, without gum, $10.

Values are for uncancelled cards; cards bearing U.S.P.S. cancels are valued approximately $1 higher.

United States Post Office
& United States Postal Service

1960 Barcelona, 1st International Philatelic Congress
Mar. 26-Ar- -

... ...International Philatelic Exhibition, Nov. ...o City. Card of 1. No. 292, inscribed in Spanish. 6.00

1970 PHILYMPIA, London International Stamp Exhibition, Sept. 18-26. Card of 3. Nos. 548-550. 4.50

1971 EXFILIMA 71, 3rd Inter-American Philatelic Exhibition, Nov. 6-14., Lima, Peru. Card of 3. Nos. 1111 and 1126, Peru No. 360. Card inscribed in Spanish. 3.50

1972 BELGICA 72, Brussels International Philatelic Exhibition, June 24-July 9, Brussels, Belgium Card of 3 Nos. 914, 1026 and 1104. Card inscribed in Flemish and French. 3.50
OLYMPIA PHILATELIC MÜNCHEN 72, Aug. 18-Sept. 10, Munich, Germany. Card of 4. Nos. 1460-1462 and C85. Card inscribed in German. 3.75
EXFILBRA 72, 4th Inter-American Philatelic Exhibition, Aug. 26-Sept. 2, Rio de Janeiro, Brazil. Card of 3. No. C14, Brazil Nos. C18-C19. Card inscribed in Portuguese. 3.50
NATIONAL POSTAL FORUM VI, Aug. 28-30, Washington, D.C. Card of 4. No. 1396. 3.50

1973 IBRA 73 Internationale Briefmarken Ausstellung, May 11-20, Munich, Germany. With one No. C13. 4.00
APEX 73, International Airmail Exhibition, July 4-7, Manchester, England. Card of 3. Newfoundland No. C4, U.S. No. C3a and Honduras No. C12. 3.50
POLSKA 73, Swiatowa Wystawe Filatelistyczna, Aug. 19-Sept. 2, Poznan, Poland. Card of 3. No. 1488 and Poland Nos. 1944-1945. Card inscribed in Polish. 4.00
POSTAL PEOPLE CARD, Card of 10 (#1489-1498) distributed to Postal Service employees. Not available to public. 14x11″. $75.00 (est.)

1974 HOBBY, The Hobby Industry Association of America Convention and Trade Show, February 3-6,

...1337. Card inscribed in 4 languages. 4.00
STOCKHOLMIA 74, International frimarksustailning, September 21-29, Stockholm, Sweden. Card of 3 No. 836, Sweden Nos. 300 and 765. Card inscribed in Swedish. 4.50
EXFILMEX 74 UPU, Philatelic Exposition Inter-Americana, October 26-November 3, Mexico City, Mexico. 2. No. 1157 and Mexico No. 910. Card inscribed in Spanish and English. 4.50

1975 ESPANA 75, World Stamp Exhibition, Apr. 4-13, Madrid, Spain. Card of 3 Nos. 233, 1271 and Spain No. 1312. Card inscribed in Spanish. 4.00
ARPHILA 75, June 6-16, Paris, France. Card of 3 Nos. 1187, 1207 and France No. 1117. Card inscribed in French. 3.50

1976 WERABA 76, Third International Space Stamp Exhibition, April 1-4, Zurich, Switzerland. Card of 2. Nos. 1434 and 1435 se-tenant. 4.00
BICENTENNIAL EXPOSITION on Science and Technology, May 30-Sept. 6, Kennedy Space Center, Fla. Card of 1. No. C76. 5.50
COLORADO STATEHOOD CENTENNIAL, August 1, Card of 3. Nos. 743, 288 and 1670. 5.00
HAFNIA 76, International Stamp Exhibition, Aug. 20-29, Copenhagen, Denmark. Card of 2. No. 5 and Denmark No. 2. Card inscribed in Danish and English. 5.00
ITALIA 76, International Philatelic Exhibition, Oct. 14-24, Milan, Italy. Card of 3. No. 1168 and Italy Nos. 578 and 601. Card inscribed in Italian. 4.00
NORDPOSTA 76, North German Stamp Exhibition, Oct. 30-31, Hamburg, Germany. Card of 3. No. 689 and Germany Nos. B366 and B417. Card inscribed in German. 4.00

1977 AMPHILEX 77, International Philatelic Exhibition, May 26-June 5, Amsterdam, Netherlands. Card of 3. No. 1027 and Netherlands Nos. 41 and 294. Card inscribed in Dutch. 4.50

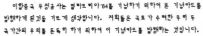

미합중국 우정공사는 필라코리아 '84를 기념하기 위하여 본 기념카드를 발행하게 된 것을 기쁘게 생각합니다. 저희들은 국토가 수려한 우리 두 국가간의 우의를 돈독히 하기 위하여 이 기념카드를 발행하는 것입니다.

지난 100 년 동안 대한민국과 미합중국은 많은 접포한 자연경관을 담은 우표를 발행했습니다. 저희들은 그러한 우표중에서 아름다운 국립공원의 경관을 묘사한 2종류의 우표를 본 카드에 담기로 선정했습니다.

이 카드에 인쇄된 한국우표는 1975년에 발행된 우표로서 '설악산' 국립공원의 장엄한 험산준령을 담은 것이어, 1934년에 발행된 미국우표는 대한국(그랜드 캐년) 국립공원의 절경을 묘사한 것입니다.

W.F.Bolger

William F. Bolger
Postmaster General

OLYMPHILEX '85

Lausanne, Suisse
du 18 au 24 mars 1985

Le Service postal des Etats-Unis a le plaisir d'émettre cette carte souvenir en l'honneur d'OLYMPHILEX '85, à Lausanne, Suisse.

L'attention de la communauté mondiale tout entière est fixée sur Lausanne, siège du Comité international olympique. Pour l'année olympique 1984 qui vient de s'écouler, les Etats-Unis ont émis les timbres illustrés, notamment le timbre de 40 cents reproduisant un gymnaste, l'un des 24 timbres commémorant les Jeux. La Suisse, quant à elle, a rendu hommage à l'importance olympique de Lausanne avec un timbre de 80 centimes.

Paul N. Carlin

Paul N. Carlin
Postmaster General

SAN MARINO 77, International Philatelic Exhibition, Aug. 28-Sept. 4, San Marino. Card of 3. Nos. 1-2 and San Marino No. 1. Card inscribed in Italian. 5.00

1978 ROCPEX 76, International Philatelic Exhibition, Mar. 20-29, Taipei, Taiwan. Card of 6. Nos. 1706-1709 and Taiwan Nos. 1812 and 1816. Card inscribed in Chinese. 4.00
NAPOSTA 78, Philatelic Exhibition, May 20-25, Frankfurt, Germany. Card of 3. Nos. 555, 563 and Germany No. 1216. Card inscribed in German. 4.00

1979 BRASILIANA 79, International Philatelic Exhibition, Sept. 15-23, Rio de Janeiro, Brazil. Card of 3. Nos. C91—C92 (C92a) and Brazil No. A704. Card inscribed in Portuguese. 4.00
JAPEX 79, International Philatelic Exhibition, Nov. 2-4, Tokyo, Japan. Card of 2. Nos. 1158 and Japan No. A674. Card inscribed in Japanese. 4.00

1980 LONDON 80—IPEX, May 6-14, London, England. Card of 1 U.S. 2¢ 1907 No. 329. Card inscribed in English. 4.00
NORWEX 80—IPEX, June 13-22, Oslo, Norway. 1975 Norway stamp and two 1925 Nos. 620-621 (Norse-American issue). Card inscribed in N...

...ribed in German. 4.00

1981 WIPA 81, May 22-31, Vienna, Austria. Card of 2. 1967 Austria and No. 1252 American Music. NSCM, National Stamp Collecting Month. Oct. 1981. Issued to call attention to special month for stamp collectors. Card of 2. Nos. 245 and 1918. Card inscribed in English. 4.00
PHILATOKYO 81, International Philatelic Exhibition, Oct. 9-18, Tokyo, Japan. Card of 2 Nos. 1531 and Japan No. 800. Card inscribed in Japanese. 4.00
NORDPOSTA 81, North German Stamp Exhibition, Nov. 7-8, Hamburg, Germany. Card of 2. Nos. 923 and Germany 9NB133. Card inscribed in German. 4.00

1982 CANADA 82 International Philatelic Youth Exhibition, May 20-24, Toronto, Ontario, Canada. Card of 2. 1869 U.S. Eagle and Shield and 1859 Canadian Beaver. 4.00
PHILEXFRANCE 82, June 11-21, Paris, France. Card of 2. 1978 U.S. French Alliance and 1976 French commemoration of American Bicentennial. 4.00
ESPAMER 82, Oct. 12-17, San Juan, Puerto Rico. Card of 3. Nos. 810 and 1437 and the U.S. Ponce de Leon

1982 issue. 4.00
NSCM, National Stamp Collecting Month, October. Issued to call attention to special month for stamp collectors. Card of 1. No. C3a. 4.00

1983 Sweden/U.S., March 24, Philadelphia, PA. Card of 3, U.S. Nos. 958 and 2036. Sweden No. 1453. 4.00
German/U.S., April 29, Germantown, PA. Card of 2. U.S. No. 2040 and German No. 1397. 4.00
TEMBAL 83, May 21-29, Basil, Switzerland. Card of 2, in German. U.S. No. C71 and Switzerland No. 3L1. 4.00
BRASILIANA 83, July 29-August 7, Rio de Janeiro, Brazil. Card of 2, in Portuguese. U.S. No. 1 and Brazil No. 1. 4.00
BANGKOK 83, August 4-13, Bangkok, Thailand. Card of 2, in Thai. U.S. No. 210 and Thailand No. 1. 4.00
NSCM, National Stamp Collecting Month. Card of 1. U.S. No. 293. 4.00

1984 ESPANA 84, International Exhibition, April 27-May 6, Madrid, Spain. Card of 2, in Spanish. U.S. No. 233. Spain 1930 issue of 40-centimo tribute to Christopher Columbus. 2.00
SALON DER PHILATELIE, International Philatelic Exhibition...

von Stephan, initiator of the first UPU Congress.
AUSIPEX 84, Sept. 21-30, Melbourne, Australia. U.S. No. 290 and Western Australian 1854 1-penny Swan River Settlement. 2.00
NSCM, National Stamp Collecting Month, Oct. 1-31. U.S. No. 2104. 2.00
PHILAKOREA 84, Oct. 22-31, Seoul, Korea. U.S. No. 741 and 1975 Korean Mount Sorak National Park. 2.00

1985 OLYMPHILEX 85, March 18-24, Lausanne, Switzerland. U.S. No. C106 and 1984 Swiss 80-centime for home of the International Olympic Committee. 2.00
ISRAPHIL 85, May 14-22, Tel Aviv, Israel. U.S. No. 566 and Israeli 1950 22-prutot Struggle for Free Immigration. 2.00
ARGENTINA 85. International Philatelic Exhibition, July 5-14, Buenos Aires, Argentina. Card of 2, in Spanish. U.S. No. 1737 and Argentine No. B27.
MOPHILA 85, Philatelic Exhibition, Sept. 11-15, Hamburg, Federal Republic of Germany. Card of 2, in German, U.S. No. 296 and German No. B595. 2.00
ITALIA 85. Oct. 25-Nov. 3, Rome, Italy. In Italian, U.S. No. 1107 and Italian No. 830.

Bureau of Engraving and Printing

1954 POSTAGE STAMP DESIGN EXHIBITION, National Philatelic Museum, Mar. 13. Philadelphia. Card of 4. Monochrome views of Washington, D.C. Inscribed: "Souvenir sheet designed, engraved and printed by members, Bureau, Engraving and Printing./Reissued by popular request". 625.00

1966 SIPEX, 6th International Philatelic Exhibition, May 21-30, Washington, D.C. Card of 3. Multicolored views of Washington, D.C. Inscribed "Sixth International Philatelic Exhibition/Washington, D.C./Designed, Engraved, and Printed by Union Members of Bureau of Engraving and Printing". 210.00

1969 SANDIPEX, San Diego Philatelic Exhibition, July 16-20, San Diego, Cal. Card of 3. Multicolored views of Washington, D.C. Inscribed: "Sandipex—San Diego 200th Anniversary—1769-1969". 80.00
ASDA National Postage Stamp Show, Nov. 21-23, 1969, New York. Card of 4. No. E4. 30.00

1970 INTERPEX, Mar. 13-15, New York. Card of 4. Nos. 1027, 1035, C35 and C38. 65.00
COMPEX, Combined Philatelic Exhibition of Chicagoland, May 29-31, Chicago. Card of 4. No. C18. 20.00
HAPEX, American Philatelic Society Convention, Nov. 5-8, Honolulu, Hawaii. Card of 3. Nos. 799, C46 and C55. 25.00

1971 INTERPEX, Mar. 12-14, New York. Card of 4. No. 1193. Background includes Nos. 1331-1332, 1371 and C76. 5.00
WESTPEX, Western Philatelic Exhibition, Apr. 23-25, San Francisco. Card of 4. Nos. 740, 852, 966 and 997. 4.50
NAPEX 71, National Philatelic Exhibition, May 21-23, Washington, D.C. Card of 3. Nos. 990, 991, 992. 4.50
TEXANEX 71, Texas Philatelic Association and American Philatelic Society conventions, Aug. 26-29, San Antonio, Tex. Card of 3. Nos. 938, 1043 and 1242. 4.50
ASDA National Postage Stamp Show, Nov. 19-21, New York. Card of 3. Nos. C13-C15. 4.50
ANPHILEX '71, Anniversary Philatelic Exhibition, Nov. 26-Dec. 1, New York. Card of 2. Nos. 1-2. 4.50

1972 INTERPEX, Mar. 17-19, New York. Card of 4. No. 1173. Background includes Nos. 976, 1434-1435 and C69. 4.00
NOPEX, Apr. 6-9, New Orleans. Card of 4. No. 1020. Background includes Nos. 323-327. 3.50
SEPAD 72, Oct. 20-22, Philadelphia. Card of 4. No. 1044. 3.50
ASDA National Postage Stamp Show, Nov. 17-19, New York. Card of 4. Nos. 883, 863, 868 and 888. 3.00
STAMP EXPO, Nov. 24-26, San Francisco. Card of 4. No. C36. 3.00

1973 INTERPEX, March 9-11, New York. Card of 4. No. 976. 4.00
COMPEX 73, May 25-27, Chicago. Card of 4. No. 245. 4.00
NAPEX 73, Sept. 14-16, Washington, D.C. Card of 4. No. C3. Background includes Nos. C4-C6. 3.50
ASDA National Postage Stamp Show. Nov. 16-18, New York. Card of 4. No. 908. Foreground includes Nos. 1139-1144. 4.00
STAMP EXPO NORTH, Dec. 7-9, San Francisco. Card of 4. No. C20. 4.00

1974 MILCOPEX, March 8-10, Milwaukee, Wisconsin. Card of 4. No. C43. Background depicts U.P.U. monument at Berne, Switzerland. 5.00

1975 NAPEX 75, May 9-11, Washington, D.C. Card of 4. No. 708. 14.00
INTERNATIONAL WOMEN'S YEAR. Card of 3. Nos. 872, 878 and 959. Reproduction of 1886 dollar bill. 35.00
ASDA National Postage Stamp Show, Nov. 21-23, New York. Bicentennial series. Card of 4. No. 1003. "...and maintain the liberty which we have derived from our ancestors." 57.50

1976 INTERPHIL 76, Seventh International Philatelic Exhibition, May 29-June 6, Philadelphia. Bicentennial series. Card of 4. No. 120. "that all men are created equal." 9.50
STAMP EXPO 76, June 11-13, Los Angeles. Bicentennial series. Card of 4. Nos. 1351, 1352, 1345 and 1348 se-tenant vertically. "when we assumed the soldier, we did not lay aside the citizen". 6.50

1977 MILCOPEX, Milwaukee Philatelic Society, Mar. 4-6, Milwaukee. Card of 2. Nos. 733 and 1128. 5.00
ROMPEX 77, Rocky Mountain Philatelic Exhibition, May 20-22, Denver. Card of 4. No. 1001. 4.00
PURIPEX 77, Silver Anniversary Philatelic Exhibit, Sept. 2-5, San Juan, Puerto Rico. Card of 4. No. 801. 5.00
ASDA National Postage Stamp Show, Nov. 15-20, New York. Card of 4. No. C45. 4.50

1978 CENJEX 78, Federated Stamp Clubs of New Jersey, 30th annual exhibition, June 23-25, Freehold, N.J. Card of 9. Nos. 646, 680, 689, 1086, 1716 and 4 No. 785. 5.00

1980 NAPEX 80, July 4-6, Washington, D.C. Card of 4. No. 573. 5.00
ASDA National Postage Stamp Show, Sept. 25-28, New York. Card of 4. No. 962. 5.00

1981 STAMP EXPO 81, South International Stamp Collectors Society, Mar. 20-22, Anaheim, Cal. Card of 4. No. 1287. 5.00

1982 MILCOPEX, March 5-7, Milwaukee, Wisconsin. Card of 4. No. 1136. 5.00
ESPAMER 82, Oct. 12-17, San Juan, Puerto Rico. Card of 1. No. 244. 5.00

1983 TEXANEX-TOPEX 83, June 17-19, San Antonio, Texas. Card of 2. Nos. 776 and 1660. 5.00
NORTHEASTERN 83, Oct. 21-23, Boston, Mass. Card of 2, Nos. 718 and 719. 5.00

1984 STAMP EXPO 84 SOUTH, April 27-29, Los Angeles, California. Card of 4, U.S. Nos. 1791-1794. 3.00
ESPANA 84, April 27-May 6, Madrid, Spain. Card of 4, U.S. No. 241 as a block of 4. 3.00
COMPEX 84, May 25-27, Rosemont, Illinois. Card of 4, U.S. No. 728 as a block of 4. 3.00

1985 MILCOPEX 85, March 1-3, Milwaukee, WI. Card of block of 4 of U.S. No. 880. 4.00
NAPEX '85, June 7-9, Arlington, VA.

Over the years, the U.S. Postal Service has published a number of limited edition philatelic products issued to commemorate various philatelic and other events. These current market values were determined through various dealers who carry these products.

Commemorative Mint Sets	Original Price	Current Market Value
1968	$ 2.50	$22.50
1969	2.50	28.50
1970	2.50	14.95
1971	2.50	7.95
1972	3.00	7.95
1973	3.00	7.95
1974	3.50	7.95
1975	3.50	7.95
1976		
1977		7.95
... With Souvenir Sheets	$11.80	$25.00
Without Souvenir Sheets	7.50	9.95
1980 Olympics Mint Set	6.50	9.95
Prominent Americans Series Mint Set	12.00	22.50
Women's Mint Set	3.00	6.00
Americana Series Mint Set	14.00	19.50
Fifty Birds and Flowers Mint Set Hardbound	17.00	17.00
Softbound	11.00	11.00
American Wildlife Album	3.50	3.50

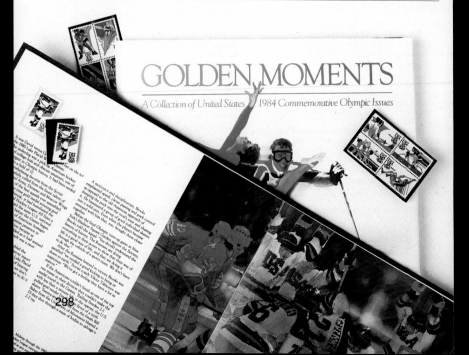

GOLDEN MOMENTS

A Collection of United States 1984 Commemorative Olympic Issues

All prices are for postal cards in mint condition.

Scott #		Mint Card
1873-98 Issues		
UX1	1¢ Liberty, brown, Lrg USPOD	250.00
UX3	1¢ Liberty, brown, Sml USPOD	50.00
UX4	1¢ Liberty, black, Wmkd	1,250.00
UX5	1¢ Liberty, black, Unwmkd	40.00
UX6	2¢ Liberty, blue	15.00
UX7	1¢ Jeff., black, faces L	40.00
UX8	1¢ Jeff., brown, faces L	25.00
UX9	1¢ Jeff., black, faces R	8.00
UX10	1¢ Grant, black	22.50
UX11	1¢ Grant, blue	8.50
UX12	1¢ Jeff., black	22.00
UX13	2¢ Jeff., black	90.00
UX14	1¢ Jeff., black	17.50
UX15	1¢ Adams, black	25.00
UX16	2¢ Adams, black	7.50
UX17	1¢ McKinley, black	5,000.00
UX18	1¢ McKinley, Oval	7.50
UX19	1¢ McKinley	22.50
UX20	1¢ McKinley, black	35.00
UX21	1¢ McKinley, blue	80.00
UX22	1¢ McKinley, blue	10.00
UX23	1¢ Lincoln, red	6.00
UX24	1¢ McKinley, red	6.00
UX25	2¢ Grant	1.25
UX26	1¢ Lincoln, green	5.50
UX27	1¢ Jeff., die I	.25
UX28	1¢ Lincoln, green	.60
UX29	2¢ Jeff., die I	27.50
UX30	2¢ Jeff., die II	15.00
UX31	1¢ on 2¢ Jeff., red	2,750.00
UX32	1¢ on 2¢ Jeff., red	35.00
UX33	1¢ on 2¢ Red, die II	5.00
UX34	1¢ on 2¢ Jeff., red	300.00
UX35	1¢ on 2¢ Jeff., red	150.00
UX36	1¢ on 2¢ Grant red	3,500.00
UX37	3¢ McKinley	2.00
1951-58 Issues		
UX38	2¢ Franklin	.30
UX39	2¢ on 1¢ Jeff., green	.50
UX40	2¢ on 1¢ Linc., green	.60
UX41	2¢ on 1¢ Jeff., dk. gr.	3.50
UX42	2¢ on 1¢ Linc., dk. gr.	4.50
UX43	2¢ Lincoln, carmine	.25
UX44	2¢ FIPEX	.25
UX45	4¢ Liberty	.75
UX46	3¢ Liberty	.40
UX47	2¢ & 1¢ Frank, rose	140.00
1962-68 Issues		
UX48	4¢ Lincoln, precan	.25
UX49	7¢ "USA"	1.25
UX50	4¢ Customs	.40
UX51	4¢ Social Security	.40
UX52	4¢ Coast Guard	.30
UX53	4¢ Census	.30
UX54	8¢ "USA"	1.00
UX55	5¢ Lincoln	.25
UX56	5¢ Women Marines	.35
1970-72 Issues		
UX57	5¢ Weather Service	.30
UX58	6¢ Paul Revere	.25
UX59	10¢ "USA"	1.50
UX60	6¢ Hospitals	.25
UX61	6¢ Constellation	.30
UX62	6¢ Monument Valley	.30
UX63	6¢ Gloucester	.30
UX64	6¢ John Hanson	.25
1973-77 Issues		
UX65	6¢ Liberty	.25
UX66	8¢ Samuel Adams	.25
UX67	12¢ Visit USA	.35
UX68	7¢ Charles Thomson	.25
UX69	9¢ Witherspoon	.25
UX70	9¢ Caesar Rodney	.25
UX71	9¢ Court House	.25
UX72	9¢ Nathan Hale	.25
1978-79 Issues		
UX73	10¢ Music Hall	.25
UX74	(10¢) John Hancock	.25
UX75	10¢ John Hancock	.25
UX76	14¢ Cutter "Eagle"	.30
UX77	10¢ Molly Pitcher	.25
UX78	10¢ G. R. Clark	.25
UX79	10¢ Pulaski	.25
UX80	10¢ Olympics	.50
UX81	10¢ Iolani Palace	.25
1980-81 Issues		
UX82	14¢ Winter Olympics	.50
UX83	10¢ Salt Lake Temple	.22
UX84	10¢ Rochambeau	.22
UX85	10¢ King's Mountain	.22
UX86	19¢ Golden Hinde	.42
UX87	10¢ Cowpens	.22
UX88	(12¢) Eagle	.28
UX89	12¢ Isaiah Thomas	.28
UX90	12¢ N. Greene	.28
UX91	12¢ Lewis & Clark	.28
UX92	(13¢) Morris	.30
UX93	13¢ Morris	.30
1982 Issues		
UX94	13¢ F. Marion	.30
UX95	13¢ La Salle	.30
UX96	13¢ Music Academy	.30
UX97	13¢ St. Louis P.O.	.30
1983 Issues		
UX98	13¢ Georgia	.30
UX99	13¢ Old P. Office	.30
UX100	13¢ Yachting	.30
1984 Issues		
UX101	13¢ Ark and Dove	.30
UX102	13¢ 84 Olympics	.30
UX103	13¢ Frederic Baraga	.30
UX104	13¢ Historic Preservation	.30

*Prices in italic indicate infrequent sales or lack of adequate pricing information.

More than 600 stamped envelopes have been issued since 1853
Represented below is only a partial listing of stamped envelope .

Scott #	Design Style	Description	Year	Un	U
U1	U1	3¢ red, die 1, white	1853	125.00	7.50
U2	U1	3¢ red, die 1, buff	1853	45.00	3.50
U3	U2	3¢ red, die 2, white	1853	400.00	17.50
U4	U2	3¢ red, die 2, buff		100.00	8.00
U5	U3	3¢ red, die 3, white	1854	1,900.00	250.00
U6	U3		1854	80.00	15.00
U7	U4	...u, die 4, white	1853	375.00	40.00
U8		3¢ red, die 4, buff	1853	675.00	60.00
U9	U5	3¢ red, die 5, white	1853	9.00	.70
U10	U5	3¢ red, die 5, buff	1854	5.00	.65
	U21	3¢ pink, white	1864	2.50	.75
U59	U21	3¢ pink, buff	1864	2.00	.50
U60	U21	3¢ brown, white	1865	21.00	15.00
U61	U21	3¢ brown, buff	1865	20.00	13.50
U62	U21	6¢ pink, white	1864	25.00	16.50
U63	U21	6¢ pink, buff	1864	18.50	13.00
U379	U85	1¢ green, white	1903	.40	.06
U380	U85	1¢ green, amber	1903	6.50	1.00
U381	U85	1¢ green, oriental buff	1903	6.00	1.25
U382	U85	1¢ green, blue	1903	5.00	1.20
U383	U85	1¢ green, manila	1903	1.50	.60
U384	U85	1¢ green, manila	1903	.35	.15
U385	U86	2¢ carmine, white	1903	.12	.05
U386	U86	2¢ carmine, amber	1903	.75	.10
U591	U137	5.9¢ brown	1982	.16	.08
U592	U138	18¢ violet	1981	.45	.18
U593	U139	18¢ dark blue	1981	.45	.18
U594	U140	20¢ brown	1981	.40	.10
U595	U141	15¢ brown & gray	1979	.35	.15
U596	U142	15¢ red, green & black	1979	.35	.15
U597	U143	15¢ blue & rose claret	1980	.35	.15
U598	U144	15¢ blue & red	1980	.35	.15
U599	U145	15¢ brown, green & yellow	1980	.35	.15
U600	U146	18¢ blue & red	1981	.45	.18
U601	U147	20¢ deep magenta	1981	.40	.10
U602	U148	20¢ dk. blue, blk., mag.	1982	.40	.10
U603	U149	20¢ purple & black	1982	.40	.10
U604	U150	5.2¢ orange	1983	.15	.10
U605	U151	20¢ red, blue & black	1983	.40	.10
U606	U152	20¢ multi	1984	.40	.10

In addition to the more than 15,000 postal facilities authorized to sell philatelic products, the U.S. Postal Service also maintains more than 369 Philatelic Centers located in major population centers throughout the country.

These Philatelic Centers have been developed to serve stamp collectors and make it convenient for them to acquire an extensive range of all current postage stamps, postal stationery and philatelic products issued by the Postal Service.

All Centers listed here are located at the Main Post Office unless otherwise indicated.

Alabama
351 North 24th Street
Birmingham, AL 35203

101 Holmes N.W.
Huntsville, AL 35804

250 St. Joseph
Mobile, Al 36601

Downtown Station
135 Catoma Street
Montgomery, AL 31604

1313 22nd Avenue
Tuscaloosa, AL 35401

Alaska
Downtown Station
3rd & C Street
Anchorage, AK 99510

College Branch
3350 College Road
Fairbanks, AK 99708

Arizona
Osborn Station
3905 North 7th Avenue
Phoenix, AZ 85013

1501 South Cherrybell
Tucson, AZ 85726

Arkansas
30 South 6th Street
Fort Smith, AR 72901

100 Reserve
Hot Springs National
Park, AR 71901

310 East Street
Jonesboro, AR 72401

600 West Capitol
Little Rock, AR 72201

California
200 Allston Way
Berkeley, CA 94504

2140 N. Hollywood Way
Burbank, CA 91505

315 G. Street
Davis, CA 95616

8111 East Firestone
Downey, CA 90241

Cutten Station
3901 Walnut Drive
Eureka, CA 95501

1900 E Street
Fresno, CA 93706

313 E. Broadway
Glendale, CA 91209

Hillcrest Station
303 E. Hillcrest
Inglewood, CA 90311

300 Long Beach Blvd.
Long Beach, CA 90801

300 N. Los Angeles St.
Los Angeles, CA 90012

Terminal Annex
900 N. Alameda
Los Angeles, CA 90052

Village Station
11000 Wilshire Blvd.
Los Angeles, CA 90024

El Viejo Station
1125 I Street
Modesto, CA 95354

Civic Center Annex
201 13th Street
Oakland, CA 94612

211 Brooks
Oceanside, CA 92054

281 E. Colorado Blvd.
Pasadena, CA 91109

1647 Yuba St.
Redding, CA 96001

1201 North Catalina
Redondo Beach, CA
90277

Downtown Station
3890 Orange St.
Riverside, CA 92501

2000 Royal Oaks Drive
Sacramento, CA 95813

Base Line Station
1164 North E Street
San Bernardino, CA
92410

2535 Midway Drive
San Diego, CA 92199

7th and Mission Sts.
San Francisco, CA 94101

1750 Meridian Drive
San Jose, CA 95101

Simms Station
41 Simms Street
San Rafael, CA
94901

Spurgeon Station
615 North Bush
Santa Ana, CA 92701

836 Anacada Street
Santa Barbara, CA 93102

4245 West Lane
Stockton, CA 95208

15701 Sherman Way
Van Nuys, CA 91408

Channel Islands
Ventura, CA 93001

396 South California St.
West Covina, CA 91790

Colorado
1905 15th St.
Boulder, CO 80302

201 E. Pikes Peak
Colorado Springs, CO
80901

1823 Stout Street
Denver, CO 80202

241 N. 4th St.
Grand Junction, CO
81501

5733 South Prince Street
Littleton, CO
80120

421 N. Main Street
Pueblo, CO 81003

Connecticut
141 Weston Street
Hartford, CT 06101

11 Silver Street
Middletown, CT 06457

141 Church Street
New Haven, CT 06510

27 Masonic Street
New London, CT 06320

421 Atlantic Street
Stamford, CT 06904

Stratford Branch
3100 Main Street
Stratford, CT 06497

135 Grand Street
Waterbury, CT 06701

Delaware
55 The Plaza
Dover, DE 19801

Federal Station
110 E. Main St.
Newark, DE 19711

11th and Market Streets
Wilmington, DE 19850

District of Columbia
Harriet Tubman
Philatelic Center
North Capitol Street and
Massachusetts Avenue
Washington, DC 20066

Headsville Station
National Museum of
American History
Smithsonian Institution
Washington, DC 20560

L'Enfant Plaza Philatelic
Center
U.S. Postal Service
Headquarters
475 L'Enfant Plaza
West, SW
Washington, DC 20260

National Visitors Center
Union Station
50 Massachusetts
Ave., N.E.
Washington, DC 20002

Pavilion Postique
Old Post Office
Building
1100 Pennsylvania
Avenue NW
Washington, DC 20004

Florida
824 Manatee Ave. West
Bradenton, FL 33506

100 South Belcher Road
Clearwater, FL 33515

1900 West Oakland Park
Boulevard
Fort Lauderdale, FL
33310

401 S.E. 1st Avenue
Gainesville, FL 32601

1801 Polk Street
Hollywood, FL 33022

1110 Kings Road
Jacksonville, FL 32203

210 North Missouri Ave.
Lakeland, FL 33802

118 North Bay Drive
Largo, FL 33540

2200 NW 72nd Avenue
Miami, FL 33101

1200 Goodlette Rd. North
Naples, FL 33940

400 Southwest First Ave.
Ocala, FL 32678

46 East Robinson Street
Orlando, FL 32801

1400 West Jordan Street
Pensacola, FL 32501

3135 First Avenue North
Saint Petersburg, FL
33730

Open Air Station
76 4th St. N.
Saint Petersburg, FL
33701

1661 Ringland Blvd.
Sarasota, FL 33578

5201 Spruce Street
Tampa, FL 33630

801 Clematis Street
West Palm Beach, FL
33401

Georgia
115 Hancock Avenue
Athens, GA 30601

Downtown Station
101 Marietta Street
Atlanta, GA 30301

Perimeter Branch
4400 Ashford-
Dunwoody Road
Atlanta, GA 30346

Downtown Station
3916 Milgen Road
Columbus, GA 31908

364 Green Street
Gainesville, GA 30501

451 College Street
Macon, GA 31201

2 North Fahm Street
Savannah, GA 31401

Hawaii
3600 Aolele Street
Honolulu, HI 96819

Idaho
770 South 13th Street
Boise, ID 83708

Illinois
909 West Euclid Avenue
Arlington Heights, IL
60004

Moraine Valley Station
7401 100th Place
Bridgeview, IL 60455

1301 East Main Street
Carbondale, IL
62901

433 West Van Buren St.
Chicago, IL 60607

Loop Station
211 South Clark Street
Chicago, IL 60604

1000 East Oakton
Des Plaines, IL 60018

1101 Davis St.
Evanston, IL 60204

2350 Madison Ave.
Granite City, IL 62040

2000 McDonough St.
Joliet, IL 60436

901 Lake Street
Oak Park, IL 60301

123 Indianwood
Park Forest, IL 60466

5225 Harrison Ave.
Rockford, IL 61125

211-19th Street
Rock Island, IL 61201

Schaumburg Station
450 W. Roselle Road
Roselle, IL 60194

2105 E. Cook St.
Springfield, IL 62703

Edison Square Station
1520 Washington
Waukegan, IL 60085

Indiana
North Park Branch
44923 1st Avenue
Evansville, IN 47710

Fort Wayne Postal
Facility
1501 S. Clinton Street
Fort Wayne, IN 46802

5530 Sohl Street
Hammond, IN 46320

125 West South Street
Indianapolis, IN 46206

2719 South Webster
Kokomo, IN 46901

3450 State Road 26, E
Lafayette, IN 47901

424 South Michigan
South Bend, IN 46624

30 N. 7th Street
Terre Haute, IN 47808

Iowa
615 6th Avenue
Cedar Rapids, IA 52401

1165 Second Avenue
Des Moines, IA 50318

320 6th Street
Sioux City, IA 51101

Kansas
1021 Pacific
Kansas City, KS 66110

6029 Broadmoor
Shawnee Mission, KS
66202

434 Kansas Avenue
Topeka, KS 66603

Downtown Station
401 North Market
Wichita, KS 67202

Kentucky
1088 Nadino Blvd.
Lexington, KY 40511

St. Mathews Station
4600 Shelbyville Road
Louisville, KY 40207

Louisiana
1715 Odom St.
Alexandria, LA 71301

750 Florida Street
Baton Rouge, LA 70821

1105 Moss Street
Lafayette, LA 70501

3301 17th Street
Metairie, LA 70004

501 Sterlington Road
Monroe, LA 71201

701 Loyola Avenue
New Orleans, LA 70113

Vieux Carre Station
1022 Iberville Street
New Orleans, LA 70112

2400 Texas Avenue
Shreveport, LA 71102

Maine
40 Western Avenue
Augusta, ME 04330

202 Harlow Street
Bangor, ME 04401

125 Forest Avenue
Portland, ME 04101

Maryland
900 E. Fayette Street
Baltimore, MD 21233

201 East Patrick Street
Frederick, MD 21701

6411 Baltimore Avenue
Riverdale, MD 20840

U.S. Route 50 and
Naylor Road
Salisbury, MD 21801

Massachusetts
Post Office and
Courthouse Bldg.
Boston, MA 02109

120 Commercial Street
Brockton, MA 02401

7 Bedford Street
Burlington, MA 01803

330 Cocituate Road
Framingham, MA 01701

385 Main Street
Hyannis, MA 02601

Post Office Square
Lowell, MA 01853

212 Fenn Street
Pittsfield, MA 01201

Long Pond Road
Plymouth, MA 02360

Quincy Branch
47 Washington Street
Quincy, MA 02169

2 Margin Street
Salem, MA 01970

74 Elm Street
West Springfield, MA
01089

462 Washington St.
Woburn, MA 01888

4 East Central Street
Worcester, MA 01603

Michigan
2075 W. Stadium Blvd.
Ann Arbor, MI 48106

26200 Ford Road
Dearborn Heights, MI
48127

1401 West Fort Street
Detroit, MI 48233

250 East Boulevard Dr.
Flint, MI 48502

225 Michigan Avenue
Grand Rapids, MI 49501

200 South Otsego
Jackson, MI 49201

Downtown Station
315 West Allegan
Lansing, MI 48901

1300 Military Street
Port Huron, MI 48060

30550 Gratiot Drive
Roseville, MI 48066

200 West 2nd Street
Royal Oak, MI 48068

1233 South Washington
Saginaw, MI 48605

Minnesota
2800 West Michigan
Duluth, MN 55806

1st and Marquette Ave.
Minneapolis, MN 55401

Downtown Station
102 S. Broadway
Rochester, MN 55904

The Pioneer Postal
Emporium
133 Endicott Arcade
St. Paul, MN 55101

Mississippi
2421-13th Street
Gulfport, MS 39501

245 East Capitol
Jackson, MS 32905

500 West Miln Street
Tupelo, MS 38801

Missouri
315 Pershing Road
Kansas City, MO 64108

Northwest Plaza Station
500 Northwest Plaza
St. Ann, MO 63074

8th and Edmond
St. Joseph, MO 64501

Clayton Branch
7750 Maryland
St. Louis, MO 63105

H.S. Jewell Station
870 Boonville Ave.
Springfield, MO 65801

Montana
841 South 26th
Billings, MT 59101

Nebraska
204 W. South Front St.
Grand Island, NE 68801

700 R Street
Lincoln, NE 68501

300 East Third Street
North Platte, NE 69101

1124 Pacific
Omaha, NE 68108

Nevada
1001 Circus Circus Dr.
Las Vegas, NV 89114

200 Vassar Street
Reno, NV 89510

New Hampshire
South Main Street
Hanover, NH 03755

955 Goffs Falls Road
Manchester, NH 03103

80 Daniel Street
Portsmouth, NH 03801

New Jersey
1701 Pacific Avenue
Atlantic City, NJ 08401

3 Miln Street
Cranford, NJ 07016

Belimawr Branch
Haag Ave. & Benigno
Boulevard
Gloucester, NJ 08031

Route 35 & Hazlet Ave.
Hazlet, NJ 07730

150 Ridgedale
Morristown, NJ 07960

Federal Square
Newark, NJ 07102

86 Bayard Street
New Brunswick, NJ
08901

194 Ward Street
Paterson, NJ 07510

171 Broad Street
Red Bank, NJ 07701

757 Broad Ave.
Ridgefield, NJ 07657

76 Huyler Street
South Hackensack, NJ
07606

680 Highway #130
Trenton, NJ 08650

155 Clinton Road
West Caldwell, NJ 07006

41 Greenwood Avenue
Wykoff, NJ 07481

New Mexico
Main Post Office
1135 Broadway NE
Albuquerque, NM 87101

200 E. Las Cruces Ave.
Las Cruces, NM 88001

New York
General Mail Facility
30 Old Karner Road
Albany, NY 12212

Empire State Plaza
Station
Albany, NY 12220

115 Henry Street
Binghampton, NY 13902

Bronx General Post
Office
149th Street & Grand
Concourse
Bronx, NY 10451

Parkchester Station
1449 West Avenue
Bronx, NY 10462

Riverdale Station
5951 Riverdale Avenue
Bronx, NY 10471

Throggs Neck Station
3630 East Tremont Ave.
Bronx, NY 10465

Wakefield Station
4165 White Plains Rd.
Bronx, NY 10466

Bayridge Station
5501 7th Avenue
Brooklyn, NY 11220

Brooklyn General
Post Office
271 Cadman Plaza East
Brooklyn, NY 11201

Greenpoint Station
66 Meserole Avenue
Brooklyn, NY 11222

Homecrest Station
2002 Avenue U
Brooklyn, NY 11229

Kensington Station
421 McDonald Avenue
Brooklyn, NY 11218

1200 William Street
Buffalo, NY 14240

Rte. 9
Clifton Park, NY 12065

Downtown Station
255 Clemens Ave.
Elmira, NY 14901

1836 Mott Avenue
Far Rockaway, NY 11691

41-65 Main Street
Flushing, NY 11351

Ridgewood Station
869 Cypress Avenue
Flushing, NY 11385

Old Glenham Road
Glenham, NY 12527

16 Hudson Avenue
Glens Falls, NY 12801

185 West John Street
Hicksville, NY 11802

88-40 164th Street
Jamaica, NY 11431

Ansonia Station
1980 Broadway
New York, NY 10023

Bowling Green Station
25 Broadway
New York, NY 10004

Church Street Station
90 Church Street
New York, NY 10007

Empire State Station
350 Fifth Avenue
New York, NY 10001

F.D.R. Station
909 Third Avenue
New York, NY 10022

Grand Central Station
45th St. & Lexington Ave.
New York, NY 10017

Madison Square Station
149 East 23rd Street
New York, NY 10010

New York General
Post Office
33rd and 8th Avenue
New York, NY 10001

Rockefeller Center
Station
610 Fifth Avenue
New York, NY 10020

Times Square Station
340 West 42nd Street
New York, NY 10036

Franklin & S. Main Sts.
Pearl River, NY 10965

55 Mansion Street
Poughkeepsie, NY 12601

1335 Jefferson Road
Rochester, NY 14692

Rockville Centre Main
Post Office
250 Merrick Road
Rockville Centre, NY
11570

25 Route 11
Smithtown, NY 11787

550 Manor Road
Staten Island, NY 10314

New Springville Station
2843 Richmond Ave.
Staten Island, NY 10314

5640 East Taft Road
Syracuse, NY 13220

10 Broad Street
Utica, NY 13503

143 Grand Street
White Plains, NY 10602

78-81 Main Street
Yonkers, NY 10701

North Carolina
West Asheville Station
1300 Patton Avenue
Asheville, NC 28806

Eastway Station
3065 Eastway Drive
Charlotte, NC 28205

301 Green Street
Fayetteville, NC 28302

310 New Bern Avenue
Raleigh, NC 27611

North Dakota
657 2nd Avenue North
Fargo, ND 58102

Ohio
675 Wolf Ledges Pkwy.
Akron, OH 44309

2650 N. Cleveland Ave.
Canton, OH 44701

Fountain Square Station
5th and Walnut Street
Cincinnati, OH 45202

301 W. Prospect Ave.
Cleveland, OH 44101

850 Twin Rivers Drive
Columbus, OH 43216

1111 East 5th Street
Dayton, OH 45401

200 North Diamond St.
Mansfield, OH 44901

200 North 4th Street
Steubenville, OH 43952

435 S. St. Clair Street
Toledo, OH 46301

99 South Walnut Street
Youngstown, OH 44503

Oklahoma
101 East First
Edmond, OK 73034

115 West Broadway
Enid, OK 73701

102 South 5th
Lawton, OK 73501

525 West Okmulgee
Muskogee, OK 74401

129 West Gray
Norman, OK 73069

76320 SW 5th
Oklahoma City, OK
73125

333 West 4th
Tulsa, OK 74101

12 South 5th
Yukon, OK 73099

Oregon
520 Willamette Street
Eugene, OR 97401

751 N.W. Hoyt
Portland, OR 97208

Williamette Valley
Salem, OR 97301

Pennsylvania
442-456 Hamilton St.
Allentown, PA 18101

535 Wood St.
Bethlehem, PA 18016

115 Boylston Street
Bradford, PA 16701

Beaver Drive Industrial
Park
Dubois, PA 15801

Griswold Plaza
Erie, PA 16501

238 S. Pennsylvania Ave.
Greensburg, PA 15601

10th and Markets Sts.
Harrisburg, PA 17105

West Avenue and
Cedar Street
Jenkintown, PA 19046

111 Franklin Street
Johnstown, PA 15901

Downtown Station
48-50 W. Chestnut St.
Lancaster, PA 17603

980 Wheeler Way
Langhorne, PA 19047

Lehigh Valley Branch
Airport Rd. & Route 22
Lehigh Valley, PA 18001

Monroeville Mall Branch
4039 Northern Pike
Monroeville, PA 15146

1 W. Washington Street
Kennedy Square
New Castle, PA 16101

28 East Airy Street
Norristown, PA 19401

30th and Market Sts.
Philadelphia, PA 19104

B. Free Franklin Station
316 Market Street
Philadelphia, PA 19106

Penn Center Station
2 Penn Center Plaza
Philadelphia, PA 19102

William Penn Annex
Station
9th and Chestnut Sts.
Philadelphia, PA 19107

Castle Shannon Branch
307 Castle Shannon
Blvd.
Pittsburgh, PA 15232

McKnight Branch
McKnight and Seibert
Roads
Pittsburgh, PA 15237

Seventh Avenue &
Grant Street
Pittsburgh, PA 15219

59 North 5th Street
Reading, PA 19603

North Washington Ave.
& Linden St.
Scranton, PA 18503

237 South Frazer Street
State College, PA 16801

7th and Ann Streets
Stroudsburg, PA 18360

South and West Wayne
Streets
Wayne, PA 19087

300 S. Main St.
Wilkes Barre, PA 18701

Center City Finance
Station
240 West Third Street
Williamsport, PA 17703

200 S. George Street
York, PA 17405

Puerto Rico
San Juan General
Post Office
Roosevelt Avenue
San Juan, PR 00936

Plaza Las Americas
Station
San Juan, PR 00938

Rhode Island
24 Corliss Street
Providence, RI 02904

South Carolina
4290 Daley Avenue
Charleston, SC 29402

1601 Assembly Street
Columbia, SC 29201

600 West Washington
Greenville, SC 29602

South Dakota
500 East Boulevard
Rapid City, SD 57701

320 S. 2nd Avenue
Sioux Falls, SD 57101

Tennessee
General Mail Facility
6050 Shallowford Road
Chattanooga, TN 37401

Tom Murray Station
133 Tucker Street
Jackson, TN 38301

501 West Main Avenue
Knoxville, TN 37901

Colonial Finance Unit
4695 Southern Avenue
Memphis, TN 38124

555 South Third
Memphis, TN 38101

Crosstown Finance Unit
1520 Union Street
Memphis, TN 38174

901 Broadway
Nashville, TN 37202

Texas
2300 South Ross
Amarillo, TX 79105

300 East South Street
Arlington, TX 76010

300 East 9th
Austin, TX 78710

300 Willow
Beaumont, TX 77704

809 Nueces Bay
Corpus Christi, TX 78408

400 North Ervay Street
Dallas, TX 75221

5300 East Paisano Dr.
El Paso, TX 79910

251 West Lancaster
Avenue
Fort Worth, TX 76101

408 Main Street
Hereford, TX 79045

401 Franklin Avenue
Houston, TX 77201

411 "L" Avenue
Lubbock, TX 79408

601 E. Pecan
McAllen, TX 78501

100 East Wall
Midland, TX 79702

10410 Perrin Beitel Road
San Antonio, TX 78284

2211 North Robinson
Texarkana, TX 75501

221 West Ferguson
Tyler, TX 75702

800 Franklin
Waco, TX 76701

1000 Lamar Street
Wichita Falls, TX 76307

Utah
1760 West 2100 South
Salt Lake City, UT 84119

Vermont
1 Elmwood Avenue
Burlington, VT 05401

151 West Street
Rutland, VT 05701

Virginia
111 Sixth Street
Briston, VA 24201

1155 Seminole Trail
Charlottesville, VA 22906

1425 Battlefield Blvd.,
North
Chesapeake, VA 23320

700 Main Street
Danville, VA 24541

Merrifield Branch
8409 Lee Highway
Fairfax, VA 22116

809 Aberdeen Road
Hampton, VA 23670

300 Odd Fellows Road
Lynchburg, VA 24506

Tyson's Corner Branch
Tyson's Corner Shopping
Center
McLean, VA 22103

Denbigh Station
14104 Warwick
Boulevard
Newport News,
VA 23602

600 Granby Street
Norfolk, VA 23501

Thomas Corner Station
6274 East Virginia Beach
Blvd.
Norfolk, VA 23502

1801 Brook Road
Richmond, VA 23232

419 Rutherford Ave. NE
Roanoke, VA 24022

1430 North Augusta
Staunton, VA 24401

London Bridge Station
550 1st Colonial Road
Virginia Beach, VA 23454

Washington
Crossroads Station
15800 N.E. 8th
Bellevue, WA 98008

315 Prospect St.
Bellingham, WA 98225

2828 West Sylvester
Pasco, WA 99301

301 Union Street
Seattle, WA 98101

West 904 Riverside
Spokane, WA 99210

1102 A Street
Tacoma, WA 98402

205 West Washington
Ave.
Yakima, WA 98903

West Virginia
301 North Street
Bluefield, WV 24701

Lee and Dickinson St.
Charleston, WV 25301

500 West Pike Street
Clarksburg, WV 26301

1000 Virginia Street
Huntington, WV 25704

217 King Street
Martinsburg, WV 25401

Wisconsin
325 East Walnut
Green Bay, WI 54301

3902 Milwaukee St.
Madison, WI 53708

345 West St. Paul Ave.
Milwaukee, WI 53203

Wyoming
2120 Capitol Avenue
Cheyenne, WY 82001

FOREIGN CENTERS
France
Theodore Champion
13 Rue Drouot
75009 Paris

**Federal Republic
of Germany**
Hermann W. Sieger
Venusberg 32-34
D-7073
Lorch/Wurttemberg

Netherlands
J. A. Visser
P.O. Box 184
3300 Ad Dordrecht

Switzerland
De Rosa International S.A.
Av Du Tribunal Federal 34
CH-1005 Lausanne
Telex No. 25524

England
Stanley Gibbons
International, Ltd.
391 Strand
London WC2R OLX

Japan
Japan Philatelic Co., Ltd.
P.O. Box 2
Suginami-Minami
Tokyo 168-91

IMPORTANT NOTE: This Index covers all issues from the 1893 Columbian Exposition issues (#230) through 1984. Listings in italic typeface refer to Definitive or Regular issues. The numbers in parentheses ( ) refer to the page number on which the stamp appears.

INDEX

INDEX

308

INDEX

INDEX

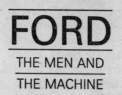

FORD
THE MEN AND
THE MACHINE

Born in Surrey in 1944 and brought up in Bristol, Robert Lacey studied history at Cambridge. His first books were historical biographies, the critically acclaimed *Robert, Earl of Essex* and *Sir Walter Raleigh*, which were published in the early 1970s while he was on the staff of the *Sunday Times*.

In 1974 he became a full-time author in order to research and write *Majesty*, his best-selling biography of Queen Elizabeth II, which came out in 1977, the year of her Silver Jubilee.

After the success of *Majesty*, the Lacey family moved to live in Saudi Arabia while Robert researched the story of *The Kingdom*. The result was a massive and wide-ranging book which, like *Majesty*, became a huge bestseller all over the world.

Princess, a largely pictorial celebration of the new Princess of Wales, followed, and Mr Lacey's book *Aristocrats* was published in 1983 in conjunction with his BBC series of the same name.

Robert Lacey went to Michigan to research *Ford*, and lived there for more than two years in Grosse Pointe, just outside Detroit, with his wife Sandi, his sons Sasha and Bruno, and his daughter Scarlett.

First Ford. Henry I and his Quadricycle of 1896

ROBERT LACEY

FORD

THE MEN AND
THE MACHINE

Pan Books

in association with Heinemann

First published in Great Britain 1986
by William Heinemann Ltd.
This edition published 1987 by Pan Books Ltd,
Cavaye Place, London SW10 9PG
9 8 7 6 5 4 3 2 1
© Robert Lacey 1986
ISBN 0 330 29879 8
Photoset by Rowland Phototypesetting Ltd,
Bury St Edmunds, Suffolk
Printed and bound in Great Britain by
Richard Clay Ltd, Bungay, Suffolk